Athlete Career Killers:

Ultimate All-in-One Success System Helps Athletes Avoid Trouble!

By David L. Brown

Reviewed by Bill Cole, MS, MA, Founder and President, IMGCA

Stop a potential disaster in a sports career before it even gets underway. Make sure that character rules the day in any young athlete's life, so they themselves don't become a character. Know how to navigate the treacherous ways of a sports career, at all levels, from all fronts. *Athlete Career Killers: Ultimate All-in-One Success System Helps Athletes Avoid Trouble*™ gives readers all of this and more. In 300+ jam-packed pages of smart strategies, *Athlete Career Killers*™ lays out a step-by-step approach to handling the inevitable pitfalls that can be thrown in the path of even the most diligent and thoughtful student-athlete or professional player.

Author David L. Brown writes from a place of wisdom. He himself was a multi-sport athlete, at a high level. He was a blue-chip prospect in football, recruited by such perennial college powerhouses as Ohio State, Wisconsin and Virginia Tech, among others. David has lived and seen the life paths of athletes up close and personal, and writes from the inside out to help protect the career paths of aspiring athletes.

Athlete Career Killers™ is street smart and athlete-friendly. Athletes and coaches of all levels, in all sports, should own this book and refer to it often. It offers practical, honest and character-driven ways to stay safe, respect others and make sport a better place. The International Mental Game Coaching Association endorses *Athlete Career Killers*™ as a vital resource for anyone in sports. Sports agents should be particularly interested in this book for their clients, and this should be mandatory reading for every college freshman athlete.

Athlete Career Killers™ is the first book dedicated to providing step-by-step solutions for improving Player Personal Conduct™ in sports. *Athlete Career Killers*™ is hard-hitting. With chapters like Clubbing, Drunk Driving, Guns, Drugs, Domestic Violence, Infidelity, Home Invasion, Gambling, Money, College Academics, and a spiritual chapter titled 3rd Down and God, this book tells it like it is to young athletes. David L. Brown speaks their language.

It is a done deal that many, if not most young athletes will go clubbing, or at least be out in the public eye at some point. *Athlete Career Killers*™ implores these young athletes to think in advance, set intelligent strategies, have contingency plans and know what to say and do when trouble shows up.

Athlete Career Killers™ is a character-driven book. Sport needs more character. This book shows us how that can be achieved. The International Mental Game Coaching Association applauds David L. Brown for this book, and for the vision he has shown for writing this superb book and his other individually titled 12-part book series.

See what other experts are saying about *Athlete Career Killers*™

"Just like any professional or college athlete would never take the field or the court without a practiced game plan, neither should they take to the social scene without proper education. Here, David has laid out the perfect game plan that all athletes need to read and embrace. Don't leave the locker-room unprepared!"

> **Bob Rathbun**
> TV voice of the NBA's Atlanta Hawks
> Motivational Speaker and Author

"All athletes should take note of the useful clubbing information found in this book. Athletes and the like should know the risks associated with nightlife and how their choices can affect their career and personal life forever. Taking the guidance that is in this book and working with an executive protection agency together can help protect you, your family, and your reputation from the pitfalls of a celebrity life."

> **Grant Linhart**
> President & CEO of Gideon Protective Services, Inc.
> (www.executive-protection-services.net)
> Current California law enforcement officer trained by retired
> United States Secret Service Agent Joe LaSorsa,
> Presidential Protection - the White House.

"An absolute must read…not only for every professional athlete, but also for everyone within his or her inner circle. David has crafted a timely and invaluable handbook to help lead athletes along their best path. I look forward to sharing its lessons with all of my players."

> **Erica McKeon**
> Senior Vice President of Bruce Levy Associates International,
> Ltd. (BLAIL), the world's oldest agency specializing in the
> representation of women's pro basketball players and coaches.

"David L. Brown's incisive comments concerning the lifestyle traps of clubbing and the liability issues of carrying a firearm are dead on! As a professional athlete you are one of the privileged few that made it to the show. Don't place everything you have worked so hard to obtain at risk by making poor decisions!"

> **Daniel W. Blake, CPO, LPI**
> Chief of Police (retired)
> President, Aegis Security, LLC
> www.aegistn.com

"I've spent the last 30 years educating people to become better athletes through mental preparation and understanding the psychological aspects of competition. David L. Brown provides necessary preparation skills to keep athletes from making devastating mistakes off the playing fields and courts. I highly recommend his books as guidance for all athletes' emotional and physical well-being. The POPS system empowers the athlete to take control of their life away from competition and keep them out of harm's way."

>**Mike Margolies**
>Sports Psychology Consultants
>TheMental-Game.com

"With clarity, logic and great insight, David L. Brown has produced a highly credible road map to assist today's modern professional and college athletes by shedding light on a wide array of off the field and court challenges, disasters and mishaps. This book is long overdue and is a must-read."

>**Forrest Dorsett**
>Founder & Principal, Dorsett Sports Marketing
>www.dorsettsportsmarketing.com

"*Clubbing*" addresses many of the dangers college and professional athletes encounter when they indulge in city nightlife. This book is a must read for all athletes due to the serious and sometimes deadly consequences that can result from a night out on the town."

>**Shaun Tyrance**
>Sport Psychology Consultant
>University of North Carolina at Charlotte

"'*Athlete Career Killers* is a great read and playbook full of tips for athletes to either avoid or (if necessary) deal with public situations where people wish to antagonize them, or worse. The examples David L. Brown gives are great depictions of real life circumstances that athletes find themselves in. David doesn't want guys to live as shut-ins, but simply to have a plan and realize the importance of practicing that plan just as they would practice during their playing careers. It's a great resource for both college and professional athletes."

>**Anthony Herron**
>Former professional football player and championship winning coach. Current television analyst for both the NFL Network and Big Ten Network. President and Co-Founder of Life Success for Athletes.

"David L. Brown's "Athlete's Career Killers" is definitely a book athletes who want to "WIN" in the sport of life should read! For the past 25 years, I have had the pleasure of spanning the globe coaching, consulting and helping amazing athletes (amateur/college/pro/superstars), teams, clubs and companies achieve their highest and best levels of SUCCESS in all walks of Life (sports, fitness, business & life). Congratulations, David, these valuable life lessons and athlete blueprints for success can and will help them ignite their champion within and live their legacy."

>**Joy Macci, PhD**
>CEO/International Tennis Specialist
>Author/Speaker/Superstar Success Coach
>www.JoyofSport.com

"David L. Brown's Athlete Career Killers is on a level that ANY athlete should read. As an athlete takes that NEXT step into their future, they should keep in mind, *ALL* organizations have people watching you 24/7. If you learn ANYTHING from reading this book know this: **Think BIG so you can become BIGGER.**"

>**James Heintz**
>Director of Football Operations
>Elite Sports Agency
>www.theelitesportsagency.com

"A very informative and proactive approach that encourages athletes to learn and practice new behaviors when it comes to enjoying life without the risk of severe legal consequences or worse. Parents, Athletic Directors, and Athletes themselves will all find this as an extremely useful tool in molding appropriate behaviors".

>**Julie Atkinson**
>Co-Host of Ridin' Dirty-The Radio Show

"This new book is exactly what professional and college athletes need. If you want to own and carry guns for your protection to go along with your new found fame and fortune, that's fine. Just seek out the proper training and attain the proper mindset involved in owning and using firearms for sporting and self-defense purposes. If you don't have the time or skill set to safely and effectively use firearms, hire professionals to protect you and your family. Quite frankly, this book is very comprehensive on the topic of guns and athletes. It should be a required read for all professional and collegiate players, coaches, and staff."

>**Grant Linhart**
>President/CEO of Gideon Protective Services, Inc.
>Current California Law Enforcement Officer trained by retired United States Secret Service Agent Joe LaSorsa, Presidential Protection - the White House.
>(www.executive-protection-services.net)

"This book is absolutely needed in the sports industry. Congratulations on the work you have done in reaching out to athletes and educating them about domestic violence. I believe that the earlier we reach out to someone, the earlier domestic violence can be prevented. I find it very touching that you have written such an important book for athletes on this subject. It is my hope that this book will increase their awareness and educate them about how to prevent domestic violence from occurring."

>**Carolyn S. Hennecy**
>Domestic Violence Awareness Advocate
>Author, Speaker
>www.orangeblossomwishes.com
>www.everydayhealth.com/blogs/emotional-wellbeing

"An essential and informative tool for athletes and anyone else, in spelling out the basics we all need in helping to prevent home invasion. This book will increase your awareness, educate you about tips you may not have known before, and is critical information for keeping your family safe."

>**Kim Castro, LPD/CISM**
>National Crime Fighting Expert
>Professional Security Manager
>Illinois State Police Executive Protection Unit

"...a must read for all professional athletes and student-athletes from middle school age through college. As a gambling recovery therapist, I recommend it for all counselors and therapists to have a better understanding of the pro athlete and student-athlete's gambling mind, and how to help him or her reduce potentially devastating life consequences."

>**James Loree, LMSW, ACSW, CAAC**
>THE CENTER FOR ADDICTION AND RELATIONSHIP RECOVERY
>Michigan Department of Community Health. Licensed Substance Abuse
>Program & Contracted Gambling Treatment Provider
>JamesLoree.com

"...a frank and refreshing, easy to read series for all athletes, or anyone else for that matter. If individuals incorporated these concepts as part of their conditioning, they would have a much higher success rate throughout their careers. They would also reap the benefits long after their careers have ended, while retaining the wealth they have worked so hard to obtain."

>**Flonnoya J. Franklin**
>Owner & CEO
>FJF Wealth Management Co.
>www.fjfwealthmgt.com

"...a great road map for student and professional athletes. It challenges your internal compass and relies on the individual to think, stay focused, and be accountable in the classroom while enjoying the true craft of the game. The concepts David uses go hand-in-hand with the work I do as an educator and life coach. It's important to impress upon each student-athlete that beyond the glamorization of athletics at the high school, college, or professional level, at the end of the day, it's really all about the choices you make. Since there is so much that makes up an individual's "Frame of Reference", it's critical that student-athletes seek out mentors, counselors, and positive support immediately, to help with time management and academic balance. The key point to remember is that Athlete Career Killers never go away. Athletes fight the battle all the way through your quest for success, both academically and professionally."

Nicholas Dillon
Certified Life Coach & Motivational Speaker
Milwaukee Counseling Services, LLC
Director of Education & Risk Services
www.milwaukeecounselingservices.com

"All the important things I didn't learn in kindergarten are in this book! It provides a simple approach to the most difficult financial situations an athlete will face during his or her academic and professional career. David's book is an easy read, designed to make readers mindful of potential financial pitfalls, along with giving them basic tools to successfully navigate through the sometimes confusing arena of personal finances. It's a must read."

Marc Brown
The Advisory Partners of Beaver, PA
Partner/Financial Advisor
Wealth Management

Athlete Career Killers

*Ultimate All-in-One Success System
Helps Athletes Avoid Trouble!*

DAVID L. BROWN

The World is Watching™

Copyright© 2010 David L. Brown. All rights reserved.

ISBN-10: 0982808925
ISBN-13: 978-0-9828089-2-4

No part of this publication may be reproduced or transmitted in any form or by any means, mechanical or electronic, including photocopying and recording, or by any information storage and retrieval system, without permission in writing from the author or publisher (except by a reviewer, who may quote brief passages and/or short brief video clips in a review.)

Neither the author nor the publisher shall have liability or responsibility to any person or entity concerning any loss or damage caused, or alleged to be caused, including bodily injuries or death, directly or indirectly, by the information contained in this book.

This book is intended for educational, motivational, self-help and how-to purposes only and contains copyrighted material. The author is making such material available in an effort to advance understanding and awareness of issues and incidents, specifically involving athletes in the NFL, NBA, NCAA football and men's basketball, Major League Baseball, the NHL, newly formed United Football League (UFL), and any other sports entity.

First Edition

Published by Parkway Press, Niles, Ohio

Printed in the United States of America

Media Interview Contact:
David L. Brown, Author
Founder & CEO
Character Athletic, Ltd.
P.O. Box 252
Niles, Ohio 44446-0252
United States
Phone: 330-307-5571
E-mail: dlbrown88@yahoo.com

Play Hard. Do Good. The World is Watching.™

www.AthleteCareerKillers.com
www.CharacterAthletic.com

Pro and college athletes, coaches, teams, leagues, athletic directors, high schools, parents, youth sports programs, sports journalists and sports fans will also enjoy reading, and benefit from the valuable and potentially life-saving information in the author's *Athlete Career Killer*™ *individual titles:*

Clubbing: Athlete Career Killer™

Drunk Driving: Athlete Career Killer™

Guns: Athlete Career Killer™

Drugs: Athlete Career Killer™

Domestic Violence: Athlete Career Killer™

Infidelity: Athlete Career Killer™

Home Invasion: Athlete Career Killer™

Gambling: Athlete Career Killer™

Money: Athlete Career Killer ™

College Academics: Athlete Career Killer™

POPS™: Athlete Career Savior™ #1 Clubbing Travel Guide

3RD Down and God: #1 Spiritual Guide for Athletes™

The author believes *Athlete Career Killers*™ should be placed in the hands of all professional athletes. All student-athletes, and all incoming freshman student-athletes who commit to continue their athletic and academic careers in a college or university football and basketball program, should also be handed *Athlete Career Killers*™ as part of an orientation program upon signing. The same with every draft class in the NFL, NBA, NHL, and Major League Baseball.

Consider this book an *investment*— an investment in your athletes, your teams, your schools, your leagues, your organizations and your communities.

Dedicated to my parents; Jimmy and Doris Brown.

To all athletes…
"Live your life to the fullest...just be smart about it."
– David L. Brown

Acknowledgments

I give honor and glory to God. None of this would be possible without Him.

To Brandon and Alýssa; I love you with all my heart...unconditionally.

To my late sister Buena; I will always remember your giving heart, spirituality, and kind nature.

To my sister Sharon; thank you for always caring.

To my brother Jim; we may live thousands of miles apart, but you are still "big bro" to me.

To my niece Danae; best wishes in your collegiate career.

To friends, family, and colleagues; thank you for your encouragement, motivation, patience, and insights.

To all athletes who conduct themselves in a professional manner and who do the right things by making good choices in your lives and athletic careers; you have my utmost respect and admiration.

Many thanks to Kimberly Martin, founder of Jera Web Creations, LLC. Kimberly did a wonderful job designing the interior of this book. She is professional and a joy to work with. Go to Self-Pub.net for all your interior book design and other publishing needs – you'll be glad you did!

Special thanks to Carrie Hodge Kibby and Theresa Martin, of McKinley Memorial & Public Library, Niles, Ohio. Your encouragement and feedback helped me a great deal along this journey.

Thank you Max, from Niles, Ohio Post Office. What a joy it was to see your smiling face and to chat with you each time I mailed my books.

Last but certainly not least, thank you Ms. Shelli Jackson, of Warren-Trumbull County Public Library, Warren, Ohio. Ms. Jackson is also a former juvenile corrections officer. Your thoughtful, kind words, humor and spiritual insights were invaluable.

The Public Library – Where Greatness Happens.™

Contents

INTRODUCTION		1
PART ONE		5

Chapter 1	Clubbing		6
Chapter 2	Drunk Driving		63
Chapter 3	Guns		91
Chapter 4	Drugs		112
Chapter 5	Domestic Violence		141
Chapter 6	Infidelity		167

PART TWO		185

Chapter 7	Home Invasion		186
Chapter 8	Gambling		210
Chapter 9	Money		228
Chapter 10	College Academics		261
Chapter 11	3rd Down And God		278
Chapter 12	Recruiting Violations		298
Chapter 13	Depression & Anxiety (Bonus Chapter)		307

About the Author	312
Personal Biography	313

INTRODUCTION

*"The history of free men is not written by chance,
but by choice—their choice."*
— Dwight D. Eisenhower

Congratulations!

You are holding in your hands the best and ultimate success system for athletes ever written.

Good choice!

Yep, that's right. You're holding the world's #1 guide that could save your life and athletic career.

This innovative and groundbreaking book contains valuable, practical and important *"best practices"* for all athletes.

This year and beyond, an athlete's dreams will come true. He/she will reach for and achieve the highest pinnacle of success in their athletic career and life. Some will be crowned champions. Sadly, it will also be remembered as a disaster for many athletes. A heart breaker. A complete disappointment.

Every day we make thousands of choices. Some choices have more impact on our lives than others. Some require more thought. Some may even require the input of others. As an athlete, you have the opportunity every day to make good choices -- the right choices, for your life and career.

What's the difference between being a champion or a chump? Character and making good choices. Yes, talent helps too, but it's diminished without the others.

As an athlete, you can choose to do one of two things with your life and athletic career: Focus or wander. If you play sports and live long enough you'll likely experience both.

Choose to focus and you have an opportunity to become great. Choose to wander and you're likely to eventually self-implode, throwing away good opportunities.

With this book, I wish to instill in you a positive mindset to the highest standards of personal character and moral conduct, from the high school level to the pros, that fans, leagues, and your teams expect from you.

This book is specifically designed to help you avoid numerous "career killers" and other social and lifestyle temptations you face each day off the field and court.

Athlete Disaster Formula

Welcome to the most volatile formula in sports. Pro or college athlete + nightclub + alcohol + 2:00 - 3:00 a.m. + guns + drinking and driving + frayed emotions + poor judgment = Big trouble!

I wrote this book specifically to help with the safety and education of all athletes who participate in nightlife. Note that when I refer to the term "clubbing," it is meant to include ALL venues of nightlife; nightclubs, bars, strip clubs, other gentleman's clubs, and parties.

It is imperative that I begin by telling you that 98% of college and professional athletes combined are upstanding citizens of good character, and DO NOT cause legal, or other problems!

Unfortunately, I GUARANTEE THIS…

As I write this, Thursday, April 15th, 2010, an athlete somewhere is making a poor decision, knowingly or not, that will be heard and read about on the web and on your favorite sports network within the next 48 hours (if not sooner)…I GUARANTEE IT!

Since you are holding this book in your hands right now, you, no doubt, have an interest in reclaiming your sanity, peace of mind, and confidence when venturing out into nightlife. And, I'd like to help. As an athlete, you've heard about the sad stories, and have seen the unfortunate headlines regarding your peers.

You probably know a teammate right now who's made some poor choices and suffered the consequences. Maybe your team or the league brought someone in to talk to you about the dangers lurking in the night, but you still have questions and concerns, and you find yourself still looking over your shoulder in fear of the unknown.

Basically, anywhere you go where alcohol is served — this book is for you.

ATHLETE CAREER KILLERS

You have good reason to be fearful. Clubbing can be scary and violent — unless you have the right tools and techniques. You don't have to feel like there's a "bulls eye" on your back 24-7. It's a problem desperately searching for the right solution. This book provides athletes a fresh, comprehensive solution for what you think you know, and what you've already been told. It's an innovative and specialized tool to help you stay safe from potential life-threatening and career killing nightlife temptations you face in today's society.

My job is to help you, as an athlete, stay safe, and allow you to keep playing the game you love. You can't help your team win if you make bad decisions when clubbing or otherwise, and later find yourself dealing with police, defense attorneys, courts, judges, prosecutors, and potential team and league suspensions.

Getting into trouble can happen in an instant — but the legal process can take much longer.

Because of this, athletes who attend clubs MUST have an effective security plan in place *BEFORE, DURING, and AFTER* you go clubbing, and potentially encounter obnoxious or intoxicated patrons who may want to cause trouble.

You also must have a clubbing game plan in place so that YOU don't end up being the one initiating and causing trouble for others!

Later, I reveal my techniques and tips, called POPS™, that will allow you to increase your awareness, confidence, and peace of mind... RIGHT NOW!

POPS™ is an acronym for *"PO'd Points"* (*"Pissed Off Points"* for adult readers).

POPS™ are all about consistent awareness, preparation, and common sense. Protecting yourself and staying safe starts with your mind, first and foremost. The same way you prepare for the next game, should be the same way you prepare yourself, friends and family BEFORE you make important lifestyle choices and decisions.

My techniques and tips will educate you on general "tendencies" of people at clubs, bars, parties, or anywhere else. I'll also educate you on how to recognize another person's "boiling points," and how to avoid potential trouble.

Much is written in the media about athletes making poor decisions, but there are few solutions that offer the total package to help you stay safe when clubbing...until now.

I don't just want to talk about your safety — I want to *show you* how to stay safe...**step-by-step.**

You can't take for granted any longer that you'll know what to do or how to react during a potentially dangerous or violent situation.

DAVID L. BROWN

I *guarantee* this book will serve as an extremely valuable tool for all athletes throughout your career and post-career. Your chances of success in using this book are greater when you exhibit an open mind and a willingness to learn.

The formula for your success is simple...

Play Hard. Do Good.™
Your Safety. My Passion.™

PART ONE

Chapter 1
CLUBBING

"What you do speaks so loudly that I cannot hear what you say."
– Ralph Waldo Emerson

Make no mistake about this -- *clubbing can kill your athletic career -- or cause someone to be injured, assaulted or killed!*

Many of the POPS tips and techniques I created for this book I tested myself — and they work. They'll work for you too — if used properly and consistently. Just like a rookie NFL athlete doesn't completely know the offense or defense during his first mini-camp and OTAs (organized team activities), but the more repetitions he gets, the more he learns. The more he learns, the better he becomes. The more confident he gets, the faster he plays and the more productive he'll be on the field.

The reason I began to do research for this book started with a sad story I saw on ESPN in mid-December 2006, involving a former high profile Chicago Bears defensive tackle. After watching that story unfold, the news of athletes involving nightclubs, guns, violence, drinking and driving and more, kept coming and coming, to the point I realized I needed to write this book.

It was reported that Chicago police searched for a man who allegedly harassed the Bear's athlete on a nightclub dance floor, on an early Saturday morning, sparking a fight that resulted in the shooting death of his boyhood friend and bodyguard. His friend died after the fight inside a popular club in the trendy River North neighborhood, police said. Witnesses told police that another man repeatedly bumped into the athlete on the dance floor, a source familiar with the investigation told the *Chicago Tribune*. The athlete's friend and bodyguard intervened, the newspaper reported, struck the man, and both fell to the floor. When club security pulled them apart, the other man pulled out a gun and shot and killed the athlete's friend, witnesses said.

To prepare for this book, I interviewed numerous athletes, coaches, high school and college athletic directors, sports agents, sports journalists, parents and general sports fans, to get their insights and opinions regarding the issues of Player Personal Conduct™ in sports today.

Opinions varied, but one thing was absolutely certain; player conduct is a consistently *HOT* topic for discussion!

I also went clubbing where the athletes hang out in Cleveland and Pittsburgh, my two major nearby cities. I went every other weekend for three months.

I saw drunks, druggies, women with agendas, men with agendas, the "hustle" of men trying to hook up with women and vice-versa. I saw the liars, the dealers, the phonies, the pretenders, the con-men and women, and the game players — all a part of the dynamic nocturnal playground known as urban nightlife. Many of the clubs I attended were in nice neighborhoods and considered upper-middle class to upscale.

The clubbing vibe I experienced during my research was exhilarating, yet scary…sexy…yet shallow. It provided a two-to-three hour short-term "escape" from the everyday hum drum. The pressure on males in clubs, bars, and parties is enormous, depending on your motives, whether you're an athlete or not. The direct competition for women is silently fierce, yet forcefully felt.

In one example, a woman approached me at the club. *I said goodbye at hello.* I sensed she was high on something.

Most of the experiences left me feeling fortunate to leave safe and sound and without incident. Some other club customers weren't so lucky. I witnessed several fights in parking lots after the clubs closed, a fight or two inside the club between guys, and women fist-fighting other women outside. I heard the echo of shots being fired outside the clubs and that eerie sound of police and ambulance sirens raging against the early morning air.

Incidents like these didn't occur every time I went clubbing, but each time I could sense emotions could potentially erupt at any time, anywhere, over the slightest thing.

We all like to party sometimes.

When you're an athlete, it's an understandable major rush for you. You're in great shape. You look good, and so, of course, the ladies are going to dig you. You're also a star on the field or on the court, and people gravitate toward that. They want to feel like they're a part of it, and so you may get a huge rush of entitlement and excitement from that experience.

Athletes want to be loved, accepted, appreciated, understood, and acknowledged. It's okay — it's part of simple human nature. You just have to make good choices and use good judgment in light of it.

There are a ton of reasons why you want to go clubbing — some you might not even be aware of. I'm going to dive into those reasons shortly. For now, I just want you to start becoming aware that you have to focus on making good choices when you decide to go out for a night.

Take, for example, the tendency of some professional athletes to carry a gun.

They do so, they say, for protection. And, granted, they have a point. No one wants to be a target, and many athletes are. There are too many examples of athletes going to jail because they used their gun, or someone used a gun on them.

Athletes must always consider this when entering a nightclub, strip club, bar, or late night party: If you believe you have legitimate reasons to carry a gun into any of the above-mentioned places…the other guy does too!

You're probably not the only one packin' for protection. Multiply one person by maybe ten to fifteen in a club and you can see how there may be a potential problem if things get out of hand, especially when alcohol is involved.

The sad fact is, if you make a poor decision, the world will know. I've done a study on it.

Nightclubs and bars can be exciting and fun for athletes to attend, but with that comes special problems. As you can imagine, an urban club or bar that markets itself to young adults in an attempt to become the next "hot" spot to be seen is bound to have a few conduct problems. Before you take one step inside a nightclub, bar, strip club, or late night party, reflect on the potential dangers and consequences and ask yourself…*is it really worth it?*

Sometimes club and bar patrons bring outside conflicts and jealousies that can erupt into potentially dangerous situations and violence. You need to know how to handle yourself if you become angry due to the actions or words of others, or YOU feel entitled to take liberties with other people because of your status as an athlete.

NEVER allow your status as an athlete to have a negative impact on your life and athletic career!

That's what this book is all about.

ATHLETE CAREER KILLERS

Update: *June 13, 2010.* I just viewed on ESPN.com a video of a Tennessee Titans quarterback getting into a fight with another person at a Dallas-area strip club early Sunday morning. I could not believe what I was watching. The Titans quarterback had numerous opportunities to just walk away, and unfortunately he did not.

The video was recorded by a security camera inside the strip club offices. No arrests were made and no charges were reportedly filed. A misdemeanor assault citation was issued to the athlete and a fine is likely.

Even though it may be considered a first time offense in regard to the personal conduct policy, I suspect the athlete will be hearing from NFL Commissioner Roger Goodell at some near point.

The point is this -- you simply *MUST* at all times, maintain your composure if someone is talking "junk" at you or making hand gestures in a club, bar or at a party. You *CANNOT* let your emotions get the best of you, causing you to do something foolish, like get into a fight with another person, risking not only your personal health, but your athletic career as well.

For example, you're at a club, strip club, bar or late night party, and someone starts "chirping" about your momma, your girlfriend, your college team, whoever, whatever.

WHO CARES!

Does this person know you personally? No. Does he know your momma personally? No. Your girlfriend? No. Will your college or pro team be offended by some fool "dissing" the team you play for? Of course not! So let it go!

Another "caught on video" incident occurred in April 2010, involving a Minnesota Vikings defensive end, who was at a tavern in Scottsdale, Arizona one evening. The original footage was recorded by another patron's video/camera cell phone and released publicly by *TMZ.com*.

The athlete was shown responding to an alleged derogatory remark another male patron made toward his girlfriend. The athlete was heard on the video yelling back at the man, something to the tune of (paraphrase), *"I'll break your neck and then write you a check."*

Again...the man making the alleged comments does not know your lady personally, *so just let it go.* It's not even worth responding to. Why give "life" to the words or gestures of an idiot in a tavern or strip club? Why give some jerk the "power" to entice you with empty words?

Your toughness and strength are displayed in your ability to *walk away* from a situation.

Simply consider the source where the "noise" is coming from. Is that person a significant and positive contributor in your life? Absolutely not.

It's not worth the trouble!

Is it sometimes difficult for you to maintain your composure and refrain from verbally retaliating against some idiot in a club or bar? *You darn right it is!* Your natural first reaction may be to take it personally and quickly respond back – but don't!

You have much more to lose than the other guy does by choosing to retaliate verbally or physically.

Try to remember the old adage, *"Sticks and stones may break my bones, but* **words** *will never hurt me."*

That may sound elementary, but it's true. Don't allow someone's shallow words to get the best of you.

I respect you as an athlete. I'm a former blue chip athlete and college football player, and I know the kind of dedication and commitment it takes to be on a team. I know what it feels like to both focus and wander.

I want to help you keep your career intact and not be potentially ruined or tarnished because you didn't have the right tools to take with you to a club to prevent possible disaster from happening.

I designed a simple to follow, but very effective program – POPS™. Until now, you've been told to be responsible, to make sure that target on your back isn't too big and bold, but you haven't had a plan. POPS™ gives you a clubbing game plan. It's one that could save your life — *literally.*

As an athlete, you have a C.H.O.I.C.E™, and it's based on…

C.ourage

H.onesty

O.pportunity

I.ntegrity

C.ommitment

E.xcellence

You will learn in this book how to recognize potential dangers while clubbing, and the "career killers" they can be. You will also learn to recognize when you yourself are about to make a poor decision, and to STOP before things get out of hand and you wind up on the front sports page in a negative and embarrassing fashion.

POPS™ will also give you a stronger voice to speak up when you see a teammate about to make a bad decision — like drinking and driving, and other potentially dangerous and career killing choices.

Ugly Headline

"Turn your wounds into wisdom."
– Oprah Winfrey

Pop! Pop! Pop!

You're all familiar with the sound of a gun fired — and the headlines that follow. Top athlete goes out and gets drunk, or high, gets in his car and something awful happens. He's shot. He gets into a fight. He is accused of sexual assault or worse, and is faced with potentially losing his career.

Take the story of a Louisville wide receiver. It was late at night on a fourth of July weekend in 2008. He's out with his fiancé. They just had a fun night of clubbing, and they're walking to their car. The next thing he knows he's being shot at -- nineteen times. It happens in a parking garage, so there's nowhere to hide.

By the grace of God, only one of those nineteen bullets hits him. But it's in the back, and his playing days may be over. The athlete told a reporter he wasn't sure why it happened or how it happened, but he is thankful he survived. He said he was at the club when someone allegedly inappropriately touched his fiancé. Words were exchanged. When he left the club, he was followed and later attacked outside a parking garage.

He later told a reporter, "The doctors said an inch to the right it would have hit my spine, an inch to the left it would have hit a vital organ."

Fortunately, doctors were able to remove the bullet shortly after the attack. He's one of the lucky ones. He's going to be able to return to the game. He gets to play again, but he also gets to live the rest of his life with that awful memory. The athlete said he's more cognizant that when he, friends and teammates go out, people know them and things like shootings shouldn't happen, but sometimes they do.

"We just have to watch what we do," he said.

He will always carry the scar in the middle of his back as a painful reminder of how quickly things can change. How many athletes can you name who have gotten into trouble, been injured, killed, or were found to have caused trouble after a night of clubbing? How many athletes can you name who have gotten arrested? How many can you name who got into a fight, hurt someone, got suspended, or lost their career because of it? One is too many.

It's the risk you take when you decide to go out for a night of clubbing.

You, as an athlete and human being, and those who are with you at the time, CAN, unknowingly or not, greatly contribute to an escalated and potentially dangerous or violent situation while clubbing!

My POPS™ tips and techniques will help you avoid possible escalated problems, and I'll tell you how saying just two simple words, repeatedly, could possibly save your life.

Shots Fired

During the early morning hours on January 19, 2009, in Midland, Texas, a Sul Ross State running back was shot and killed at a nightclub.

According to public police reports, the athlete died "...after he was shot multiple times in the body and the legs," just before 4:00 a.m. at the Pleasures Club, said Sgt. Lupe Bretado of the Midland Police Department. He was 23, and died at Midland Memorial Hospital.

Three people were later charged, each with one count of murder. The athlete was a star running back at Permian High School before going to Sul Ross, the *Odessa American* reported on its online edition. He rushed for 909 yards on 152 carries and scored 10 touchdowns in his first season with the Lobos, making the American Southwest All-Conference team.

Athletes at all levels — high school, college and the professional ranks — are perpetuating or finding themselves victims of troubling circumstances and violence at an increasingly alarming rate.

What makes this even more upsetting is that when most people hear that an athlete was shot in the wee hours after a party, they don't wonder about his race.

Most don't want to admit that, for the most part, we are talking about African-American athletes.

The logical question is why this continues at such a startling rate — and what can be done to curtail it. The next question is why African-American athletes find themselves disproportionately involved in trouble and violence. I'm not looking to blame the victim, I just think that this issue needs to be explored, discussed and addressed head-on. Athletes of all races at some point in their careers go out and have a good time. On the face of things, there's nothing wrong with that. Should it be that different from a factory worker wanting to blow off some steam on a Friday or Saturday night?

Unfortunately, under the surface, there exists a culture that glorifies violence and danger in many of the venues that these athletes choose. "Chillin'" with your "homies" from your old neighborhood that might have ties to the street game is alluring and dangerous — and may seem to help these athletes maintain their "street credibility" off the field and court. Athletes often quickly find themselves in a tense environment — competing for women and becoming a potential target for others trying to prove something.

After a few drinks, words are exchanged, tempers may flare, punches get thrown and weapons are brought into the mix.

Adding to the situation is that African-Americans typically socialize in environments that blur economic or class lines. A number of African-Americas are the first members of their families to graduate from college or land an attractive career. By leaving the neighborhood, they may return to face a certain stigma, or feel the need to overcompensate to "fit in" with their old friends.

What are the choices? To run the risk of having their ethnicity challenged because they went off to school? This accomplishment may cause them to be perceived as "too good" to hang out with the very people they grew up with — some of whom have taken markedly different directions with their lives.

Unfortunately, athletes and scholars we send off to school often find themselves without a support system when they return home. This is one of the first places that we, as a society, fall short. Millions of words have been written about the challenges African-Americans face when they excel at something, but it's time to do more than write about it. When we don't support them, an atmosphere ripe for trouble and violence grows.

Athletes bear the brunt of this because they are more exposed, more celebrated and often targeted in our society.

While the questions around why this continues are simple, the answers are not. It's a complex issue that will not go away without some serious dialogue. It's time to start asking questions more loudly, forcing our communities to ensure that more African-American athletes are given room to succeed without the threat of violence, murder and devastation.

Responsibility

"You can avoid your responsibilities, but you can't avoid the consequences of avoiding your responsibilities."
– Famous moral axiom

If someone has been drinking at a club, bar, or party, DO NOT look at them funny, DO NOT stare them down, DO NOT talk to their lady or look her up and down in an exaggerated manner, DO NOT contribute in any way, shape, or form, to a situation which might cause a dude to act a fool toward you…or you toward him, or others.

I'll later show you how POPS™ can help you keep your emotions in check.

Tragic Circumstance

A Jacksonville Jaguars offensive tackle was shot and critically wounded outside an apartment building in September 2008, as he and a former teammate waited for two women they had met earlier at a nightclub, police said.

The athlete, then 26, and his friend were waiting in a Cadillac Escalade when a gunman fired into the vehicle, said Jacksonville Sheriff's Office spokesman Ken Jefferson. The athlete was shot several times, but it wasn't clear where he was hit. The shooting happened around 2:45 a.m. in a middle to upper-class neighborhood just west of downtown Jacksonville. The players had gone to the apartment complex so the women could drop off their car, authorities said.

A 6'-7", 345-pound linemen, he was the third NFL player to be shot in the past 18 months. A Washington Redskins star safety was fatally shot during what police said was a botched burglary attempt at his Miami-area home in November. A Denver Broncos cornerback was killed when his rented limousine was sprayed with bullets minutes after leaving a New Year's party at a club in 2007.

The Jacksonville Jaguar athlete is now paralyzed below the waist, and one leg had to be amputated. Doctors said he suffered fourteen bullet wounds to the back, left groin, left leg, and right buttock.

In addition, a bullet severed his spinal cord, causing the paralysis.

The amputation was the result of damage to his left leg and groin, where blood clots formed.

Five bullets alone were removed from his urinary bladder and the athlete also had bouts of pneumonia, infections and renal failure. He has undergone physical therapy to learn how to move from his bed to a wheelchair.

He will never walk again, a doctor said.

"He has extreme grief for a lifetime of dreams he won't be able to fulfill," his agent told reporters.

Professional and college athletes being victimized by violent crime — or perpetrating it — is becoming a major social issue. In many ways, this has become a lifestyle issue. The lines are no longer clear — the above-mentioned Jaguar athlete was shot in a nice neighborhood. He and a former teammate had been at a club (presumably a nice one) and were returning to the home of two women they met while they were out.

It's a delicate issue. Obviously, the person or people who pulled the trigger are the criminals here, and the Jaguar athlete is the victim. But athletes are finding there's a pattern to a lot of the trouble.

These athletes are seemingly being targeted at nightclubs. Is the atmosphere at clubs, bars and parties so charged that any small slight or suggestive look can result in attempted murder? I say yes. There doesn't always have to be a reason, and the problem isn't limited to high-profile athletes. Does this have the potential to turn pro athletes into hermits? Will it ramp up the idea that every athlete needs an armed 'posse' to match the equally armed bad guys doing the targeting?

Every sports league runs rookie seminars that go over possible scenarios. Clearly, young professional athletes should be able to go out for dinner and a few drinks wherever they want. But it's just as clear that alcohol, egos, a sense of entitlement, women, poor judgment, and late nights/early mornings fuse to create a highly combustible compound.

One thing, and maybe only one, is for sure: this is no longer just an image problem for a team or a league. This is a problem that is drifting perilously close to becoming a crisis, if it hasn't already reached that point. And, it's time to focus on how it affects the young men involved, and give them the opportunity of a plan, before, during, and after clubbing.

I hope you're reading this and thinking, *You know, maybe I shouldn't go out to the clubs.*

There's always going to be someone who is jealous, crazy or mentally off-balance, and if you get into altercations, anything can and will happen. But if clubbing you must — club responsibly, and take POPS™ with you.

If you're making millions of dollars with your body, you better take care of it and do your best not to put it in harm's way. You can still have fun — just don't go places where you know drunk, rowdy people will be around competing for women and attention.

If you are truly concerned about becoming a target, as well you should being a public figure and celebrity, I'm all for you being aware of that potential threat. But, if you think you're a target, and you're trying to avoid being a target, then please don't go to a place where you might become *target practice*.

Let's be honest, a nightclub, for example, is the last place an athlete should go to **A-V-O-I-D** being a target.

> *"Character is made by many acts; it may be lost by a single one."*
> – Unknown

A Cleveland Browns wide receiver was charged with killing a pedestrian while driving drunk after a night out at a swank South Beach nightclub on April 1, 2009, in Miami. An arrest warrant charging him, age twenty-eight, with DUI manslaughter was filed in the March 14, 2009 accident that killed a fifty-nine-year-old man.

The athlete's blood-alcohol level after the crash was .126, well above Florida's legal limit of .08, according to results of a blood test. It was later determined he also had marijuana in his system at the time of the accident. He was also charged with DUI, which carries a possible six-month sentence, plus fines and community service for first offenders.

"Whenever a deadly accident occurs and a driver is impaired, families suffer," Miami-Dade State Attorney Katherine Fernandez Rundle said in a statement. **"I can only repeat this message over and over: if you are going to drink, don't drive."**

An additional police affidavit filed Wednesday said that on the morning of the crash, the athlete was drinking at a nightclub in a posh hotel on South Beach. The athlete later agreed to plead guilty to a DUI manslaughter charge, and also reached a financial settlement with the deceased man's family to avoid a potential lawsuit.

The athlete served twenty-four days of a thirty-day jail sentence. Shortly after his guilty plea, he was suspended indefinitely, without pay, by NFL Commissioner, Roger Goodell.

Through excerpts of a letter released by the NFL to the media, Goodell wrote: "The conduct reflected in your guilty plea resulted in the tragic loss of life and was inexcusable. While the criminal justice system has determined the legal consequences of this incident, it is my responsibility as NFL commissioner to determine appropriate league discipline for your actions, which have caused irreparable harm to the victim and his family, your club, your fellow players and the NFL."

The athlete is currently attempting to revive his career, making the best of a second chance by signing a one-year contract with the Baltimore Ravens.

A Big Gun Story You Probably Heard About

Guns are NOT your Friend!

A Miami Dolphins linebacker defends athletes' need for guns…

In an interview that was aired on *ESPN First Take* in 2008, the Dolphins linebacker said some NFL players feel the need to have a firearm to defend themselves and their families.

"Everybody has their mistakes, but that's exactly what they are….Until you've been in that situation, when you've been robbed at gunpoint, or you've had a gun waved in your face, or had your house broken into before, or been carjacked, you really don't know what it's like," he told the show's host.

A well known former New York Giant wide receiver was injured in the early morning hours of November 29, 2008, in a nightclub in Manhattan, when a .40-caliber Glock he was carrying in his jeans slipped down his leg. As he grabbed at it, he accidentally pulled the trigger and shot himself in the thigh.

The Giants suspended the athlete for the final four games of the regular season and placed him on the non-football injury list. He was released by the team in April 2009.

The Dolphin linebacker had his own scare on Aug. 30, 2003, when he was with the Pittsburgh Steelers. He decided to fly out to see Colorado State, his Alma-mater, face Colorado. Afterward, he went to a Denver bar with some friends and, while standing in a parking lot with about 150 other people, got caught in the middle of a shooting. Denver police said the athlete was an innocent bystander, and that the shooting, which left one dead and five others wounded, was possibly gang related. The athlete was struck in the buttocks by a .9 mm bullet, which lodged in his right thigh.

"When you get out of a situation like that, and you've been in harm's way, the first thing that goes through your mind is, I'd rather get caught and take the little penalty from the media, whatever the situation may be, than not have a chance to save my life," he later told a reporter. "It's tough out there, so I'm not gonna say I condone what happened. It was a mistake being there."

The Dolphin linebacker said he does not have a bodyguard, but acknowledged that he owns a firearm, and has a permit to carry a concealed weapon in California, but not in Florida. "I'm not saying I'm walking down the street with a handgun on my hip," he said. "I'm not doing it for show. It's not fun. Hopefully, in my lifetime, I never have to use it."

NFL Commissioner Roger Goodell, who discussed the situation, said the NFL has a strict gun policy but also must manage it against the constitutional right to bear arms. "The real issue to me, is when the players feel they're unsafe, they shouldn't be there," Goodell told reporters.

"So get out, don't be there. If you feel the need to have a firearm to be some place, you're in the wrong place."

No one is suggesting that athletes become prisoners in their homes and avoid the public. Young men like to go to clubs to relax, but they have to be smart about it.

A loaded gun in a public place is never the answer.

As a world-renowned scholar and purveyor of human behavior, USC Sociology professor Todd Boyd, has clearly come to recognize all distinctions.

"For me, part of this controversy lies in the ignored reality that there lies a twisted push for gun rights all across this country," Boyd told a reporter. "Right after the Obama election, all you heard about were all the people who were going out buying weapons in anticipation of amended gun laws. I'm not defending athletes, but people still want to signal out and separate athletes — particularly black athletes — when they're involved in these kinds of incidents when the reality is there's a huge gun culture that exists within our entire population."

ATHLETE CAREER KILLERS

NFL Athletes and Others Share Thoughts on Guns
2008

"We're not like Joe or Sally. We definitely have a big red target on our backs. They know our salaries. You can go on web sites and find our salaries. I just never go anywhere alone. I just try to be with people who I know are thinking security first."

* * *

"My message is… 'If you have to go somewhere where you feel you've got to carry a handgun, you don't need to be going to that spot. Let us help you go somewhere else.' …We had a little, let me say, dip in the thing or a blip on the radar there for a bit (spoken by an NFL head coach), but I just wanted to remind the guys to keep doing things as pros and be smart, and understand, don't take your life, your career and other things at risk."

* * *

"It's real. People are allowed to carry guns, it's in the Constitution. So people want to protect themselves. But you've got to do it legally."

* * *

"The whole country has a problem. No education on them, and people can buy them anywhere now, off the street, and don't have to have a license or anything. I think when it's done the right way, and you know about it, and you register it, then it's okay. But you get guns in the wrong people's hands, it's a problem."

* * *

A Houston Texans director of security said, "We discourage guys from having guns, but if they choose to own guns, handguns, we just make sure they get the proper training, that they're licensed so they're carrying it legally. We also have (Houston police) officers come in and talk to the guys about gun safety, and just gun awareness. Make sure that they know that most of the time, having a gun in a situation just escalates the situation, where not having a gun might not lead to a drastic outcome."

* * *

"I've just never been in a circumstance where I've felt that (lack of security). It's never happened to me or my family. But you know people know where you live or where you're gonna be. If someone wants to get to you, they can. That's when you start feeling a little scared."

* * *

One player commented on why NFL players carry guns, "Why not? Everybody else is. It's all right to have possession to protect ourselves. We're a high target. We have plenty of people who point us out. They know where we live. They know exactly when we're gone. They know exactly what our schedule is. They know exactly what we make because it's printed out every year. We are a target. Our whole business, our personal life and professional life, is always out there in the media. So why not?"

* * *

"Unfortunately, the NFL is a microcosm of society, so, of course, there are going to be some guys out there who are into guns and into the extremes just because it is maybe looked at as being cool. That's the unfortunate part of it. With maturity that changes, but you're talking about twenty to twenty-one year-old guys who come into this league."

* * *

A wide receiver told the story that when he was nine years old, his older brother was shot and ended up a paraplegic. He stated, "It's heavy on my heart that an athlete has to feel that uncomfortable to carry a weapon with him. You hate to see guys in such a silly situation."

* * *

"As an athlete, you always have extra scrutiny. To whom much is given, much is expected, so you have to understand the position you're in and carry yourself accordingly."

* * *

"If I'm going somewhere by myself, if I'm going out or something, I'm going to have security and have somebody with me. I'm not going to do it myself, but to each his own."

* * *

"You can't bring a knife to a gunfight, so sometimes you think you have to protect yourself with a gun. Me, personally, that's not something I want to do, but some guys feel that way, and not that it's right or wrong, but you've got to protect yourself. You should be able to go out and have a good time as well."

***

"Personally if I've got to carry a gun, I don't need to go out to public. It's probably a place I shouldn't be at. Playing in Pittsburgh, the way the city and fans are, I don't think we have a need for that. Always when you go out, you need to be aware of your surroundings and what not."

***

"We've got to continue to educate ourselves. We can't get bored, saying 'That's the same old message.' Sometimes it may take two or three times for the message to register. That's just life. We've got to keep reinforcing player safety. Choosing the right place to be, the right time of night, etc. We've got to realize we are part of society's rules on top of the NFL's. That keeps us in the same fish bowl."

***

"That's the no-win situation when we get attacked by someone in a club. Do we fight back, standing a chance of getting sued? Do you fight back and stand a chance of somebody looking for you after the club or the next few weeks looking for you? Or do you just take it?"

***

"Any time that you introduce a gun into any situation, that's a scary situation, no matter what it is. The scary thing is, that a lot of these guys don't understand or don't know how to use a gun. It's new to them. They think, 'Shoot first, ask questions later.'"

***

"If you're an NFL player and you go out in public or you go out on the town, you're a target. Women come up to you. Guys want to challenge you to show how tough they are. If you're going to be out there, you have to learn how to walk away from situations. Too many young players haven't learned how to do that."

Headlines Athletes Don't Want

"Avoiding a fight is a mark of honor; only fools insist on quarreling."
– Proverbs 20:3, NLT

DAVID L. BROWN

A New Orleans Saints defensive end posted $10,000 bond on May 22, 2008 in Blakely, Georgia, after his indictment on an involuntary manslaughter charge stemming from a February nightclub fight in which a woman died. The athlete himself was stabbed in the neck during the February 3 fight. He was charged by a Grand Jury that also charged another person with felony murder and killing a fetus in the shooting death of another woman at the club, who was pregnant. She died after being taken to the Southeast Alabama Medical Center in Dothan. The athlete and another person had allegedly gone to a club in Blakely, not far from the player's hometown of Colquitt, and somehow got entangled in the fight.

* * *

On June 18, 2008, an Arizona Cardinals running back was among five people arrested after a fight at a nightclub in Rocky Mount, North Carolina. Police said an off-duty officer called for assistance around 1:30 a.m. Wednesday after the fight broke out at the nightclub. The then twenty-five-year old athlete was charged with disorderly conduct.

* * *

It was determined on June 26, 2008, that a Detroit Lions' top draft pick would serve one year of probation and pay $52,000 in medical expenses after settling an assault charge stemming from a 2007 bar brawl that resulted in a patron being seriously injured, according to *The Boston Globe*.

The 6'-7" athlete and a former college teammate, were both charged with assault and battery with a dangerous weapon for their roles in the brawl. The charges against them would be dismissed if they completed the terms of their probation and stayed out of trouble as part of the settlement they reached with an injured patron.

It was alleged that the athlete and his former teammate intervened in a dispute between the bar's co-owner and a patron. The co-owner, a Massachusetts State Police Sergeant, wanted the patron and his friends to move so the athlete and a group of his teammates could sit down.

According to *The Globe*, the patron, a software engineer, testified during a preliminary hearing that the athlete grabbed him in a two-arm choke hold and dragged him across the bar's dance floor while two other athletes repeatedly punched him. The patron also testified that he and the athlete crashed into a table and that he lapsed in and out of consciousness while the athlete and another person kicked him. The patron suffered a broken neck and other injuries, according to the report.

ATHLETE CAREER KILLERS

NFL Commissioner Speaks
June 25, 2007
PALM BEACH GARDENS, Fla.

After Commissioner Roger Goodell spoke to rookies for about ten minutes about making good decisions, a Washington Redskins rookie quarterback asked an innocent yet telling question: "What exactly can we do?"

The simple answer: Think. But in the complex world of the NFL, where instant money meets youth in an environment that mixes sports and corporate life, asking people to think isn't always easy.

"This is about the decisions they are going to have to make, and this is a big transition from college," Goodell told a reporter. "I think we're providing some tools for them, but the big focus for us is how do we expand this? How do we make it better? We want to continually promote these messages and help the players make good choices.

"I'd be naïve to think that everyone is going to understand this and that we're not going to have any discipline matters going forward. But again, I think we are making the players more aware of the standards of behavior and, secondly, we're giving them more tools and resources to make better decisions. Hopefully, that's going to have a great impact."

"The man means business," said a New England Patriots safety to a reporter, and former University of Miami standout, who was involved in a shooting before his final college season, and involved in a brawl during that campaign. "If you get in trouble now, it's because you don't care."

Goodell told reporters that players becoming targets was "a big issue." "We have to do everything we can to educate our players of the simple things they can do to protect themselves."

Anywhere, Anytime

No matter where professional athletes are — at home, out with friends, in their cars, in a limo — they know they could be targets. They, perhaps, have never been more uneasy about their personal safety than they are right now.

"There's no question we're targets," said a Chicago Bears tight end to a reporter. "We're high-profile people. They want what you have, and they're willing to do whatever they have to do to get it."

One NBA forward told a reporter, "You always want to feel like you're safe, but that doesn't seem to be the case anymore. If these things keep happening like they're happening, you'd be a fool not to take necessary measures to protect yourself and your family."

That's a point each professional sports league has been making for years, be it at annual rookie symposiums or in constant updates from league and team security personnel throughout the season.

Robert Gadson, head of security for the NBA Player's Association, sent a memo to all NBA players, urging them to review their security procedures and scrutinize everything from the height of the bushes in front of their homes to the people with whom they surround themselves to the type of home security system they have.

"Our players, their work schedule is public knowledge, the amount of money they make is public knowledge, they're easily recognizable and they're rich," said Gadson, who spent 23 years as a New York police detective. Even if athletes aren't targeted more often than the average man on the street, extra security might provide a sense of calm for them.

After all, we live in an internet driven society. All sorts of personal information — someone's phone number, address, or even a satellite image of an athlete's house — can be found on the Web. And once your salary increases, so does the anxiety.

A two-time Super Bowl winning quarterback's public persona isn't limited to game days. Does his being a high- profile athlete give fans an invitation into his life? If there's a line that shouldn't be crossed, where is it? With no easy answers, this high profile QB is one of a growing number of athletes who uses bodyguards when going out. He told a reporter that, much like in a collapsing pocket, you sometimes can't tell what's coming until it's too late. He spoke about the time he found himself alone, and it was scary.

He said he didn't have anybody with him, when suddenly a guy brandished a weapon in his face. The QB said he tried to keep his cool and talked his way out of it. People later showed up and helped him get rid of the guy. That's when he said he decided to have someone with him all the time.

Having a bodyguard doesn't make you weak. I'm sure 99% of the guys in the NFL and NBA could handle themselves in a fight. The issue is protecting yourself and what you have — your name, health, family, money.

An athlete might go a whole lifetime and not encounter one thing. Or you may encounter ten things in one weekend.

You never know.

Security doesn't mean a guy holding your hand as you're walking through a crowd. They're just there to keep an eye out. You have to interact with people. You have to shake hands, say hello, take pictures, sign autographs. You can't always be watching what people are doing behind you, and there's been more than one occasion when an athlete was grateful to have a security guy — or two, or even three, with him.

> **Note**: Your personal security, friends or family members whom you go clubbing with, are not there just to protect you from OTHERS -- they also need to be focused on protecting the public from YOU! Sometimes athletes go clubbing, drink, surround themselves with enablers, feel entitled, start acting a fool, and potentially place other innocent club or party goers in danger. If an incident occurs, you soon will find yourself on the front sports pages, on popular TV sports networks and the internet, defending yourself from potentially or allegedly being accused of committing a crime.

Clubbing + alcohol + drunkenness + entitlement and ego + enablers + poor judgment = the likelihood that if trouble finds you and it's clear that you played a part in initiating it, your league commissioner may have no choice but to announce..."*Mr. Athlete -- you are suspended indefinitely and without pay.*"

Don't let this be you!

Also, if you are in the field of personal security, are a friend of an athlete, or a family member, and you're holding this book in your hands right now, make a pledge to yourself and to the athlete that you will do your best to help him/her make good choices and avoid getting caught up in doing something stupid to, or with other people while clubbing. Of course, the ultimate choice of action belongs to the athlete, and him or her alone. But you can do your part to help them make good decisions while clubbing -- keeping everyone safe.

DAVID L. BROWN

Choices

"The only difference between where you are right now and where you'll be next year, at this same time, are the choices you make."
– David L. Brown

Will you take the knowledge this book offers and apply it — right now? Or will you just blow it off?

Make the right C.H.O.I.C.E. and stay safe. Know that precaution guarantees nothing.

A late Denver Bronco cornerback had a limo. He was with friends. He was trying to do the right things. And he still got targeted. Guys have to know that sometimes it doesn't matter what you do — there's always something out there that could harm you, but you should still diligently prepare yourself.

"A well-known teacher of spirituality once said that your character is the sum total of yourhabits. Your habits are the sum total of your choices. Making the right choices strengthens your good habits, while poor choices only diminish them."
– David L. Brown

I viewed a January 2009 interview done by an ESPN reporter, interviewing an infamous former Dallas Cowboy defensive back and punt returner, shortly after the athlete's release by the Dallas Cowboys.

The ESPN reporter asked the athlete why he felt the need to go to a nightclub to drink.

The athlete responded that, it was because he was an alcoholic.

I commend that athlete for admitting his alcoholism and entering himself into a program to help him conquer his repetitive demons. However, I strongly believe he had two choices on the day he decided to go to the nightclub.

One, he made the choice to go. Two, he made the choice to drink and get drunk. Now, my question is this: why did the athlete feel he had to go to a nightclub to drink? He could have made a better choice by deciding to stay home and get drunk on his living room couch, thus avoiding all the legal trouble he found himself in. Plus, police officers are not going to come to his house and arrest him for getting drunk in the privacy of his own home.

He made poor decisions that day, which will ultimately and collectively decide his professional career in the NFL.

We All Make Mistakes

Learn to allow your mistakes to sink in!

When you do this, you will come to a point where you can sense when a mistake is coming your way. For example, when practicing your jump shot in basketball practice, your coach might tell you that you're not bending your knees enough to generate power on lift-off, and you're not spreading your fingers apart wide enough on your dominant shooting hand, thus the reason your form is out of whack. But when you can "feel" that mistake yourself as soon as it happens, you're in a better frame of mind to not let it happen again. The point is, in order to avoid mistakes you have to allow yourself to feel them, openly and honestly.

Do you think your coach is going to tag along with you while you're clubbing to make sure you stay out of trouble? Nope. How about the owner of the pro team you play for? No way. Maybe the athletic director of your college team? Not a chance.

Therefore, you must be responsible for yourself — period.

The dictionary defines a mistake as "an error in action, opinion, or judgment caused by poor reasoning, carelessness, and insufficient knowledge." In other words, most mistakes are not intentional. They result from lack of training, experience, knowledge — or just plain stupidity.

I believe that every mistake is an opportunity. When an athlete makes a mistake, he should ask himself these questions:

1. What can I do to keep this from happening again?
2. What did I learn from this mistake?
3. If I don't want to make this mistake again, what do I need to change?

If you make a mistake, can you recover, redeem yourself, and rebuild your athletic career? Maybe. Our country is forgiving and open-minded to second chances. However, if you make repeated, unacceptable bad choices, any future opportunities to continue your career could be limited.

It's a privilege to play your sport, not a given.

Why put yourself, your family, your teammates, and your league through all that anguish and embarrassment? In today's sports society, it's not enough just to be good on the field and court — you have to be good off it as well.

Parenting an Athlete

> *"As a parent, I vow to instill in my children the basics of character, humility, kindness, a good attitude, giving back, helping others having their own faith and spirituality, integrity, and being their own persons to create the life they want for themselves, on and off the field and court."*
> – David L. Brown

For Dads on teaching their child athletes about character…

> *"Dads, teach them to play with courage, sportsmanship, passion, character, and work ethic. Then watch them strive to be the best, on and off the field and court."*

For Moms on teaching their child athletes about character…

> *"Moms, teach them patience, respect, integrity, responsibility, and self-confidence. Then watch them grow as a person and athlete."*

For coaches/role models on teaching character to children and players on all athletic levels…

> *"Coach, teach them discipline, purpose, focus, mental toughness, and perseverance. Then watch them shine and become good people and athletes."*

You Can Make a Difference

Throughout their career, many fine athletes who have worked hard and behaved responsibly have quietly sacrificed — in wins, playoff opportunities, possibly even Super Bowls and championships, due to the irresponsibility of teammates. They may not come out and say that publicly — so I did.

ATHLETE CAREER KILLERS

True Story, 2008, Youngstown, Ohio

On one early and sunny Saturday morning, I drove a local, high profile high school athlete to a nightclub in our area. He is currently being recruited to continue his athletic career by Ohio State, Pitt, Michigan, Penn State, and Notre Dame, among others.

Beforehand, I didn't tell him where we were going, but I did tell him I had an important point I wanted to make and that it would be up to him to choose to ignore it or consider it. We stood outside the club and chatted for a moment.

He then asked, "So, what are we doing *HERE?*"

I asked him to look closely at the building, to study it for a while. I then asked him to name five *POSITIVE* outcomes that would enhance his life and athletic career by walking through the doors of that club someday, or any other club on a Friday or Saturday night.

He thought for a moment and then smiled, at which time I asked him to exclude "hot babes" from the list, because he can mingle with attractive, professional, grounded, intelligent women at better venues than nightclubs, strip clubs and bars.

After making that exclusion, he could not name one positive thing that could enhance his life and athletic career. What he did come up with was a long list of *NEGATIVE* headline grabbing, career killing, home life destroying, personal and family heartache, that he may never be able to fully recover from.

My message to him was clear. *Do not put yourself in that position.*

Going clubbing is never — let me repeat this — going clubbing is *NEVER* going to impress the coach (who'll be the one the media hammers all season long with questions about you and your lack of good judgment if something bad happens). If trouble finds you, it won't increase your marketing and earning potential when a company may want to hire you to pitch their products.

It won't help you gain respect from teammates who may privately think you're a jerk.

It will never impress the team owner who gave you that big contract. It will never cause young kids to worship you (who later will be disappointed and stop wearing your jersey, and whose parents will then despise you). And it will never help you gain respect within your family and community.

Your legacy is essentially etched in stone and when your playing days are over. People won't remember your amazing skills and accomplishments — they'll remember the negative headlines.

Is it worth giving that all up for a few hours of fun at a club, bar, or late night party? And, by the way, if you happen to have, or some day will have, a club built into the lower level of your home — the same principles apply. Yes -- *I watch "MTV Cribs" too!*

> *"Character Durability: an athlete's ability to consistently demonstrate high character and moral conduct throughout his entire career on and off the field and court."*
> *– David L. Brown*

It's All About Respect

Winter, 2008

I took a drive to a local police department in my nearby area. My mind was on research, specifically reality versus perception. I wanted to talk to officers coming out of the building to get some insights about reasons that would cause people to act violently.

This is what I found out.

Time and again, the number one reason officers gave me was the perception of being…*DISRESPECTED*.

The Dictionary defines the word "Disrespect" this way:
1. An expression of lack of respect.
2. A disrespectful mental attitude.
3. A manner that is generally disrespectful and contemptuous.
4. Have little or no respect for or hold in contempt.

Being "dissed" may make one feel devalued as a human being. A guy at a club you encounter may "feel" like you just spit in his face, even though you didn't. It's perception we're talking about here. Perception can be a dangerous and deadly reality from another person's standpoint in regard to you and clubbing.

Being disrespectful, in my opinion, is the worst attitude an athlete can have. It is your enemy when dealing with people at clubs, bars, and parties. If you want trouble with another dude, just have him "perceive" that you're dissing him and see how quickly stuff can happen.

I commend our athletes. Most mind their own business when they go out and don't look for trouble but, unfortunately, things do happen sometimes.

ATHLETE CAREER KILLERS

Did you know #1:

A recent police study on guns concluded that officers who waited longer between practicing their shooting skills were found to be much slower in their reaction time when drawing their weapon in the real world. The study revealed it generally takes a longer time to react to a situation, and then draw the gun.

Even if you carry a gun and can quickly draw it, your accuracy may be minimal.

A gun can easily get tangled up in your clothing and then…*pop, pop, pop* — you could be dead. So make the right choice, use common sense, and don't carry.

Did you know #2:

During research with the local police, I also asked them:

Where's the best place on a person's body to take a bullet if they had to? The leg? No. Head? Certainly not. Buttocks? Surprisingly, no. Abdomen? No. Chest. No way. Neck? Are you kidding? Shoulder? No, too close to the neck. Back? No…a bullet can pierce through your back, travel from back to front, and damage vital organs along the way.

Answer: The arm. Why? Because there are no vital organs nearby to cause sudden life-threatening damage.

Okay, so you get the message of this book, right? Now what?

Number one, be a steward of good character and use common sense everywhere you go. Be prepared for anything, but don't put yourself in situations that could be potentially dangerous or deadly.

Like in sports, you arrive at camp and work on fundamentals of the game, honing your skills along the way. Your personal safety fundamentals should be honed with the same attitude.

Continue to treat others with respect. Surround yourself with good energy and positive people.

I want to help make clubbing safe for you, your friends, and your family; before, during, and after.

If Clubbing You Must — Club Responsibly.™

It's time to make a plan. A clubbing plan. A plan of action. Action that you MUST take to make your life safer.

Gain back your peace of mind and confidence. Make good decisions — consistently.

As an athlete, you're physical. It's been that way practically your entire life. Your physicality on the field and court personifies who you are and what you do. It's almost a part of your DNA. Without it, you would not be the athlete you are. The point is, it's very difficult sometimes to turn that off when the game is over.

That physical nature you have come to depend on generally stays with you away from the game. It is what it is. That being said, it can be used against you, and you can contribute to it being used against you, but you have a choice to allow it to happen or not.

There are two main ways to get negative headlines off the field and court.

One, you act a fool. Two, the other person acts a fool.

It doesn't matter if you're an All-Pro, future Hall of Famer, just won the Super Bowl, an NBA title, college championship, or whether you're an obscure athlete on the practice squad, sitting at the end of the bench in basketball, a college All-American, or a walk-on.

If you make a poor decision, it will generate significant media attention for you, your family, your teammates, your coaches — the entire organization.

It's one of the worst trickle-down effects in sport. It starts with you, and the choices you make.

Introducing POPS™

What They Are and How They Could Save Your Life

PO'd Points™ (POPS) are the understated silent club killer.

I want to begin by informing you I believe a PO'd Point (POP) is very different from anger. A POP is calm, sneaky, calculated, and thought out. It's usually acted upon over a period of time, rather than the immediate angry outburst we're accustomed to hearing about. A person who encounters an athlete at a club and exhibits a POP may feel inferior in some way to the athlete. He may perceive an athlete as "bigger than life."

To bring that athlete down to his personal "comfort zone," he may pull a gun, a knife, or confront you in order to, in his mind, "humanize" you as an athlete.

POPS™ are silent killing cousins to anger. The dictionary defines anger as: A strong passion or emotion of displeasure or antagonism, excited by a real or supposed injury or insult to one's self or others, or by the intent to do such injury.

We all know there are varying degrees of anger. The first definition is extremely important, and one that every athlete should be aware of. Let me repeat a key point, then expand on how it could contribute to being a life or death situation for you.

"A strong passion or emotion of displeasure or antagonism, excited by a *REAL OR SUPPOSED* injury to one's self or others, or by the intent to do such injury."

Recall the information I spoke on earlier about the definition of disrespect, or being "dissed." Disrespect and PO'd Points™ are definitely related, yet keenly different. Most of us can easily tell when someone is externally ANGRY. Anger generally accompanies telltale body language, screaming, yelling, flailing arms, obscenities, etc.

You basically know when someone is angry. But PO'd Points™ often start internally.

They can be sneaky, and a person doesn't even have to show any facial expression or body language to indicate they're PO'd. Even a simple smirk on someone's face is no indication, but you should pay attention to it.

A person doesn't have to look "PO'd" in order to feel that way based on their own internal "perception," real or imagined, of being disrespected in some way.

PO'd Points™ can be every bit as dangerous as any level of anger. I think people sometimes assume that a person has to be clearly physically angry in order to cause them to act violently. Not true. A person could very well shoot you because they're simply "PO'd" in a calm way. You never know what a person's anger threshold is. You don't know what little thing could push them over the edge.

My tips and techniques will educate you on general "tendencies" of people at clubs, bars, parties, or anywhere else. I'll also educate you on how to recognize them, avoid them, and stay safe.

POPS™ are all about consistent awareness and using common sense. Protecting yourself and staying safe starts with your mind, first and foremost.

The same way you prepare for the next game should be the same way you prepare yourself and your friends BEFORE you go clubbing. It's important not to become complacent with your awareness and your security plan while clubbing.

You must use my tips and techniques on a consistent basis for success.

Think about how any given situation may apply to you, or someone you know, like a teammate, friend or family member.

What personal social and lifestyle challenges are you currently facing?

If you're looking for **solutions** -- keep reading.

Before Clubbing

*"It's not always easy to do the right thing, but do it anyway.
It could save your life and athletic career."*
– David L. Brown

1. Have the right attitude. Just as you put on your "game face," put on your "club face." When your buddy calls and wants you to go clubbing with him, make sure he understands that you have a "game plan" for the evening to keep everybody safe — just in case. Explain your clubbing safety plan in detail to everyone you know will be with you. Make sure they take it seriously.
2. Understand the moment you step outside your home, you're an instant public figure and a potential target.
3. Leave your best bling at home. Go clubbing in a minimal amount of jewelry you can afford to lose, to avoid standing out. The same with your vehicle. The less bling your vehicle has, like lavish custom rims for example, the better.
4. Inform at least two to three other friends or family where you're going in case you need a ride afterward, or your vehicle is blocked, or some fool decides to mess with you. Make sure they have your cell phone number. If you can't reach them in person, leave a voice mail.
5. Know who your friends and family members are friends with. Don't be afraid to ask them who their friends are if you don't know them and have never met them, or maybe met them briefly once or twice. Will they be meeting you at the club later? Will they come by your house and later leave with you and your other friends? Will they bring other people with them you may or may not know?
6. Invite friends and family strong enough to tell you…*NO!* You're an athlete, maybe a high-profile athlete. You may have gotten used to having your way without anyone in your inner private circle questioning your decisions. Take those who will tell you you've had too much to drink, and WILL take your keys

from you, or who will gladly intervene if they see you about to make a foolish mistake, like leading an obviously intoxicated female to a private area, etc. It could save your life and athletic career. You want to surround yourself with people who truly care for you, not enablers. What's an enabler? One who enables an athlete to persist in self-destructive behavior by providing excuses, or by helping him avoid the consequences of his/her behavior.

7. Call each club you may attend in advance, or have your security or a friend do this for you. Ask the owner or manager if there is a section for VIPs, and where it's located — ground floor, top floor, front of the building, back of the building? Ask in advance if there is a side or back door where *"celebrities"* can enter and exit. Yes, athletes are celebrities.

8. Guns. Don't carry them with you! But if you absolutely feel you must, be legal, licensed, and properly trained to use it. Carrying a loaded weapon can cause more potential harm than it can keep you safe. A loaded weapon can cause an already escalated situation to quickly get out of control and become deadly.

9. Let your security person carry a gun if you feel the need. Make sure your security people are also licensed and properly trained. I highly recommend clubbing with at least *TWO* professionally trained security people. It's not enough just to have a bodyguard, you have to have a plan. Even though you may have security with you, your number one protector is…YOU! Don't slack on yourself and let your guard down for a moment!

10. Consider purchasing an armored vehicle that you keep at home at all times — really. Consider it an *investment*. If you're going clubbing with a group of people, make arrangements ahead of time to travel to and from the club in an armored limousine, car or SUV. If the *President of the United States* rides in one, you should too. You're not the President, but you are the president of your own life and athletic career.

11. Know beforehand what routes you're taking to the club AND back home. Take the quickest one available, and make sure they're different. Huddle with your security team, friends and family beforehand, to make sure everyone is on the same page.

12. Inside your house. Before you walk out the door, spend a few moments gazing around the house and remember how things are situated and located. For example, is your master bedroom door open or closed when you leave? Is the light on

or off in the kitchen? Is the light on or off in the front entryway? Taking a mental photo of how your house looks inside as you walk out the door will be important for when you return home. Also, if you had friends over earlier, or someone was working on the house inside or out, make sure all the windows are locked. It's easy for someone to unlatch a window and return later. Living in a gated community complete with security cameras, so that every face entering the grounds can be identified, is also strongly recommended, but is not 100% foolproof.

13. Outside the house. Will you be leaving a front patio/porch light on? Is the back yard well lit? If you have kids and it's summer, are their bikes still in the yard? If it's a snowy winter day, take time to view your own tire tracks and footprints as you pull out of your driveway, whether you're backing out or not. Are yours the only set of tracks and prints when you leave? Maybe friends or family stopped by earlier…that's fine, just know that. Make sure you close the garage door and remember you closed it. Make sure the side garage door is also locked. It's all about awareness and common sense.

14. Outside perimeter. Check or have your security people thoroughly check the perimeter of your home. Some fool could be waiting in the shrubs for you to leave. Don't just focus on the ground level…look up into the trees, on the roof, and check the other side of perimeter fences, if you have them.

15. Make sure you activate your home alarm system before you walk out the door! I suggest purchasing a remote home alarm system that is NOT connected to your regular home electric system. If your electric is cut off by an intruder, your remote alarm system will still work and alert police of potential danger.

16. Carry only one credit card to pay for food, tips, or other items. Keep things simple. Carry a small amount of money with you because you don't want to be seen pulling out a large wad of cash, which could draw unwanted attention and increase your chances of becoming a target. Leave the house a little earlier than you normally would. You don't want to be predictable in your routine.

17. Once you walk out the door and enter your vehicle, make sure you lock the house doors behind you. Don't speed off in a hurry to get to the club. Drive slowly while leaving your neighborhood. Be keenly aware of who is on the streets and what their demeanor may be. Notice who may be walking on foot and if they're intentionally trying to avoid being noticed in any way. Notice cars parked on the street near your home that you may not recognize.

18. Drive through your neighborhood. Stop a couple of blocks away, wait ten minutes, then backtrack to your house as if you forgot something. Again, be aware who's walking on the streets or vehicles you have never seen before. Do not pull into your driveway, just slowly drive by. If your intuition tells you all is fine, then carry on and proceed to your club destination…safely. If anything seems suspicious, call the police. Be observant, but don't try to take matters into your own hands.

19. On your way to the club, realize that many people who will also attend have been drinking alcohol and/or doing drugs long BEFORE they arrive. So, before they even get there, they're likely already intoxicated, high, or both.

20. Consider the construction of the building you'll be attending, especially if it's more than one story high. Is the building new? Old? Is it structurally sound? How do you know? If you knew a bridge was in poor condition, would you drive over it? I bet you wouldn't, and neither would I. No one ever thought the Dallas Cowboys indoor dome-like practice facility would collapse on Saturday, May 2, 2009, seriously injuring a special teams coach, leaving a team scout paralyzed for life, and causing serious injuries to others. Anything can happen — anytime — anywhere, bad weather or not, which was determined to be the culprit of that collapse, in part due to severe high winds. Be the athlete who's prepared for anything.

21. Don't forget to buckle up on your way clubbing, or you may get pulled over and ticketed for not wearing a seat belt. Most states now have seat belt laws, so buckle up!

22. Don't drink alcohol before you go clubbing and then get in a vehicle and drive to a club, party, or bar. If you do, you are asking for trouble — and it will find you. There is no acceptable level of alcohol consumption that makes it safe to drive — *ever*.

23. The bad guys don't always need guns to do damage in your life. Your social security number or a pre-approved credit card application from your trash, could be all they need. Be extra careful with your personal information in your home, and when you're away. Identity theft is the nation's fastest growing crime according to recent FBI statistics, and identity theft/fraud is the fastest growing category of *Federal Trade Commission* (FTC) complaints. Don't be the next victim — protect yourself.

24. Think of your personal safety as preventive maintenance. You work out during the off-season. You train and stay in shape so you can avoid wear and tear on your body and to hopefully reduce injuries during the season. POPS™ is the same way — you have to train your mind, change any bad habits, and prepare yourself each and every time you're in the public's eye.
25. For more information on purchasing an armored vehicle:
    http://www.iacarmormax.com
    http://www.armoredcars.com
    http://www.armoured-vehicles.com
    http://www.bukkehave.com

While Clubbing

> *"One of life's most painful moments comes when we must admit that we didn't do our homework, that we are not prepared."*
> – The late Merlin Olsen, former NFL great

1. Check your ego and potential sense of entitlement at the door.
2. When you go clubbing, you're NOT attending a club full of your peers, meaning other athletes. The majority of the folks that attend are everyday people, working everyday jobs, with everyday problems and issues. Expect somebody to eventually act a fool when you go clubbing — just have your POPS™ plan ready when it happens. And also have it handy just in case YOU are tempted to act a fool, or are provoked in doing so in any way. POPS™ will serve as a timely deterrent in those and other circumstances.
3. Don't be fooled or seduced by a club located in a nice neighborhood or area. Bad things can still happen. Don't assume you're totally safe in the V.I.P. section either. You still always have to be aware of potential danger and not let your guard down.
4. The parking lot. Just like when you go to the mall or store, you exit your vehicle, take a few steps, then intuitively turn around to take a mental photo of where your car is parked. The same principle applies when clubbing. Remember where your car is parked.

5. Valet parking. Ask the valet attendant the location he/she will be parking your vehicle. Take the time and wait for them to park it, and take a mental photo of where it's located. It wouldn't hurt to get the valet's name also.

6. You want your security people to conduct themselves like the security people you see on the sidelines at your games. You know, the folks wearing the bright color college or pro security shirts or vests, who face the stands the whole game? Even if there's a last-second touchdown, or a shot to win the game, they are trained to NOT turn and watch the action. Their job is to watch the crowd in the stands at all times. Your security people should have the same focus. Their job is to watch the crowd in the parking lot, inside the club, and when leaving the club. Their job is NOT to dance, drink, and party with everybody else. Their job is to protect YOU — period.

7. Inside the club, always maintain a positive attitude and be nice. It sounds simple, but you'll be amazed how positive the results will be. People will tend to mess with you if you come off arrogant and disrespectful. Confidence is a deterrent.

8. You're a celebrity — and to a degree, an entertainer. Give each person you happen to encounter a quick moment of your highest energy level. When approached for autographs and hellos, look them in the eye, smile, shake hands, and *quickly be on your way.*

9. Statistics show, as the night wears on, the chances of an escalated incident increases dramatically. Do not leave when the club or bar closes! Make it a part of your safety plan to leave well before closing, at least two-hours.

10. The two words I mentioned earlier that could save your life when encountering someone, are…"I'm sorry," or "I apologize," "My bad," "My fault" — however you want to say it. This is an important part of your POPS "club etiquette" safety plan. As simple as it may sound, take this seriously. You want to avoid a potential problem, not ignite one.

11. Athletes can use my techniques to dramatically minimize your role and contribution in a potentially dangerous situation. For example, if you encounter someone who's been drinking and you happen to bump into him/her on the dance floor by accident, or they accidentally bump into you, if they seem agitated, tell them immediately — *"I'm sorry."* DO NOT wait for them to do this. You take the initiative! Be the bigger person. Sometimes you have to swallow your pride to stay alive.™

12. You want to say *"I'm sorry"* at least *SIX TIMES* — repeatedly. Why? Because when a person is in the early stages of POPS, drinking, annoyed, and maybe incoherent, he won't likely hear you say it the first three times because he might be too busy running his mouth talking junk back at you. You have to say it at least six times in order for him to truly listen. Be sincere when you say it. You could say something like, *"I'm sorry, man, my bad."* or *"I apologize, my fault."* Let him know you're cool with things, and wait for confirmation that he is too, then *quickly* walk away, or move to another part of the dance floor. You may not see him as a threat to YOU — but he might see you as a threat to HIM.
13. If someone recognizes you're an athlete, give him an autograph ONLY if he requests one, take a quick photo ONLY on request. Do it QUICKLY and be on your way! Do not linger for half-an-hour talking about last night's game. Your focus is to stay safe. As an athlete, you easily recognize momentum changes in a game. The ebb and flow of a guy's POPS, who's been drinking, can be difficult to quickly recognize — unless you use my success system and techniques. You are never going to know 100% what someone is going to do and when. You can't get into their minds to see how they tick. But you CAN equip and prepare yourself for the worst.
14. Don't be confused about the difference between being a random, or non-random target. Realize that you CAN, unknowingly or not, contribute to someone acting a fool toward you. Do not allow yourself to get into a verbal battle with anyone. Don't talk back to people, glare at them in a disrespectful manner, or make any perceived negative gestures. It's not worth it, and can escalate very quickly. Always treat people with respect, even though they may not return the courtesy.
15. Alcohol and clubbing. Less is better. None is best™. Use common sense and set boundaries. Don't even think about driving if you've been drinking!
16. Women and clubs. The ladies can definitely be a potential distraction to your clubbing safety plan -- if you allow yourself to lose focus. Treat women you meet with respect at all times. **After all, *she's someone's daughter — possibly a young child's mother.*** Ask yourself what your true plan is for the evening. Are you going clubbing to meet women, or are you going with your girlfriend, wife, or significant other? Maybe you just want to relax and have a good time with your buddies without hassles or drama? Know your reasons, and be honest. If you go clubbing with the intent to meet and leave with a woman, be certain she didn't

come with her man. He could show up later unexpectedly, or another man could become interested in her too. Testosterone and alcohol can be dangerous and deadly when mixed with competition for women at clubs, bars, and parties. What might be her motive for hooking up with you? Is it the lure and excitement of meeting, then possibly leaving with a high profile pro or college athlete? Is she looking for a long-term relationship? A possible financial windfall? A short-term fling? A one-night rendezvous? Don't forget to consider sexually transmitted diseases and AIDS. Have a smart safety plan for **sex**, if that's your intent. Be responsible. Protect yourself — and her.

17. Leaving the club. When you are ready to leave, before closing, position yourself in the middle of your two security people. Why? They will provide a shield for you. Walk through and out of the building at a preferable distance of at least three feet between you and them, back to front. If anyone tries to get to you for a last minute autograph or some fool wants to act crazy, you'll be insulated between two big bodies. Don't slack on positioning and distance. Just like in a game, if you're not in the right position, it's difficult to execute the offense and defense. Try to leave as quietly and unnoticed as possible. This includes your friends or family. You don't want to draw unnecessary attention to yourself by being loud.

18. Make sure all friends or family are accounted for. If they decide to stay, be aware of it, and find out how they'll get back home if they initially got a ride from you. Make arrangements to have someone else pick them up, if needed. You don't want to back track to the club later to pick anyone up, if you can help it. That's too risky.

19. Make sure not to leave your cell phone, Blackberry, or anything else at the club important enough to have to go back for — especially anything that would contain personal contact information, like addresses and phone numbers.

20. While at clubs, bars, and parties, don't accept a drink from anyone except a bartender, and observe the drink being mixed. Don't leave your drink unattended or share drinks, because someone might slip a drug into it that will make you unconscious or sick, and vulnerable to assault. If you are in doubt about a drink, get a new one, or better yet -- just don't drink at all.

After Clubbing

> *"Only in growth, reform and change, paradoxically enough is true security to be found."*
> *– Anne Morrow Lindbergh*

1. Leaving the club. You want to always leave well BEFORE closing -- at least two hours.
2. Be aware of your surroundings when you're outside the club. Scan the area and get a quick sense of the vibe, the number of people lingering, and noise and argument levels. For example, be aware if bouncers are having trouble clearing the parking lot because of drunk people. Avoid distractions like talking and texting on your cell phone when leaving.
3. Leave quickly. Do not linger outside the club or bar talking to people, signing autographs, taking photos, etc. Remember where your vehicle is parked after taking that earlier mental photo, or get to the valet *quickly*, get in your vehicle when it arrives, put your seat belt on — and leave.
4. If a friend or family member are at home, make a quick call to let them know you're on your way there.
5. Beware if anyone is following you. Your security people and your driver should also be aware of this. Just like you depend on your teammates to do their jobs to win a game, you must also depend on and expect your security people and driver to do the same.
6. Police are aware what time clubs and bars close. Their radar is heightened between 1:00 and 3:00 a.m. Drive home at posted speed limits. Don't be drunk while driving. You will get caught... eventually. It doesn't take much to exceed most state legal limits for DUI and DWI. If you know you've been drinking after clubbing — **DON'T DRIVE!** Remember the friends you informed earlier of your evening plans? Call them to pick you up if you've been drinking, or call a cab. Both the NFL and NBA offer toll-free numbers their athletes can call to get a free ride home. Don't be afraid to take advantage of those and other services offered by your league and team. It could save your life and athletic career. My motto for athletes is, if you're drinking and driving — you're not striving.™

7. If you decide to drive **(I know you won't)**, avoid talking and texting on your cell phone, as this causes distractions and can be dangerous, whether drinking or not. Consider a "hands free" phone option.
8. Avoid club and bar hopping — going from one venue to another. Remember, the later the evening, the higher the risk factors.
9. Take the quickest route back home, but take a different route than you did on arrival.
10. If you happen to get pulled over by police for ANY reason, my advice — *chill, baby, chill!* Cooperate and be professional. If you have nothing to hide and have done nothing wrong, you should be fine. Don't allow your emotions to get the best of you in this situation. You want to get home safely, not spend the night or weekend in somebody's jail.
11. Arriving home. Home invasion involving athletes is REAL! When you're driving home, I suggest driving straight home. *I apologize if this sounds juvenile*, but if the club or bar closed at 3:00 a.m., and you left at 1:00 a.m., stopping somewhere else to have a nightcap, attend another club or party, or even stopping at a restaurant to grab a bite to eat only increases the risks. Why bother? Drunk people are also out clubbing, partying, drinking and driving, and will be frequenting restaurants and other places too. How many times have you heard or read about an altercation in a parking lot in the wee hours of the morning? I have — I've seen it.
12. When you arrive back at your neighborhood, drive slowly. Be aware of who may be on foot and what they may be doing.
13. Do not immediately pull into your driveway. Drive slowly past your home, looking intently at the outer perimeters to make sure everything is the same as you left it. Take note of outside lights you left on before leaving. Make sure they're still on. Bad guys like to unscrew light bulbs to avoid being detected. Look at windows carefully, making sure none seem broken or any screens missing or damaged. Look at doors, including garage doors, front and side. Make sure they're not ajar or damaged in any way.
14. Drive around the block again, maybe twice. If things feel good and look good, proceed to return home. If not — call the police.
15. If it's winter, notice if foot and tire prints in the driveway are the same as when you left. If it's not winter or it doesn't snow where you live, outside front and rear lights, windows and doors will be your initial check points.

16. Once inside the garage, do not immediately get out of your locked vehicle. Leave it running momentarily. (Warning: DO NOT let your vehicle run for a long period of time, to the point where a significant amount of carbon monoxide may accumulate inside your garage! This could be very dangerous -- even deadly!) Check your side and rear view mirrors quickly yet thoroughly, to ensure the garage door has safely and fully closed behind you and no one has slipped in undetected before it closes. The reason you should briefly remain in your vehicle once inside your garage, is because if you pull into your garage, turn your headlights and vehicle off, exit your vehicle and THEN close your electronic garage door, you leave yourself vulnerable and potentially exposed to an attacker who is now in the process of entering your garage before the doors close securely. Due to its mechanical nature, garage doors generally take a bit of time to fully close once opened, thus affording a bad guy who may be hiding unseen at the side of your home, plenty of time to slip inside your garage before the door closes.

Let's say a few days ago, prior to this clubbing evening, you opened your garage door, only to realize you didn't really need to. The door gets to about half-open before you hit the button again to re-close it. Even at mid-level -- it will *STILL* take some time to fully close securely! *Test your own garage doors at home.* Grab a watch or verbally count, one-thousand-one...one-thousand-two...one-thousand-three...and time how long it takes your garage doors to open, and close fully. Then test them again at various levels of open and closed. Write down the closest estimated amount of time that it takes -- *and remember it!*

Pass that information on to your loved ones at home -- it could save a life some day.

Understand that a potential attacker or home invader can crawl or roll on the ground and into your garage before the door fully closes, catching you completely by surprise. A bad guy only needs a crack of an opening to do damage in your and your family's lives. Be prepared for anything.

Here's another potential scenario. If you immediately begin the process of closing your garage door upon entering, and you fail to thoroughly survey the interior of your garage after turning your headlights and vehicle off, and have already exited your vehicle, you could become exposed to an attacker, who may have earlier broken into your garage and is now lying in wait for you to return home.

In my expert opinion, with your interior garage lights now on, I believe it's best and safer to *briefly* remain in your vehicle while it's still running, and conduct a quick, thorough *"due diligence"* check inside your garage before exiting your vehicle.

While inside the garage, your vehicle will serve as protection for you in case an attacker attempts an assault. If that's the situation you find yourself in, at least you're still *INSIDE* your vehicle and can quickly start it back up and exit the garage, or use whatever object available inside your vehicle to protect yourself from an attacker.

If you have nothing inside your vehicle for protection and you feel it's taking far too long for that doggone mechanical garage door to fully open back up again, after someone has gained entry inside your garage and is attempting to assault you, the seconds that pass may seem like hours!

Once the garage door has reopened, drive out (or back out) of the garage as quickly as you can and call 9-1-1. I've actually read about people who didn't wait for the garage door to reopen and plowed right through it in order to get to safety!

Hey – whatever it takes! Make the best safety choice for you and your family. You can always replace a garage door, but you and family members can't ever be replaced.

Why do most garage doors generally open and close so slowly anyway, you may be thinking?

One word -- *SAFETY*.

We have all heard and read about tragic stories all across the country involving children being hurt, seriously injured, or killed by unforgiving closing garage doors. These days, many garage doors come installed with infra-red beam "sensors" that can detect objects (or humans) in its path, and will immediately reverse direction and open back up.

Unfortunately, the bad guys are also well aware of this fact, and can and will, use modern garage door technology and its deficiencies against you, so be careful.

17. After conducting a quick interior check of your garage with your vehicle running, turn your engine OFF but continue surveying the interior. Leave your headlights on momentarily before exiting your vehicle (this normally won't run your battery down), in case the interior lights have timed out. But be warned, bad guys take light fixtures and bulbs out inside the garage too! Make sure the

inside entry door from the garage hasn't been tampered with. If all looks safe, turn off your headlights and proceed inside your home. If you feel something is just not right, *quickly* get back in your vehicle, lock the doors first, hit the garage door remote control button, restart your vehicle, turn your headlights back on...and leave! Hopefully, it won't take forever for that darn garage door to open back up! Once you are on the street or road, call the police right away.

18. Immediately reactivate your home alarm system once inside your home after determining all is fine in the garage.
19. The garage tips and techniques listed above can also be applied to preventing *home invasion!* See Chapter 7 for more details.
20. If you choose to own a gun, your home is the best place to keep it. If it's there, you will become empowered to use it in case an intruder enters or is already inside your house. Use common sense, and by all means protect yourself and your family if you have to. Make certain that any guns, knives, or other weapons inside your home are safely locked away in an area not accessible to youngsters and teens if you have kids.
21. Pets are great for home security. Dogs, big or small, are wonderful deterrents to home invasion. If you don't have one, consider it. A dog doesn't have to be big and mean to be effective. I used to have a miniature dachshund. On the other side of a closed door, she had the bark and growl of a much larger dog.
22. Now that you're inside the house, safe and secure, you can relax and get comfortable, right? Wrong. There's still work to be done inside your home. Keep reading for more inside the house tips later in the book. As with most things worth doing, the more you apply these tips and techniques, the better your awareness will become. The more intuitive you are, will greatly improve your confidence, help you sleep better at night, and reward you with a sense of control in your life and athletic career.
23. POPS™ are about preparation, awareness, and confidence — not fear. Being fearful means you're not prepared. Being prepared and having confidence allows you to make decisions more quickly and correctly in case of trouble. It allows you to keep your emotions at an even keel so you can think clearly and make good choices, even in the midst of a bad situation. Being nervous before, during, and after clubbing is okay. That's not being afraid. It just means you care. You don't have to live in fear. You should always be prepared. POPS is similar to

sport — the better prepared you are – the more you know – the faster you play. The better decisions you make — the more successfully you'll execute your game plan.

24. If you happen to be walking to or from a destination and you think you're being followed, cross the road and walk confidently to another busy area, shop, business, or well-lit house and call the police.

25. Carjacking is scary and potentially deadly. There have been more than a few reported incidents of carjacking and attempted carjacking involving professional athletes. It is a serious threat to your personal safety. If you are ever confronted by an armed carjacker, don't resist. Give up your keys, money, and jewelry without resistance. Don't argue, fight or chase the guy. You can be seriously injured or killed. Call the police immediately afterward. When driving in the city, make sure windows are rolled up and doors are locked, especially at stop signs and stop lights.

26. Share this book with a teammate, coach, members of your organization, and family members. College athletes can also share this book with their athletic directors. The only way you can help reduce clubbing trouble and potential violence is to continue to educate everyone involved and spread the word.

More POPS™ to Be Aware of

1. He's calm. Don't let calmness fool you. It can be dangerous.
2. He has a slight or exaggerated smirk on his face.
3. He walks away and does not immediately retaliate.
4. He's seen shortly thereafter having a discussion with his friends at the club, looking and pointing toward you.
5. He leaves the club area you're in after a short period of time without incident.
6. He's seen back in the area again, acting agitated or suspicious.
7. He continually tries to make eye contact with you. He could want you to know what's coming, but doesn't want you to know when.
8. He literally tells you he's coming back later — and does.
9. He says nothing, does nothing, then leaves, but does not come back into your immediate area. He could possibly be waiting for you somewhere, and attempt to confront you there or follow you in your vehicle when you leave.

10. He talks smack, curses at you, makes hand gestures, but is not overly agitated or angry at this point. He then leaves and is nowhere to be seen when you leave the club.
11. He damages your vehicle outside the club, then leaves. Be careful, he may not be satisfied with damaging your car, and things may escalate at some point later.
12. He doesn't say anything to you, but tells the friends you came with of his intentions.
13. He looks you in the eye from a safe distance and seems calm, without saying a word to you. This is when the POPS period is heating up. He's trying to rationalize his own perception of you disrespecting him and how he might react to it. His buddies might be egging him on to "do something about it." **Peer pressure** is strong at clubs, bars, and parties. Add alcohol, and people feel invincible and fearless. It makes them do stupid things they normally wouldn't do — or maybe they would.
14. He tries to get information from other people at the club about you and who you came with (security, how many friends, male and female, etc.), in an effort to determine who might be carrying a weapon.
15. You look in his eyes. Your gut tells you his attitude and demeanor is saying, "Okay, now I'm pissed off."
16. You may think he's smart enough NOT to mess with you in a public place with plenty of witnesses. Maybe. Maybe not. He might have a buddy confront you later that night, or at some point in the near future. If there was an incident or war of words between the two of you, maybe nothing escalated. You may have long forgotten about it after a few hours, or couple of days — but he didn't. You might be making a trip to the golf course to play a few holes and some fool steps up on you with a gun. These kinds of bad guys won't wait too long to make their move. Don't take anything for granted — just be prepared for it.
17. He's clearly been drinking and acting a fool.
18. He's clearly been drinking and *NOT* acting a fool. A mellow drunk dude can be just as dangerous.
19. He wants to be famous or known in the community for messing with you, the athlete. This is his *"fifteen minutes of fame,"* his sick legacy, and you're his target. He can't do it without YOU.

20. He's seen you at a club before, and views it as an opportunity to settle things. Maybe he just doesn't care what goes down.
21. Men generally will commit the act of shooting a gun, more so than a woman at a club. If a woman shows POPS, she'll likely have her male friend or boyfriend confront you, but beware of female POPS also! If a woman gets in your face in a club and the two of you exchange words, **I guarantee** soon after, either her "girlfriends" she came with, or other males who are total strangers, will come to her defense. Now everyone's anger is directed toward YOU! It's the *"Damsel in Distress"* clubbing theory. It's a no-win situation for you -- so keep your mouth closed and your emotions in check.

Ten Perceived POP™ Reasons

1. He thinks you looked at him funny. (Really, it doesn't take much.)
2. He thinks you looked at his woman, were trying to talk to his woman, looked his woman's body up and down in an exaggerated manner, or commented on his woman in a negative or positive way, which he, or she, perceived as disrespectful.
3. He thinks you're in competition with a woman he wants to hook up with. He feels inferior to you, your status as an athlete, your wealth, and fame.
4. He's had a bad day, bad month, or bad year. He may feel that he has a lousy life, is unhappy, and can't see any daylight. He has a chip on his shoulder and low self-esteem.
5. He thinks you "dissed" him in some way, shape, or form. It doesn't matter that you didn't do anything wrong. What matters is his perception of being disrespected, real, or imagined.
6. You're an athlete, he's not. You're wealthy, he's not. You're well known, either in the local community or nationally, he's not. You could have any woman you want, he can't. You live a great life and have tons of opportunities to continue doing so as a college or pro athlete — he doesn't.
7. He thinks you're another arrogant athlete who believes you can do anything you want and people will still love and cheer for you. He's disgusted with that mentality, but would sell his soul to the devil to trade places with you for a day. Basi-

cally — he's desperate. Desperation is dangerous at clubs, bars, and parties — especially when mixed with alcohol or drugs.
8. He lingers in the parking lot after the club closes, or lingers when you leave the club.
9. Watch out for groups of people. Bad guys generally like to roll with a group of people. Misery loves company.
10. We, the upstanding public and sports fans, can easily access your salary on the internet — so can the bad guys.

More Clubbing Safety Tips

1. When you're inside clubs or bars, be aware of where rear and side exits are located.
2. The moment you step foot inside that club, reduce your distraction level. This might sound simple, but you'd be amazed at the number of things you get distracted by. Like your cell phone, Blackberry, iPod, or exaggerated conversations with friends.
3. Be aware of people around you on the dance floor and elsewhere. Take note of the vibe they give off. Be keen to people that seem surly, annoyed, or agitated.
4. If the building where you're clubbing has multiple levels, try to stay on the first level. You don't want to waste time taking the elevator or the stairs if trouble breaks out. You want to get out as quickly as possible.
5. If you're clubbing on the first level, don't go too deep inside. Stay within a good distance from the entrance and side or rear exits if you possibly can.
6. Remember, you want to have a good time, but you also want to have a good safety plan in case a situation occurs.
7. You should insist your personal security *NOT* drink at all while clubbing. I've heard one too many stories of personal security losing their focus because they were partying just as hard, if not harder, than their client! Because it is distributed so quickly through the body, alcohol affects the central nervous system, even in small amounts! It also affects several parts of your brain. In general, it contracts brain tissue and depresses the central nervous system. When alcohol reaches the brain, it interferes with communication between nerve cells and can significantly suppress nerve pathways. What does this mean? Alcohol reduces

your reaction time -- substantially. That's something you don't want if trouble breaks out.

8. Before you go to the club, make sure your personal security have been thoroughly trained to respond and effectively handle an escalated situation.

9. Make sure you and your personal security are properly and legally licensed to carry a gun in the state in which you are attending the club. If not licensed in that state, avoid clubbing!

10. If you haven't been properly trained to carry a concealed weapon — c'mon, man, don't carry the weapon on you!

11. You don't have to be a target in order to prepare yourself. You could be enjoying yourself with friends at a club or bar and a situation breaks out with other club goers that has absolutely NOTHING to do with you. Be prepared for other situations not directly related to you, and exit quickly.

12. If something does break out that is NOT related to you, leave! Don't hang around to find out what happened to who, who said what, who did what and why. Many times tensions are still high, and things can escalate worse AFTER the police or club security get involved. *Yes, I watch the show "COPS" too!*

13. When in doubt, don't! If the thought of needing to carry a gun with you to a club, bar, or party makes you feel uneasy — just stay home!

14. Your attitude is the control center of your life. If you have a good attitude about safety, you'll make the right decisions. Follow my tips and techniques. You'll enjoy a better life, have more confidence, and attain the peace of mind you've been searching for.

15. You're young, big, strong, tough, and playing at the college, NFL, or NBA level. You may feel invincible. You can easily correct a mistake at practice and in a game, but you might not get a second opportunity when clubbing.

16. No one deserves to have a gun pulled on them, shot at, or assaulted just because you might look at someone funny, or talk trash to them at a club, bar, or party. If something bad does go down, you may have contributed to that incident in some way without even knowing it.

17. Your first and most important contribution to an incident like that may be to avoid clubbing in the first place. If clubbing you must — club responsibly.

18. *DO NOT* follow a woman back to her place after clubbing! Do not drive a woman back to your place either — no matter what! This could be deadly in a heartbeat.

If you met her the night of clubbing and you both choose to leave together, that's fine, you're adults. However, you might not be aware of other circumstances you could encounter once you get to her place, or yours. There could be a jealous ex-boyfriend waiting, a husband you didn't know about, a guy she met at the club, bar, or party that same night. Someone could be targeting you, or her. He might have followed you to her place, or her to yours. You can imagine the increased chances of someone getting seriously injured or killed in this situation. Throw in alcohol (again), maybe drugs, high emotions, guns, and you now have yourself a distasteful and combustible recipe for potential disaster.

19. Well, you say, maybe a nice hotel room would be a better choice? I don't believe so. Again, too dangerous. It's just not worth the risk these days — and you're smarter than that, right? I know you are.

20. Due diligence and women. Due diligence is a term you must be familiar with — now. It is used for a number of concepts. We'll focus on the "people" concept of the term. It involves the voluntary performance of an investigation of a person or persons. It refers to the care a reasonable person (you) should take before entering into an agreement with another party (her). Due diligence is a way of preventing unnecessary harm to you AND her. Here's a sports example. Your coaching staff conducts due diligence on the next opponent in an attempt to uncover tendencies that can be exploited to your team's advantage in the course of a game, by creating mismatches. What advantage for you is uncovered when meeting women at clubs and bars? *Avoiding* mismatches and staying safe and alive! Sometimes you win, sometimes you lose. Make sure you know who you're waking up to the next morning.

21. If you're tempted or enticed to talk smack with someone at a club, bar, or party — DON'T. Save that for your next game. If you choose to allow yourself to become distracted and lose focus in a game, it may cost your team a win. If you allow yourself to get distracted and lose focus clubbing — it could cost you your athletic career...even your life.

22. People at clubs, bars, and parties don't tend to settle their differences with their fists anymore. These days they carry guns or knives. They will use them without any regard for your well being whatsoever.

23. Your physical size and strength are no longer an obstacle for the bad guys. They use guns as their equalizer these days.

24. What's your best defense when clubbing? Your mind. Who's your mind's best friend? Your attitude.
25. Worry is of your own creation, perceived or otherwise. Fear is nothing more than the response you have chosen. When athletes have the proper tools, preparation, and the right attitude, fear and worry are minimized. Choose to be aware. Choose to be informed. Choose to prepare and stay safe the right way — and continue playing the game you love. The POPS success system for athletes allows you to change your previous nightlife habits for the better. You're simply not going to allow anyone to push your emotions over the edge, which would be detrimental to you, your family, your team, and your league, right? POPS teaches you how to lay a good foundation for all nightlife experiences. As athletes, you have to THINK about security, which should be a focal part of your safety plans during your entire career and post-career.

Stayin' Alive Safety Tips

1. Make it a point to thoroughly research clubs and bars prior to attending (due diligence). Choose those that stress the importance of ID checks at the door. Teens trying to sneak into clubs and bars with fake IDs are likely to cause trouble if they do get in. Also, buying rounds of drinks for underage patrons, unknowingly or not, could get you in a heap of trouble fast!
2. Choose clubs and bars that invest in discretely placed security cameras. Whether cameras are located inside or out, they are a major deterrent to trouble, but they also could potentially exonerate or convict you if accused of committing a crime.
3. Keep eyes and ears open — and hands free. It is important to be alert to who and what is around you. Headphones or ear buds may give the impression that you are less aware. Headphones also cut you off from your surroundings and make it very easy for an attacker to sneak up on you, so keep the headphones and ear buds off, inside and outside.
4. When driving, if you, or someone who's driving you, believe you're being followed, reverse your direction — it will take them a much longer time to turn around, and they will likely just continue on to find a different target.
5. If you're ever in a situation where a bad guy pulls out a gun (I pray not), run away in a zigzag pattern. Look for cover, but mostly concentrate on gaining dis-

tance. Putting distance between you gives you protection against weapons. How? It is difficult for even the best marksman to hit a moving target, so be a moving target. Hitting anything more than fifteen yards away is difficult. By pulling a weapon he has threatened your life, and you must believe he means it. Get out of the situation before he completes his threat. The odds are more on your side with every yard you gain in distance.

6. Practice your POPS™ clubbing safety plan often. In an emergency, the mind is often frozen with indecision. The body carries through if you have practiced or trained for this emergency. Practice out loud. Practice what you need to do in every detail. Include your friends and family too.
7. Keep your head up and look confident when you're walking anywhere. Your posture can make all the difference in how you are perceived by a potential attacker. If you are looking down, seem distracted, or look afraid, you are more likely to become a target. Why? An attacker makes you as an easy target when your body language tells him that you are fearful. Keep your head up, be aware of what is going on around you, and keep your gaze fixed at nose level.
8. Have your keys ready at all times when you approach your vehicle. Check inside your vehicle first, before entering. Do this even if driving a short distance.
9. While traveling in your vehicle and coming to a stop, leave enough room to maneuver around other cars. Drive in the center lane if it's available. Avoid driving alone. Don't stop to assist strangers, especially after dark.
10. When parking and leaving your vehicle, never leave valuables in plain view. Always look around before you get out. Make sure you lock the doors and the windows are rolled up.
11. While approaching your vehicle, be sure to walk with purpose, and stay alert.
12. Beware of the *"Bump and Run"* scenario. No…not that bump and run technique a cornerback in football operates with. I mean, a car, usually with a driver and at least one passenger, rear ends or "bumps" you in traffic. You quickly get out to check the damage and exchange information. Either the driver or one of the passengers in the other car jumps in your car and drives off or attempts to rob you. If bumped by another vehicle, make sure there are other cars and vehicles around before getting out of your car. If the situation leaves you uneasy, write down the plate number (if visible), the car's description, and motion the other

driver to follow you. Drive to the nearest police station or well-lit area. Always take your keys with you when leaving your vehicle.

13. At home, experience reveals three basic concepts repeatedly: The appearance that an occupant is present and is attentive to the condition of the property is, in itself, a potent deterrent to would be criminals. Physical security equipment is worthless unless used. The component in any security system most likely to fail is the human one. Keeping your residence well lit and well kept, and giving the appearance of being home (being in and out, and active inside) is the first fundamental step toward preventing crime there.

14. When in a parking lot, look at the cars parked on either side of your vehicle. If a male in a vehicle is sitting alone in the seat nearest your car, or if you are parked next to a van, always enter your car from the side opposite the other vehicle.

15. If you have encountered a violent situation, the most important thing is to react immediately. If the bad guy has a gun but you are not under his control, take off running! Experts say he will only hit you, a running target, four out of every one hundred shots. And, even then, it most likely will not be a vital organ, so don't be afraid to RUN — it's okay.

16. Make non-threatening eye contact. It may be your first instinct to lower your gaze as you walk to and through a club, bar, or party, but looking straight into the face of potential bad guys is the better option. Eye contact may scare him off because he may fear you'll be able to identify them later.

17. Believe in yourself. When you believe in yourself, you'll trust your wisdom and your mental strength. You'll trust your perceptions, and you'll believe you have the right to your emotional and physical well-being.

18. Understand the reality — and face it. Many athletes understand the realities of nightlife but some don't face it full on. Completely see and accept reality and you'll be miles closer to being safe and being in charge of your life.

19. Trust your intuition. If you forget everything you learned from this book, remember this one thing — if your intuition alarm goes off, there IS something wrong. Trust it, and act upon it to increase your personal safety.

20. Focus on what you CAN do. You have the power to make a difference through your daily actions. While you cannot control every outside circumstance, you can choose how you respond to them.

21. Stay calm under pressure. How can you stay calm and make better decisions if you find yourself under pressure? It is normal for most people, let alone athletes, to get upset and overwhelmed when they feel under pressure. When you are centered, you are most able to assess the situation, figure out what your options are, and make thought out decisions rather than just reacting. So keep your emotions in check.
22. Protect yourself from a threat. Self-defense includes more than knowing how to hit or kick. It also includes knowing skills and behaviors that can prevent a problem in the first place. For effective self-defense, pay attention to your tone of voice and choice of words. Pay attention to your body language and facial expressions. Projecting an attitude of awareness and confidence is a powerful clubbing self-defense skill. Are you glaring at someone and making disrespectful gestures? This makes you look like an aggressor. Most communications with others will work best if your body is upright and your face is calm. Dealing with a conflict works best if your voice, tone, words, body, and expression are firm, polite, strong and clear.
23. Protect yourself from an attack. Your first choice is to leave a confrontation, if you can, by simply walking away. In an attack, you might have to be willing to risk a possible injury in order to escape. If someone is pointing a gun or waving a knife at you, it is safer to run away most of the time. If someone is grabbing you with a gun to your head, remember that the gun is a lot more dangerous when it is pointed *at* someone rather than *away* from someone. If someone is holding a knife to your throat, you might want to grab the knife, even if it means cutting your hands.
24. POPS™ is about being confident and being prepared — not about fear. Don't let fear imprison you. I believe personal safety for all athletes is now everybody's business. By setting aside our own discomfort about speaking up, and by risking the displeasure of someone else when we do, we are sending a powerful message to our young athletes that your well being is our top priority.
25. After you have finished reading this book — go back and read it again! Use it often as a reference point.

ATHLETE CAREER KILLERS

Away Game Safety Tips

Nothing wrecks getting out and having a good time on a road trip more than getting hurt, robbed, or arrested. When athletes travel on the road, they might not recognize potential dangers that would be obvious to them at home. They may not have the resources that would normally be available to them at home.

When traveling, different is not wrong, and people in different places have different ways of doing things. If you treat people with respect, kindness and patience, most of them will respond with the same.

The good news is that most dangers are avoidable if you keep the following POPS™ personal safety tips in mind during road games.

1. Be proactive. Carry this book with you to away games, or carry the condensed POPS™ clubbing travel guide version — you'll be happy you did.
2. Avoid stress by planning to travel at a relaxed pace instead of hurrying to do everything.
3. If clubbing on the road, figure out where you are going in advance.
4. Most times, you are safer with people whom you approach rather than with people who approach you. That said, there are many kinds people you will encounter on the road who might offer their help for various reasons. Thank them, but notice whether they are acting in a way that makes you even a little bit uncomfortable. Is someone just being helpful? Or are they trying to get too close to you? Are they being too pushy? You can interrupt someone and leave politely by saying, *"Sorry, gotta go. Thanks!"*
5. Carry yourself with awareness, calmness, and confidence during road games, making sure you notice what is happening around you in all directions. Don't stare at people, but look around with a "soft eye." Keep assessing your environment if you've got some free time before or after a game. Neighborhoods can change quickly from one block to the next. Places that are safe by day are not always safe by night. Isolated places are usually less safe than places where there are more people around. Places where gangs hang out are to be avoided at all times. You want to stay away from people who might select you as a target because they feel you are on their turf.
6. Move away from people whose behavior is unexpected, especially if it seems to be oriented toward you. Leave ANY TIME you feel uncomfortable. This might

mean walking into a shop, crossing the street, leaving a restaurant, mall, bar, or nightclub — or changing your plans and going to where more people are. Your intuition is one of the best tools you have for protecting yourself, as well as at home. Don't ignore it.

7. If you're walking on foot and anyone for any reason starts walking with you and talking, make sure that this is something YOU are choosing. Scan in all directions in case this person has a friend who is approaching from behind you. You can disengage by going into a store or by saying firmly, *"Sorry, no!"* or *"No thank you!"* Use peripheral vision and keep your awareness on where that person is after they have left your immediate area.

8. If someone tries to pick a fight with you, deescalate the confrontation. Walk away from insults rather than getting into an argument. If somebody claims you did something wrong, apologize. This does not mean that you agree, but that you are sorry that this person is upset. Remember the POPS™ *"I'm sorry"* self-defense technique, and be friendly while you leave, even if the other person is acting a fool.

9. Do what you can to prevent robbery or personal injury, but remember that *YOU ARE MORE IMPORTANT THAN YOUR STUFF!* Your stuff can be replaced. You cannot. After you have given up your stuff, do not just stand there. Without waiting to see what the robber is going to do next, run to safety. In some places, thieves might try to harm you rather than have you report the robbery.

10. Carry a cell phone that works locally. Any safety plan that involves a cell phone should also have a backup plan. Cell phones, while convenient, do not always get good reception in all areas, and your battery may be weak. Having a backup safety plan that does not rely on cell phones is important for your personal safety when traveling at home or on the road.

11. At your hotel during away games, be able to close securely the places you are sleeping. Make sure you can lock the door well from the inside, or use a rubber doorstop. Sometimes, even hotel employees will steal from guests. Think before you open your hotel room door instead of just assuming that the person at the door is safe.

12. If you feel you must carry a gun with you during away games, know the local laws of the city you're in and respect them. Getting arrested is just not worth it. Check with airlines ahead of time, and make sure you understand the rules

about what you can carry with you and what you can't in airports and on airplanes.

13. Let people who care about you know where you are and what you are doing, both for your personal safety during away games, and their peace of mind at home. Give people at home your itinerary and how to get hold of you. Let them know when your plans change. Call family members or other people who might worry about you. Emotional safety for the people who love you lies in their knowing that you are okay. Taking a few minutes to give someone who might be worrying about you the gift of peace of mind is just plain smart and the right thing to do.

14. Forget the *"it won't happen to me"* attitude. It CAN happen to you. Don't allow yourself to be in denial.

15. Preventing clubbing trouble and/or violence is not the only area in an athlete's life where getting help makes a difference. Whether you are dealing with a personal safety issue or facing any other challenge, knowing how to ask for help from others is a fundamental life skill. Even though it may feel that way sometimes, it is important to remember that you are not alone. You do not need to re-invent the wheel. You do not need to face problems by yourself. By reading this book and applying the tips and techniques I have listed, you can bring more protection, comfort, information, resources, and understanding into your life...right now.

16. Why bother learning about safety? Fed up with feeling uneasy every time you think about going clubbing with friends? Do you feel afraid because off all the terrible headlines you've heard and read about regarding other athletes, maybe even a teammate? How would you feel if you were more confident about your ability to stay emotionally and physically safe? What would your life be like? POPS™ shows you, step-by-step, how to protect your emotional and physical safety and can change your life. The courage, self-respect and power that you need to keep yourself and your family safe, lies within you — it always has.

17. Now you can fight back by applying POPS™ tips and techniques when you go clubbing. Applying all your new wisdom makes the possibility of an attack much less likely. But it still might happen.

18. You should not be afraid to ask questions about your personal safety. Seek advice on whom to contact for professional licensed instruction on how to properly use a weapon, if you feel you must carry one, and do so responsibly.
19. Always travel with someone you know and trust when you go clubbing, and make sure you carry your POPS™ game plan with you. Remember — not many good things happen after midnight.
20. If you're the recipient of a crime while you're playing on the road, don't be embarrassed to report that you have been victimized.

Update! New photo policy for athletes:

Athletes should consider NO LONGER allowing photos or pictures of yourself to be taken in a social setting with ONLY females, unless she is your wife, girlfriend, or a member of your family. If an athlete allows a photo or picture of him to be taken with a female other than his wife, girlfriend, or family member, another male or males MUST also be included in the photo or picture taken! If the person requesting the photo or picture refuses this, no photo or picture should be allowed to be taken without the expressed consent of the athlete. Reason: To help reduce potential misrepresentation and false allegations of sexual misconduct or abuse, and any other false allegation made against an athlete.

Implement this new photo policy in your clubbing lifestyle safety game plan -- NOW!

You have no doubt seen teammates and other athletes in photos and pictures on the internet at a club, bar, or party posing with a woman (or women) whom they had just met. A few different examples I viewed recently shows a woman snuggled up close to an athlete. Another photo shows a woman cheek-to-cheek with an athlete. Yet another shows a woman with her hands draped around an athlete's neck and waist. I also found a photo of an athlete who had picked up a young woman in his arms, holding her. It was later confirmed these were women the athletes had just met that night/early morning.

My professional advice: *STOP ALLOWING THIS* (unless the woman is your wife, girlfriend, or a family member, and you agree to it)!

If you have allowed this in the past -- let it be your last -- starting today!

If you are falsely accused of any form of misconduct, or YOU knowingly or not, initiate misconduct, the photos will be plastered all over the internet and you'll be considered guilty in the minds of public opinion.

Buying Rounds of Drinks

Stabilize the Streets™: If at a club, bar, pub, strip club, or party, DO NOT buy rounds of drinks for friends, family or patrons! You're only asking for trouble. Also, unbeknown to you, some club and bar patrons may be *underage!* Buying rounds of drinks for underage persons can cause you lots of problems and embarrassing headlines. These people may later make the potentially deadly choice to drink and drive once they leave.

The point is, you just can't be too careful these days with your social life.

These tips will further assist you in changing your mindset regarding the lifestyle you lead away from the game. They will encourage you to continue to be cognizant of making good choices each day, and help you increase your individual *Player Social Development*™.

Laddering

Laddering™: When at a club, bar, party or elsewhere, it's when your eyes climb up and down a woman's body, as if you're climbing up and down a ladder. Don't do this, or do it in an *exaggerated manner*, as it can easily be perceived as being disrespectful to her (or to her man!) if seen. "Laddering" can cause conflict with another person or people, which could lead to an ugly incident -- and a negative headline in the news involving you.

Benefits

If you can benefit from just one tip, technique or piece of advice from the nearly 500 or so listed throughout this book, that one tip, technique, or piece of advice could be the one that saves your career and life. Don't be the athlete who has his good name dragged through the mud by the media, creating negative headlines that your children and family will have to live with for a long time.

When making a choice on where you go and who you mingle with in your social life — just because you feel like doing it doesn't mean it's the right thing to do.

I hope this book will assist the *NFL, NBA, NCAA, NHL, MLB* and other sport organizations, in maintaining their value and strong brands for all involved for many years to come. I encourage leagues, teams, college and universities, high schools, parents, sportswriters, and agents to share POPS™ tips and techniques with their athletes.

Consider it – Veggies for the Mind.™

It's the best success system for athletes ever created, and a program that works.

Make it your success system.

POPS™ can also be easily integrated in coordination with your current athlete safety and security programs, creating an even broader safety and security foundation on which to educate and build.

Preventing a potential problem is far more efficient than fixing a problem afterward. POPS™ helps prevent problems from happening and, in the long run, it saves athletes, teams and organizations time and money — and it could save a life.

Stay in the game — it's your C.H.O.I.C.E.

Chapter 2
DRUNK DRIVING

"The price of greatness is responsibility."
– Winston Churchill

Of all the headlines you may read and hear about regarding athletes making poor choices, drunk driving is arguably the most common. This much we know as fact: an athlete chooses to drink and drive — period.

I must say — most college and professional athletes DO NOT drink and drive, and I applaud you. But maybe you know a teammate that has…or might in the future.

Driving under the influence (DUI) of alcohol or drugs is an astoundingly preventable crime.

Unfortunately, too many athletes neglect to plan ahead or underestimate how impaired they are, and later get behind the wheel after drinking.

You rarely hear about athletes being stopped on the road by police after they've been drinking at home. Drunk driving generally happens after an athlete has been drinking at a club, bar, or party, then makes the wrong choice to drive.

Each time an athlete makes a good choice to not drink and drive, they say "no" to many other bad ones.

Make no mistake about this, if you make a mistake, you may no longer have a place on your team when you come back — if you come back. There will be plenty of high character, talented athletes hungry and waiting to take your position on the team.

It's a privilege to play your sport. You should never take that for granted.

The *NFL, NBA, MLB,* and *NHL* have programs generally referred to as *"Safe Ride"*, *"Player Protect"*, or *"Corporate Security"* services. If an athlete makes the judgment that he is not in condition to drive after drinking at a club, bar, or party, he can call a number provided by his team or league and have someone pick him up and drive him home.

Many teams pick up the tab for the ride. Other teams require athletes to pay out of their own pocket, but the call is *NOT* reported to your team and your name remains anonymous and confidential.

Heck, the NFL even has a similar program for their non-players!

The cool thing is, in most cases, your friends get to ride free too!

Naturally, however, athletes do have built-in barriers against using these type of services, so let's address a few of them.

Barrier #1: You don't want to leave your expensive Corvette or Mercedes overnight in a club parking lot, and have to get a ride from a buddy back to the club to pick it up the next morning.

> **Solution**: Have two people come to pick you up. One person can drive you home, the other person can follow in your car. Or, instead of driving your Corvette to a club, for example, take the Buick.

Barrier #2: Your team or league says it's confidential and your name won't be disclosed, but you fear somehow, someway your name will get leaked out to the media.

> **Solution**: Get it in writing from your team or league that guarantees your anonymity. Keep a copy of the agreement at home for your records.

Barrier #3: Privacy issues. What you do with your friends on a Friday or Saturday night is your business and not your team or league.

> **Solution**: We're living in a different environment these days. Media is 24\7 and watching your every move anyway, so why not just be smart about it and do the right thing regardless of who knows about it?

Barrier #4: You're young, fit, muscular, and believe your body can absorb a few drinks enough for you to drive home safely.

> **Solution**: Again, alcohol and driving share absolutely nothing in common – so be smart and don't drive if you've been drinking.

Barrier #5: You think it will be an inconvenience to teammates, friends or family you came with.

> **Solution**: Let's say you drove everyone to the club in your vehicle. That makes you the QB for the evening. Your teammates, friends or family are

your offensive linemen. Without them protecting you from the "rush" of alcohol consumption, you're likely to get sacked every time. My point is, the people you're with also have to be responsible and not allow you to drive if you've been drinking. You may think about scrambling from the pocket, but if you do, at least head for the sidelines and get out of bounds by handing the keys off to a sober friend instead of trying to take on a linebacker who's itching to knock your head off (*an unfortunate accident or DUI charge*).

So, *DO NOT* be afraid to use these services! They are only meant to protect you.

Female athletes appear to be more vulnerable than male athletes to the many adverse consequences of alcohol use. Women achieve higher concentrations of alcohol in the blood and become more impaired than men after drinking equivalent amounts of alcohol. Research also suggests that women are more susceptible than men to alcohol-related organ damage, and to trauma resulting from traffic crashes and interpersonal violence.

I often read books and articles from psychologists and sports writers about the problems facing athletes today. However, no one offers tips, techniques, or a step-by-step program of substance, except *Athlete Career Killers™*, that athletes can implement into their daily lives.

I'm weary of reading books and articles about the *problems* — let's give athletes a plan of action that results in **solutions.**

It starts with these four things:
1. Acknowledgment
2. Attitude
3. Education
4. Change in habits

You must first acknowledge a change is necessary. You must have the right attitude to receive a different mind-set, which education offers. You then must change your habits based on that education.

If you don't remember anything else from this chapter, remember this: **alcohol and driving share nothing in common** — *ever.*

And you should also remember, guilty or innocent, public perception is a powerful and impacting entity.

If You're Drinking and Driving — You Ain't Striving™

> *"The hope for our athletes, who have extraordinary power in our society and upon our youth, is that they will also exhibit extraordinary trust, character, and integrity."*
> *– David L. Brown*

When an athlete is in the moment of a night out drinking, it can seem like the only way to get home is to "tough it out" and drive yourself home afterward. A drunk driving conviction is not worth it. Consider taking a cab, or call a sober friend to pick you up. There's always another option to drinking and driving, and it will always be the better one.

> **Important note:** When you go out for a night of fun with your group of friends or family, make sure you choose in advance someone whom you know well, trust, and is responsible, to be the designated driver for the evening. Discuss this important and potentially life-saving assignment long before you decide to go out. The person you carefully choose must completely understand his/her inherent responsibility for the safety of all those involved -- and take it seriously!

> I read about a sad story not too long ago, whereby a group of young adults were out having a good time on a Friday night. A designated driver had been chosen for the evening. The designated driver drove the group to a club, dropped them off, and was scheduled to return later and pick everyone up. However, after dropping the group off at the club, she proceeded to drive to a nearby bar to have a few drinks.

> Later that evening, she was summoned by phone to come back to club and pick everyone up, as previously agreed. The young woman arrived at the club and the four other merry club-goers, believing they were doing the right thing by having a designated driver, piled into her car and off they went! Tragically, ten minutes later, the young woman selected as the designated driver, ran a stop light and the group's car was blind-sided by a semi-trailer truck, killing all five passengers.

The message is clear. If you choose a designated driver for yourself or your group of friends or family, make sure they understand the importance of their responsibilities and refrain from consuming ANY alcohol for the e-n-t-i-r-e evening.

Law enforcement in all 50 states take drunk driving very seriously. You should too.

Some states, like Arizona, have what they call "extreme DUI," where there is a blood alcohol content (BAC) of .15% or higher within two hours of driving.

The actual number of high school, college, and professional athletes who drive while under the influence of drugs or alcohol is impossible to estimate — until they get caught.

Don't Be a Fool–Drinking and Driving Isn't Cool™

And remember — *"buzzed"* driving is also drunk driving.

State by state DUI/DWI/OWI laws

<u>Note</u>: The state DUI laws listed below pertain to general laws of each state at this writing. DUI laws are constantly evolving. Some state laws may have changed since this book went to print. Research the laws frequently in your state for updated laws and penalties.

The choices you make today will impact you, your family, and your team for years to come.

Arizona

- Arizona DUI laws treat drunk drivers seriously. Arizona state laws include provisions for installation of ignition interlock devices for first-time drunk driving offenders and increased penalties, such as for "extreme DUI" cases involving a BAC (blood alcohol content) above .15.

Alaska

- Residents of Alaska can be charged with DUI while operating any motor vehicle, be it a car, truck, snowmobile or even a boat. DUI charges in Alaska are treated seriously by local police.

Arkansas

- Arkansas DWI cases are not treated lightly. The state requires ignition interlock devices for some first-time DUI offenders, as well as higher penalties for drivers with a BAC above .15.

California

- California DUI law doesn't discriminate. Even movie stars and athletes can get pulled over. The long-term impact of a DUI conviction in California can be devastating to your athletic career in any number of ways.

Colorado

- Colorado DUI laws are some of the most nuanced in the nation. Like most states, Colorado carries stiff penalties for drunk drivers with a BAC above .08. But, Colorado can also charge drivers with DWAI, driving while ability impaired. A BAC of .05 or greater gives rise to an inference of impairment. Both charges carry penalties that can leave a lasting impact on any convicted driver.

Connecticut

- A Connecticut DUI charge shouldn't be taken lightly. There is a mandatory jail sentence for a DUI conviction in Connecticut, even if this is your first offense.

Delaware

- Delaware DUI laws can carry stiff penalties, including harsher penalties for higher BAC levels.

Florida

- Florida DUI charges can lead to a number of tough penalties. Florida law stipulates mandatory jail time, fines, and the use of ignition interlock devices in many DUI cases.

Georgia

- A Georgia DUI conviction carries a laundry list of penalties. Even if this is your first offense, you could be facing jail time, loss of license, steep fines, community service, and alcohol rehab classes.

Hawaii

- A Hawaii DUI conviction can have you saying "Aloha" to your freedom, your driver's license, and thousands of dollars.

Idaho

- Idaho DUI laws are clear: Drunk driving punishments will include jail time, fines and driver's license suspensions. But for anyone convicted of drunk driving in Idaho, the penalties could last longer.

Illinois

- Recently, legislators beefed up the DUI laws in Illinois. The drunk driving laws now carry increased penalties, including fines and jail time. First offenders may even be required to use ignition interlock devices on their cars.

Indiana

- Indiana DUI laws clearly outline the penalties for offenders. A drunk driving conviction in the state can lead to jail time, ignition interlock devices, and even alcohol treatment classes.

Iowa

- In Iowa, drunk driving is charged as Operating While Intoxicated, or OWI. And while Iowa may use a slightly different name, their penalties for the crime are just as serious as the rest of the country. Iowa OWI laws call for mandatory jail time, thousands of dollars in fines, and license suspensions. There are increased penalties for drivers with a BAC above .10, like the use of ignition interlock devices. Iowa DUI laws call for alcohol treatment for anyone convicted.

Kansas

- Kansas DUI laws are very specific in outlining the punishments for drunk driving. The state has minimum jail sentences for all levels of conviction, as well as use of ignition interlock devices and required alcohol safety education programs.

Kentucky

- Kentucky is the home to one of the country's largest breathalyzer manufacturers. So it's no wonder the Bluegrass State has such tough DUI laws. A DUI in Kentucky can result in jail time, driver's license suspension, and heavy fines. State laws also allow for the use of ignition interlock devices.

Louisiana

- A DWI in Louisiana can be a costly offense. Drunk driving laws in the state call for fines, jail time and loss of license, all of which are typical state DUI laws. However, Louisiana also has aggressive treatment requirements for anyone convicted of DUI, and the state may also seize and sell your vehicle if you are convicted multiple times of DWI.

Maine

- Maine OUI (operating under the influence) laws are the real deal. A drunk driving conviction can result in jail time, fines and a suspended driver's license. Simply refusing to take a breathalyzer test may also result in fines and jail time.

Maryland

- Maryland drunk driving laws are very nuanced. You can be charged with a DUI even if your blood alcohol level is below .08. A BAC above .08 could be classified as a DWI (driving while intoxicated). Both charges carry tough penalties that could include fines, suspended license, and jail time.

Massachusetts

- Massachusetts DUI laws have some of the highest maximum penalties in the country. This means that if you are charged with drunk driving in Massachusetts, be it an OUI or DUI, you could be facing years in jail and tens of thousands of dollars in fines.

Michigan

- Michigan DUI convictions can leave a nasty, long lasting mark. In the short term, a DUI in Michigan can lead to jail time, fines, and loss of license.

Minnesota

- Minnesota DWI laws mandate jail time, fines, and even vehicle forfeiture for drunk driving convictions, depending on the circumstances. Minnesota laws also call for harsher punishments for drivers with a high BAC. Drunk driving charges in Minnesota can seem intimidating. There are filing deadlines, court appearances, regulations, and the threat of life-altering punishments for a conviction.

Mississippi

- Mississippi laws make it clear: A DUI is a serious charge. The statutes in Mississippi mandate fines and a suspended license for first DUI offenders. Multiple offenders are looking at mandatory jail sentences.

Missouri

- Missouri DWI laws are some of the most intricate in the country. Missouri's driver's license point system can cause penalties for DWI, DUI or DUID (driving under the influence of drugs) to compound quickly. Even if you have no other driving violations, a DUI conviction can be costly, resulting in loss of license, jail time, and heavy fines.

Montana

- Montana DUI laws are tough. The state imposes a variety of penalties on convicted drunk drivers. These penalties include jail time and fines, but Montana also requires the use of ignition interlock devices in some cases.

Nebraska

- A drunk driving conviction in Nebraska can result in jail time, hundreds of dollars in fines, and loss of your driver's license.

Nevada

- Nevada DUI laws call for immediate penalties for a DUI conviction, such as jail time, fines, community service, license suspension, and completion of an alcohol program.

New Hampshire

- New Hampshire DUI laws carry strict minimum penalties, even for first offenders. A DUI conviction in New Hampshire can mean minimum fines, loss of license, and mandatory enrollment in an alcohol intervention program.

New Jersey

- A DWI in New Jersey can put you face-to-face with serious penalties. New Jersey DWI law calls for jail time, fines, and driver's license suspension for drunk driving convictions.

New Mexico

- New Mexico DWI laws are among the toughest and most aggressive in the nation. Even a first-time drunk driving offense can lead to steep penalties, including jail time, ignition interlock use, driver's license revocation, probation, community service, and attendance at an alcohol treatment program.

New York

- New York's drunk driving penalties include jail time, hefty fines, and driver's license revocation. A second DWI arrest can be charged as a felony.

North Carolina

- North Carolina DUI laws mean business. There are mandatory, minimum jail sentences for convictions. Multiple DWI convictions can lead to years in prison, and permanent revocation of your driver's license.

North Dakota

- North Dakota DUI laws mandate minimum fines, loss of license, and alcohol evaluation programs for drunk driving convictions.

Ohio

- Here in my great state of Ohio, DUI laws are strict and swift. Simply being charged with a DUI could get you a 90-day administrative license suspension. This penalty doesn't include the court-ordered license suspension that is likely if you are convicted of a DUI. Other Ohio DUI and OVI (operating a vehicle intoxicated) penalties include mandatory jail sentences and heavy fines.

Oklahoma

- Oklahoma DUI laws are no joke. Your first conviction is a misdemeanor offense that can include one year in jail and a $1,000 fine. A second offense could put a felony on your record, and may mean a five-year jail sentence.

Oregon

- DUI in Oregon, sometimes known as DUII (driving under the influence of intoxicants) is a crime that can leave a lasting mark. First time convictions may carry a hefty fine and installation of ignition interlock devices.

Pennsylvania

- A Pennsylvania DUI can impact the rest of your life. Even one conviction could affect your ability to continue your athletic career.

Rhode Island

- Rhode Island DUI laws are some of the country's most detailed. They include different punishment levels, depending upon a driver's blood alcohol content (BAC). DUI penalties start with jail time, large fines, license suspension, and community service. Higher BAC and multiple DUI arrests will quickly increase the penalties to include mandatory jail time, seizure of vehicle, and required enrollment in alcohol programs.

South Carolina

- South Carolina DUI laws seek to penalize drunk drivers in a number of ways. The drunk driving laws call for fines, jail time, license suspensions, and ignition interlock devices.

South Dakota

- South Dakota DUI laws are clear cut. DUIs are considered class one misdemeanors. Conviction on drunk driving charges could lead to jail time, fines, and a suspended license.

Tennessee

- Tennessee DUI laws define clear punishments for drunk driving convictions. Convictions may come with mandatory jail sentences, significant fines, and driver's license suspensions.

Texas

- Texas DWI laws aren't to be messed with. DWI penalties in Texas include mandatory jail sentences and thousands of dollars in fines.

Utah

- Utah laws are serious. A DUI in Utah could result in jail time, large fines, and a suspended driver's license. For DUI cases involving a higher BAC, ignition interlock devices may be required following conviction.

Vermont

- Vermont DUI law includes fines, suspended license statutes, and alcohol education requirements.

Virginia

- Virginia DUI laws are tough. They carry increased penalties for higher BAC levels and minimum fines. Breath test refusals may be treated as civil or criminal charges.

Washington

- Washington DUI laws are harsh and intricate. The penalties for a DUI conviction may include a mandatory jail sentence, fines and ignition interlock device use — even if this is your first DUI. The laws also include higher penalties for drunk drivers with a higher BAC. In some cases, a BAC above .15 will double the minimum punishments for a DUI conviction.

Washington, D.C.

- Laws aren't just made in Washington, D.C., they are also strictly enforced. Just like in any other state, you can be charged with a DUI in Washington, D.C. Drunk driving in the District of Columbia can result in jail time, fines, community service, and even ignition interlock devices on your car.

West Virginia

- West Virginia DUI laws call for long sentences for DUI offenders. In addition to fines and jail, West Virginia DUI laws call for driver's license suspensions to have lengthy minimums—10 years in some cases.

Wisconsin

- A Wisconsin DUI case can cause you substantial grief. The state's OWI, operating while intoxicated statutes, include additional fines for all drunk driving convictions.

Wyoming

- Wyoming DUI laws are straightforward. Drunk driving convictions can put you in jail and saddle you with steep fines.

Note: The *ignition interlock system* mentioned above prevents a vehicle from starting until the driver successfully passes a blood alcohol concentration test. Before the vehicle will start, the driver must blow into the BAC (blood alcohol content) tester. If the breath test shows a driver's BAC to be above a set limit, usually around .02-.04%, the starter on the vehicle will lock and the driver can't use the vehicle. If a driver's BAC is below that level, then the vehicle will start and operate normally. Some ignition interlock devices require breath tests to be performed at random intervals while the vehicle is being used. This is to ensure no one enters a car sober and then begins drinking.

Less Is Better. None Is Best™

When you are pulled over on suspicion of driving under the influence, you'll be asked to take a breathalyzer test.

You may also be asked to take field sobriety tests. Then, if the officer believes that you are intoxicated, you'll be arrested.

In many areas, you will not be eligible to post bond until your blood alcohol content level has dropped to a prescribed level. In most states, you'll receive a court date before you leave the jail, although in some areas you may receive notice of the hearing date by mail or by some other means after you've posted bond.

"A safer you is a safer me."
– Unknown

NFL Commissioner Roger Goodell is taking aim at NFL employees — players and non-players alike — who commit alcohol-induced crimes. Goodell sent a letter to all NFL teams in July, 2009, and released via *SI.com*, warning employees he will enforce the league's alcohol code of conduct just as vigorously as he does with league athletes.

"I want to use this opportunity to remind all NFL personnel — both players and non-players — that the prohibitions on alcohol-related misconduct, including DUI, apply to everyone," Goodell wrote to teams.

"In the past few years, I have not hesitated to impose discipline, including suspensions, on club and league employees who have violated the law related to alcohol use. Every club should advise its employees of their obligations and our commitment to hold people accountable for alcohol-related violations of law."

The NFL has prioritized preventing its players and employees from DUI infractions, which Goodell called an "embarrassment" in his letter.

There are many situations and scenarios that can lead to an athlete DUI arrest. Three primary circumstances may include a crime observed first-hand by a police officer. This may be the most common and most obvious circumstance that leads to a DUI arrest. If a police officer personally witnesses a traffic violation or a driver exhibiting drunk driving symptoms, the driver will be pulled over for suspicion of DUI.

After field sobriety tests or a breath test to determine the driver's blood alcohol content, a DUI arrest may occur.

If facts and circumstances lead an officer to reasonably believe that a person has, or is about to commit a crime, that person may be arrested. The officer's reasonable belief is called "Probable Cause," and may be sufficient grounds for a DUI arrest in some situations.

"Probable Cause" DUI arrests generally happen when a person has been noticed driving erratically, smells of alcohol, and/or refuses a breath test to determine their blood alcohol content.

After a DUI arrest, suspects are generally taken to the police station or local jail and booked. This process includes recording details about the crime and the suspect, including fingerprints and a mug shot.

Personal property, such as keys and cash, are also confiscated at this time, and are usually returned when the suspect is released unless they are held as evidence. In some cases, bail may be posted immediately, or a suspect can be released on their own recognizance, which means they sign a promise to appear for their court date. In other cases, the suspect will be required to wait in jail for a hearing before a judge to determine the amount of bail.

The severity of a DUI penalty may depend on a variety of factors, including:

- Which state you were arrested in. (State laws differ.)
- Whether your BAC was higher than a certain level. (Varies by state.)
- Whether you have been previously convicted of drinking and driving.
- Whether you had a child in the car, and/or whether you had other passengers in the car.

If an athlete is convicted of DUI, either through a guilty plea, jury verdict, or accepting a plea bargain, there are various sentences you could receive.

Each state's DUI laws outline DUI sentencing guidelines, but in every state the consequences of a DUI conviction can be very serious.

The penalties of a DUI conviction could include:

- Fines
- Jail time
- Prison time, if the DUI results in injury or death
- Probation
- Suspended sentence, to take effect if probation or other conditions are violated
- Suspension of driver's license
- Forfeiture of vehicle
- Community service
- Drug or alcohol treatment programs

What a First DUI Offense May Mean for You

If you are charged with your first DUI, you should not go into your case with the attitude that you won't face harsh penalties if convicted just because you are a first time offender or high profile athlete. Don't assume that because this is your first DUI charge you can avoid harsh penalties. Many states have mandatory penalties for first offenders that can have a lasting impact on your life and athletic career.

Examining DUI Second Offenses

If you didn't learn your lesson the first time around, a DUI second offense could mean a harsher reality. Law enforcement strives to make sure you feel the burn if you are found to be a DUI second offender. DUI second offense punishment comes down a little harder. With a DUI second offense, most states will typically increase the penalties if it is within five years of your first offense. A DUI second offense may mean more jail time, larger fines and a longer license suspension, as well as additional penalties.

DUI Felony or Misdemeanor?

While every state has the same general blood alcohol content limit, each state has different penalties in place for conviction of a DUI offense. Typically, however, a DUI offense is a misdemeanor. With that said, felony DUI is still a possibility. The severity of the penalty depends on many factors, including the number of offenses, the level of blood alcohol registered in the breath test, and whether other drivers are injured in an accident with the DUI offender.

Felony DUI

Though some states classify DUI convictions with aggravated charges as gross misdemeanors, or simply misdemeanors, most states have provisions to convict a DUI offender as a felony for drunk driving that result in severe injury or death. Often, this charge is called reckless homicide or vehicular homicide if the accident results in the death of another driver or passenger.

Before You Drink—Take Time to Think™

What's the difference between DUI misdemeanor and felony?

The main difference in terms of penalties for a misdemeanor as opposed to a felony is where the prison sentence will take place. A misdemeanor requiring incarceration will be served at the county jail; a felony must be served at the state prison.

Misdemeanor Charge for DUI

Drinking and driving charges may result in either DUI misdemeanors or DUI felonies. Typically, an athlete receives a DUI misdemeanor for your first, second or third DUI offense. Felony charges typically result after a third DUI offense, or if you were involved in a car accident that caused bodily injury or property damage. Penalties for DUI misdemeanors are generally less than felony DUI penalties, but they vary state-by-state.

The severity of the charges usually depends on whether you have had any prior DUI misdemeanor charges, and include:
- Monetary fines
- Probation
- Mandatory alcohol counseling
- License suspension and/or restricted driving privileges
- Jail time

Understanding the DUI Manslaughter Charge

DUI manslaughter charges are generally brought to the table when a driver is arrested for DUI and has caused an accident that resulted in the death of another person. Although DUI manslaughter laws vary from state to state, there are two versions of vehicular manslaughter that typically apply in these DUI manslaughter cases:
- Vehicular manslaughter with gross negligence: charged when a driver was DUI and drove extremely recklessly.
- Vehicular manslaughter with ordinary negligence: charged when a driver was DUI and violated a traffic law, but was not extremely negligent. It can also mean that a driver failed to use reasonable care to prevent injury and/or death. If convicted of DUI manslaughter with gross negligence, a driver faces severe penal-

ties, which typically includes at least 10 years in prison for each person killed. A DUI manslaughter with ordinary negligence conviction typically brings a sentence of up to 4 years imprisonment for each person killed.

In addition to facing long-term imprisonment, other penalties for DUI manslaughter can include heavy fines, loss of driving privileges, and a felony record that can't be wiped clean in most states. The laws vary in each state, so it's important that athletes keep abreast of your current state laws.

Obviously, legal and financial consequences aren't the only cost in a DUI manslaughter case. Sadly, there are countless stories of lives cut short due to drinking and driving. One error in judgment by an athlete can result in life changing circumstances for everyone involved in a DUI car accident.

Most athletes don't get behind the wheel intending to hurt someone, but impaired judgment can lead to you making bad decisions. Protect yourself — don't put yourself in a position to be arrested for DUI and possibly receive a DUI manslaughter charge.

Drinking and driving is a serious risk. If you've been drinking, don't get behind the wheel!

DUI Probation Conditions

Stipulations of DUI probation vary state to state, but most DUI probationers are required to periodically check in with a DUI probation officer and follow a strict code of behavior to avoid being sentenced to penalties that are more serious.

DUI probation conditions may include:
- Wearing an alcohol-monitoring device
- Submitting to random sobriety tests
- Limiting driving privileges
- Paying court costs or fees as ordered
- Avoiding any major moving violations or criminal violations
- Attending alcohol counseling
- Submitting to alcohol evaluations

DUI Probation Violations

Remember, when you are sentenced to DUI probation, it is an alternative to the judge sentencing you to prison or jail time.

There may be serious consequences if you happen to violate DUI probation. Consequences can vary in severity, but may include incarceration for the remainder of the probation time, loss of driving privileges, extension of the probation period, fines and/or mandatory community service — and your athletic career could be over quickly.

Life After DUI For Athletes

A DUI conviction can have a much greater affect on your life and athletic career than you realize. Not only will a DUI conviction show up on your driving record, it can influence your career long term, and substantially reduce your earning power and longevity as a college or professional athlete.

Breathalyzers — if you refuse, you lose!

An athlete can be cited for driving under the influence after refusing to take a breathalyzer test, and possibly have your license suspended for one year for refusing to take it. Refusing a breath test in most states may be used as presumptive evidence in a DUI case. Although a breathalyzer test and blood alcohol content are interchangeable, there is a very important difference. A breathalyzer doesn't read your BAC, but estimates it.

It's possible for an athlete to be convicted of DUI even after passing field sobriety tests or not appearing impaired if your BAC is .08%. Following a DUI conviction, you may face many DUI penalties like license suspension, fines, probation, or jail time with the possibility of a prison term.

Don't Try to Fool a Breathalyzer!

One of the most popular questions people ask about drinking and driving is whether it's possible to fool a breathalyzer. The short answer is no, but that hasn't stopped people from coming up with all sorts of ways to try to beat the system during a DUI stop.

Harsh DUI penalties are being enacted in almost every state, which make many people panic when pulled over for drinking and driving.

Eating can help you sober up in the long run, but it won't help you beat a breath test. People have tried eating strong foods like onions, coffee grounds and breath mints, all without any luck. Strong substances will often mask the odor of alcohol on your breath, but that doesn't make the alcohol content disappear.

When you blow into a breathalyzer, the device will still be able to read the alcohol in your breath.

When it comes to DUIs, there are no shortcuts for anyone, including athletes.

When you're out drinking and it's time to head home, you may wish you could become sober in order to safely drive your car, since penalties for DUI convictions can be very severe. But, in reality, there's no quick fix for drunkenness — just a lot of dangerous myths about what activities can minimize your impairment enough to drive.

The Sobering Myths

- Drinking black coffee: Caffeine will not help your liver metabolize alcohol, and neither will any of the other ingredients in coffee. Drinking coffee while drunk may actually have a negative effect: you may feel more alert and capable of driving when, in fact, you're still impaired.
- Taking a cold shower: Unless your liver hops out and takes a shower with you, this will have no effect on your level of drunkenness. Like drinking caffeinated beverages, though, it could give you a false sense of alertness.
- Getting some fresh air: Like taking a cold shower, this may make you feel better — and even less impaired — but it has absolutely no effect on your blood alcohol content (BAC) or liver.
- Exercising: While exercise does help the body eliminate some alcohol through sweating and breathing, the amount is negligible and won't affect your BAC. In fact, because alcohol impairs motor skills, a drunk person engaging in vigorous exercise may actually end up hurting him or herself by falling or bumping into something.
- Eating food: Eating before you begin drinking can slow the absorption of alcohol into your bloodstream, but eating after you drink will have zero effect on your drunkenness.

- Drinking lots of water: Drinking liters of water once you're bombed will not make you okay to drive home; however, alternating a glass of water with a glass of alcohol throughout the night can help you consume less alcohol, and so avoid becoming too impaired to operate a vehicle. Ample water consumption also helps minimize hangover symptoms after drinking.
- Mouthwash: It may be able to slightly mask the smell of alcohol on your breath, but like any other strong substance, it won't lower the breathalyzer readings. Mouthwash contains a small amount of alcohol that could potentially *increase* the amount of alcohol registered on the breathalyzer. If you haven't been drinking at all and use mouthwash, depending on when you used it and how much you used, it could even register a false positive on a breathalyzer.

The Sobering Facts

The human body processes alcohol at a rate of about one drink (that's one beer, one shot of liquor or one glass of wine) per hour.

Factors like how much food you have in your stomach, how quickly you drink, your height and weight, your gender, and whether or not you alternate booze with water also factor into your overall level of alcohol impairment.

But the only thing that will return you to sobriety is...*time*.

If you plan on drinking, follow these basic rules of thumb:
- Drink responsibly/moderately, which means no more than what your body can process. Set boundaries for yourself.
- If you don't do the above, assign a sober and responsible designated driver who completely understands their role and responsibilities.
- If you don't do the above, please call a *"Safe Ride"* service, taxi, a sober friend or family member to come and pick you up.

ATHLETE CAREER KILLERS

College Athletes and DUI

> *"You must be willing to accept responsibility for your mistake, learn from it, and consider it a blessing in disguise. Only then can you bounce back from adversity to become a better person and athlete."*
> – David L. Brown

DUI penalties for college athletes extend far beyond sentencing.

The impact of a DUI conviction on the life of a college athlete is readily apparent, and the effects of a conviction can spread much further. Recent news coming out of our nation's colleges and universities has been full of DUI arrests involving NCAA athletes, coaches and administrative personnel.

Those arrests often result in suspensions and dismissals. It is easy to see their negative results. From the college freshmen on the verge of their athletic careers, to Hall of Fame coaches, any arrest and conviction illustrates the drastic effects that a DUI can have on everyone.

One unique aspect of a career in college athletics is the amount of media publicity when things go wrong.

The dismissal of an athlete or a coach for driving under the influence can tarnish the reputation of an otherwise vaunted sports program and hurt a team's chance of success, not to mention the impact on the careers of the individuals involved. In recent weeks and months, several high-profile athletes and coaches have faced the consequences of their actions to the detriment of their schools and programs.

If there is a lesson to be learned from these highly publicized and well-documented DUI cases, it is that the consequences of a DUI conviction can not only have an impact on your life, but on those around you as well. While you might not play football or basketball on a national stage, you will still have to face the repercussions of a DUI conviction in ways that you might not realize now. The consequences go far beyond those direct penalties imposed by the court.

Allow me to reinforce my basic point to all athletes — college and pro. *Stop driving drunk!*

This also applies to coaches and all executive sports personnel. Being a college or professional athlete carries a lot of responsibility. Athletes are held to a higher standard on and off the field and court, which is generally accepted by society. An athlete's mistake will be more scrutinized by the media.

Are Athletes Fully to Blame?

College sports have been substantially supported by alcohol companies that advertise during television and radio broadcasts. But some athletic officials and health advocates aim to put an end to those sponsorship dollars, *CNN/Money* reported Sept. 3, 2008.

According to *Sports Business Journal*, beer and other alcohol companies spent $50 million advertising on college sports broadcasts in 2008.

In addition, 45% of Division 1A football schools received direct sponsorship dollars from alcohol companies, while another 25% received indirect money through advertising. Leading the effort to rid college sports of alcohol advertising are the athletic directors and head coaches of some high-profile schools. They join a campaign that is backed by the *Center for Science in the Public Interest* (CSPI) and the *Center on Alcohol Marketing and Youth*.

Prescription Drugs:
The Overlooked Danger for DUI

In discussions surrounding DUI, driving under the influence of drugs is often overlooked in favor of the much more widespread driving under the influence of alcohol.

Many states have recognized the danger of driving while impaired by drugs and have coupled strict drug possession penalties with DUI penalties specifically targeted toward those convicted of driving while high on drugs.

However, despite these legal measures targeted toward drugged driving, prescription drugs are often missing as part of the discussion by lawmakers, public officials and drivers alike.

The fact is, an athlete using prescription drugs can cause impairment as great or even greater than using illegal drugs, which can be dangerous to both the driver as well as others on the road.

Another consideration when discussing athletes and prescription drugs is that some prescription drugs enhance alcohol absorption rates and, therefore, can affect your body's processing of any alcohol that you have consumed. This can lead to a potentially dangerous misperception of your level of intoxication.

Drugs like codeine, Percodan, Xanax, Valium, and a host of other drugs are labeled with instructions to avoid these drugs when operating a motor vehicle.

However, when treated as a recommendation on a prescription bottle, some athletes may not realize that criminal penalties can result from impairment, just as with illegal drugs and alcohol. An athlete trying to beg off by pleading ignorance won't work when the danger is listed right on the medication — judges in a DUI case won't buy it.

In some cases, an athlete may have proclaimed the idea that using prescription drugs just to get a high in place of illegal drugs makes them safer.

Oxycodone products, Vicodin, Dexedrine, and many other drugs crop up at nightclubs, bars, strip clubs, and parties as drugs of choice. However, when impaired and behind the wheel, it doesn't matter what drug the driver has taken — any potential damage or accidents are treated the same way.

Prescriptions drugs, while useful in the recommended dosages given by licensed physicians, can be as deadly as any illegal drugs available.

The consequences of athletes driving while under the influence of these powerful prescription drugs can be harsh. Whether or not it was intentional, driving under the influence of prescription drugs will be viewed unfavorably by the law and can result in fines, jail time and loss of driving privileges, and even further criminal penalties — and then it's — *"hello league suspension"* and possibly *"bye-bye athletic career."*

A Note about Drowsy Driving

Most sports fans are well aware of the dangers posed by driving under the influence of alcohol or drugs — part of the reason that criminal penalties for those convicted of DUI are getting steeper and steeper.

But alcohol and drugs aren't the only things that can impair an athlete's ability to safely operate a vehicle. Drowsy driving, or driving without getting adequate sleep can be just as dangerous as driving drunk.

In a country where athletes are pulled by the demands of being pro and college players, sleep is often the first "luxury" to be dropped when you need to squeeze more activities onto your calendars. Depriving the body of quality rest hours, though, could have deadly consequences for you.

Sources indicate that going 18 hours without sleep leads to a level of impairment equal to that of someone with a blood alcohol content of .08%, the legal limit nationwide.

Part of the problem of drowsy driving is that there's no way to test for it. If an athlete has been drinking alcohol, police can use a breathalyzer test to measure the concentration of alcohol on your breath, which can help determine your level of impairment. But if you haven't slept enough lately, that won't show up on any roadside test police can administer.

Like drunkenness, reports indicate that sleepiness slows reaction time, decreases awareness, impairs judgment and, therefore, increases the risk that a tired driver will cause an accident.

Worse yet is driving drowsy AND intoxicated!

Unlike DUIs, drowsy driving can be impacted by a number of factors, including medical conditions an athlete may have, medications being taken, career and family demands, and the amount of sleep an athlete gets.

Experts suggest taking precautions to guard against driving while tired, especially if you're planning on taking a long trip.

Here's what athletes can do to prevent drowsy driving:

- Get a full night's sleep the night before leaving. That means 8 to 10 hours of uninterrupted slumber.
- Take breaks on the road. Some experts suggest allowing for 15-minute breaks for every two hours of driving.
- If possible, alternate drivers, if one is available, to give everyone a chance to rest.
- Drink coffee or other caffeinated beverages.
- If you get on the road and feel yourself drifting off, pull over somewhere safe, drink a cup of coffee and take a 15 to 20 minute break, or get out of your vehicle and stretch your legs out while the caffeine kicks in.

Driver impairment doesn't always come in a bottle. Athletes should be cautious whenever you operate a vehicle.

All athletes have a **C.H.O.I.C.E**™ and it's broken down like this:

Courage: Having the courage to step away from another drink when you know you've had too much. Having the courage to NOT get in your vehicle and drive when you've been drinking. Having the courage to make these choices consistently, without hesitation.

> *"It's about having the courage to do what's right, instead of what's easy."*
> – David L. Brown

Honesty: Being honest with yourself, and listening to that small still voice inside that warns you before you make a poor decision. Being honest and not putting yourself on a pedestal, and knowing you're human and will make mistakes.

> *"A true friend will tell you the truth to your face — not behind your back."*
> – Sasha Azevedo

Opportunity: To play your sport is a privilege, an honor, and a blessing. It's an opportunity to play the game you love and have worked hard to excel in, which can easily be taken away from you in an instant if you don't make the right choices every day.

> *"Opportunities always look greater going than coming."*
> – Unknown

Integrity: Having the integrity to admit your mistakes, and having the courage to change your attitude and habits.

> *"Integrity is telling yourself the truth.*
> *And honesty is telling the truth to other people."*
> – Spencer Johnson

Commitment: Displaying true commitment to being the best person you can be, on and off the field and court, for yourself, your family, your teammates, coaches, and your organization.

> *"Individual commitment to a group effort — that is what makes a team work,*
> *a company work, a society work, a civilization work."*
> – Vince Lombardi

Excellence: Striving for excellence in your life and career each and every day, yet knowing success is a journey, not a finish line.

"We are what we repeatedly do. Excellence, then, is not an act, but a habit."
– Aristotle

"Champions do not become champions when they win the game, but in the hours, weeks, months and years they spend preparing for it. The victorious performance itself is merely the demonstration of their excellent championship character."
– T. Alan Armstrong

You must also have **S.M.A.R.T.S**™ to succeed:

S.afety
M.ission
A.ttitude
R.esponsibility
T.rust
S.acrifice

It's a safety mission based on a good attitude, accepting responsibility for your actions, trusting yourself to do the right things, and making the right sacrifices to attain success along the way.

Play Hard. Do Good. The World is Watching.™

Chapter 3
GUNS

Think Before You Carry!™

Some athletes carry a gun. It's a fact. No sense being naïve about it. It's your right as an American citizen. Just make sure you're licensed, trained, and of a sound mind when making the decision to carry or use it.

When not, athletes and guns can be a horrible mix.

An infamous former New York Giants wide receiver pleaded guilty August 20, 2009, to a weapons charge and agreed to a two-year prison term for accidentally shooting himself at a Manhattan nightclub in the early morning hours of Saturday, November 29, 2008. The wide receiver pleaded guilty to one count of attempted criminal possession of a weapon, a lesser charge than he initially faced.

Under the plea agreement, he agreed to a two-year prison sentence and two years of supervised release. With time off for good behavior, legal officials speculate the two-year sentence could be reduced to 20 months. Sentencing was set on September 22, 2009. He could be freed as early as spring, 2011. He will be monitored during an additional two years of supervised release.

Upon release from federal state prison, the athlete will be 34 years old. It may be an uphill battle to resume his NFL career.

The athlete and a former teammate were at a popular Manhattan nightclub.

While walking up a flight of stairs to the VIP section, the gun, tucked into the designer black jeans he was wearing, slipped down his pant leg, and as he reached through the outside of his jeans to keep the gun from sliding down further, he accidentally pulled the trigger and the gun fired, shooting him in the right thigh. The athlete later told a reporter that the sound of the gun firing was not heard due to high noise levels at the crowded club.

Shockingly, the athlete also told the reporter that nightclub security knew he had the gun, and he was allowed to enter the club anyway, through the metal detectors, after being patted down by hand.

When the reporter asked the athlete why he was not wearing a holster to contain the weapon properly, the athlete replied, "Bad judgment."

The gun was not licensed in New York or in New Jersey, where the athlete lived, prosecutors said. His license to carry a concealed weapon in the state of Florida had reportedly expired in May, 2008.

The athlete's attorney told reporters the case was "a perfect example about how bad judgment can have very serious consequences."

The athlete, then 32, and his wife, were expecting a child, a baby girl, around Thanksgiving, 2009. Unfortunately, he will not be there to witness and take part in that special moment in a father's life. He also has a young son.

He caught the winning touchdown for the Giants over the New England Patriots in the final minute of *Super Bowl XLII* (Super Bowl 42).

Here's the time line regarding this unfortunate story:

- November 29, 2008: The athlete suffered an accidental self-inflicted gunshot wound to the right thigh at a nightclub in Manhattan.
- December 1, 2008: Charged with two counts of second degree criminal possession of a weapon.
- December 2, 2008: Suspended by the New York Giants football team.
- March 31, 2009: Case delayed until June 15, 2009.
- April 3, 2009: Released by the New York Giants.
- June 15, 2009: Case again delayed until September, 23, 2009.
- July 29, 2009: Testified before Grand Jury.
- August 3, 2009: Indicted by Grand Jury.
- August 20, 2009: Plead guilty to one count of attempted criminal possession of a weapon.

Afterward, NFL Commissioner Roger Goodell suspended the wide receiver indefinitely, a ban that will run concurrently with the prison term he agreed to in the guilty plea.

The NFL released this public statement to the media: "[*athlete's name*] is not under contract to an NFL team. In light of his plea today, Commissioner Roger Goodell has suspended [*athlete's name*] and informed him that he is ineligible to sign with any team until he completes his jail term. Commissioner Goodell said [*athlete's name*] will be reinstated and eligible to sign with an NFL team upon the completion of his sentence. [*athlete's name*] was notified on June 26 that Commissioner Goodell had initiated a review of the matter for potential discipline under the NFL's personal conduct and weapons policies."

One must now wonder if his NFL career is over.

If an athlete can't be trusted to make good choices OFF the field and court, how can your teammates, coaches, and your organization trust you to make good choices ON the field and court?

They can't — and they won't. And, soon after, the world will be reading that you were released from your team.

That's the reality of the consequences from the choices you make.

Even non-athlete trained professionals make mistakes with guns.

In Orlando, Florida, April 2004, a federal drug agent shot himself in the leg during a gun safety class. The *Drug Enforcement Administration* agent (DEA), was giving a gun safety presentation to about 50 adults and students organized by a youth golf association, witnesses and police said.

According to the police report, the federal agent drew his .40-caliber duty weapon and removed the magazine. He then pulled back the slide and asked someone in the audience to look inside the gun and confirm it wasn't loaded. Witnesses said the gun was pointed at the floor, and when the federal agent released the slide, one shot fired into the top of his left thigh.

In May 2009, a twenty-six-year-old Phoenix gun-safety advocate veteran, accidentally shot himself in the head while demonstrating gun safety, the *Arizona Daily Star* reported. The man was explaining to two others the necessity of keeping guns unloaded in the house.

To demonstrate, he placed his own gun, which he thought was unloaded, to his head and pulled the trigger. He was pronounced dead at a local hospital.

If these tragic events can happen to a highly trained federal agent and a veteran gun safety advocate, it can happen to you. If you're a young athlete, find a good mentor who will provide guidance and wisdom to help you with your decision making. Be the athlete who chooses to be proactive by using good judgment each and every day.

Off-topic note: Many people ask me about dog fighting and the infamous former Atlanta Falcons, now Philadelphia Eagles quarterback.

I doubt you'll hear about another dog fighting story in sports for a long, long time.

There is a tremendous negative spotlight surrounding the subject of dog fighting. The mere utterance of the word sends chills up the spine — and makes the hairs on the back of one's neck stand up.

Nationally and around the world, people are intensely disgusted with anyone who has any involvement in such vile acts.

This much is clear — people take dog fighting and cruelty to animals *personally*.

Dog fighting is a profound *Athlete Career Killer*™. As far as another athlete being caught and charged with dog fighting, I just don't believe you'll hear of it again anytime soon. Incidents involving clubbing, drunk driving, guns, drugs, domestic violence, infidelity, home invasion, gambling, and money problems are far more common headlines you will read about regarding professional and college athletes.

I'm a huge dog lover. I abhor dog fighting — or any other type of animal cruelty. Unfortunately, dog fighting still exists to some degree underground. I'm hopeful the proper authorities will put an end to that senseless and heartless crime for good.

As for the athlete himself — he paid his debt to society. He got punished for his crimes. The rest of his career in the NFL, on and off the field, and as a human being, is now up to him.

I hope he'll cherish this blessed second opportunity and commit to making good choices going forward.

Remember...

> *"Opportunities always look greater going than coming."*
> – Unknown

Before You Buy or Carry a Gun

NBA Commissioner David Stern said he advises his athletes to leave their guns at home when they go out in public.

"I don't think it's necessary to walk the streets packing a gun," Stern said during a teleconference to reporters. "I think it's dangerous for our players." "It's a pretty widely accepted statistic that if you carry a gun, your chances of being shot by one increase dramatically," he said.

"We think this is an alarming subject that, although you'll read about players saying how they feel safer with guns, in fact, those guns actually make them less safe. And it's a real issue," the NBA Commissioner told reporters.

The NBA Commissioner's office has definitely made it clear that it wants to set the highest standard of personal conduct for its athletes.

You may be an athlete looking for your first self-defense handgun. Or you might be a lifelong "gun person." Either way, this book is for you.

Guns are among the deadliest of hand-held weapons because they are effective and widely available. Consequently, they are also the weapons of popular choice by violent criminals. By the same token, guns are a lethal means of self-defense in the hands of properly trained citizens.

Given that, what's an athlete to do? It's a complex and personal dilemma. It has to start with education and open communication.

You're an athlete holding this book in your hands right now, and you're considering buying a gun for home or personal protection. You must be beware of common mistakes associated with your reliance on this weapon. It's alarming how many people become frightened or angry about violence and crime in our society and rush right out to buy a firearm.

In some cases, this emotional reaction can be fatal.

Athletes may assume the mere possession of a firearm will guarantee your safety. This assumption forms a fallacy of dependency and the sole reliance on a particular weapon for personal protection. While a gun may augment your personal protection, no single weapon, self-defense technique, or security alarm system is the definitive answer — by itself.

Here are twelve things athletes should consider when thinking about purchasing a gun.

1. Why do you want a gun? Do you want a gun for protection, or to go hunting, for example?
2. If you want it for hunting, do you know how to hunt? Do you have a place that is safe for hunting nearby? Do you have a hunting license?
3. Often, the reason some athletes or coaches carry a gun is cultural. Whether you came out of a tough neighborhood or you're from a small rural town, guns may

have been a common part of your life growing up. Owning or possessing one or more for protection or hunting is not a big issue for you.

4. Consider the safety of having a gun in your home. If you decide to have a gun in your home, it should be locked up. Your children, if any, should not have access to it. You should not store the bullets and the gun in the same place.
5. If you buy a gun for safety or for hunting, take a gun safety class. Attend regular target practice at a shooting range. If you don't know how to properly handle a gun, it becomes a potential danger to you and your family.
6. Are you willing and mature enough to take on the added responsibility and accountability that comes with owning and carrying a gun?
7. Liability issues come with owning a gun. Find out what they are. Make sure you are taking every precaution available.
8. Teach your children, if any, and other family members about gun safety.
9. Can you carry a concealed weapon in a certain state or community?
10. Can you carry a concealed weapon across state lines?
11. What guns are allowed, and what guns are outlawed?
12. What are the ramifications of carrying an unlicensed firearm?

It's a personal choice for each athlete.

Once you make the choice to own or carry a gun, you must be responsible for the safety of yourself and those around you. Gun ownership is guaranteed and protected by the Second Amendment. This immediately provokes hard debate and fiery discussions when any type of control or restriction on gun purchases or ownership is proposed.

Informing yourself about the facts regarding gun ownership and the risks involved is just plain smart.

All self-defense weapons have limitations. Consider, for example, the limitations of a handgun.

You can't take a handgun everywhere. Legal restrictions and disregard of the law aside, you still can't carry a handgun everywhere you go. If you don't take my word for it, try slipping one past airport security or into a courthouse. These aren't the only types of limitations.

Criminal predators are smart. They rely on the element of surprise. They get the drop on you before you can get to your gun. It happens all the time, even to law enforcement officers. Guns also jam, run out of ammunition, misfire, and can easily get tangled up in your clothing when drawn.

Athletes must ask themselves — is it worth it?

Not all violent situations justify the use of a gun. For example, a hostile confrontation with an enraged but unarmed motorist won't justify self-defense with a weapon. The bottom line is, as athletes, only you can accept the full responsibility for your self-defense, and you must have a variety of self-protection measures to meet the myriad of potential conflicts.

You must be equipped and prepared to rely on all available means. Most importantly, you must also rely on your intelligence, common sense, and emotional calm.

Firearm ownership is a controversial issue that has generated tremendous national concern, sports or not.

Some pro gun activists believe that law-abiding citizens have an absolute Constitutional right to bear arms, with restrictions. Their opponents, on the other hand, believe that guns are the root of all evil and must be eliminated to address criminal violence in our society effectively.

Again, what's an athlete to do?

As long as there are deadly and vicious criminals, there will be an availability of firearms.

However, I don't believe that everyone should own a gun. It's difficult to disagree with the position that gun ownership should be restricted to law abiding athletes who are willing to make the time and commitment to safe, responsible ownership. You just have to be smart about it, be legal, and be trained.

The decision for athletes to own a firearm for personal protection or not, warrants considerable personal thought and honest reflection.

Here are six important questions to consider:
1. Do you live alone?
2. Are there children in your household?
3. What experiences have you had in handling guns in the past?
4. What type of gun is right for you?
5. Have you ever fired a gun?
6. Are you willing to take the time to obtain a license and learn the skills needed to handle a firearm safely?

I encourage you to sit down and have a serious face-to-face talk with yourself in the mirror before you consider buying or carrying a gun.

Remember these scary truths about firearms:

Many gun owners are killed accidentally by their *own weapons*. Handguns and shotguns contribute significantly to the death or injury of friends and family members yearly.

The *NFL, NBA, NHL, Major League Baseball*, the player's associations, the *NCAA*, and law enforcement authorities, all have policies and programs that continually educate athletes to recognize the dangers of owning and carrying a gun, including rules stating athletes must not possess a gun or any other weapon at any time and at any location that you are performing any service for your team or your specific league.

For example, you are strongly prohibited from carrying a firearm into your locker room, or into the arena, stadium or sports facility you play at.

The pro leagues conduct yearly rookie symposiums and transition programs for their young athletes to acclimate them to the nuances of being professional athletes, on and off the field and court.

This goes without saying, but I'll say it anyway. Please do not attempt to transport or conceal a weapon of any kind in your luggage or on your person, knowingly or not, licensed or not, in an airport. How many stories have you heard about athletes getting caught with a weapon in this manner? It will be discovered by airport security, and you'll have a career-long worth of baggage (*no pun intended*) to explain.

It's just not worth it!

Pro and college athletes, if you own a gun, or have possession of a gun, I encourage you to inform your college or university, your pro league, and your team about it. Allow them the opportunity to help you become a responsible, licensed, and trained gun owner and handler. Take advantage of your school or league's immense resources that help you stay safe. It's all about open communication and two-sided dialogue.

Help your team help you. It's the smart and safe way to go.

The Pros and Cons

You must fully understand your local, state, and federal laws that apply to gun ownership, and be aware that if you transport a weapon from one place to another, for example, across state lines — a different set of laws may apply in a different location.

In some circumstances, the mere presence or showing of a firearm may allow you to gain control and command over a robber or attacker without firing your weapon. Consider the story of a Yonkers, New York man, who was making a call at a public phone one evening, when a robber came out of nowhere and demanded his wallet. Instead, he reached into his front pocket and came out with his licensed .38 revolver.

The criminal fled empty-handed. A gun can tilt the balance of power significantly in your favor — if your attacker is unarmed.

Now, let's *flip the script*.

A Texas man and his wife were walking out of a restaurant early one evening, when a man approached them, nervously asking for directions. Frightened and sensing danger, the husband pulled out his Glock 23 .40 caliber handgun. A struggle ensued. The other man, with the intent to rob the couple, was also carrying a weapon. The two men held their weapons in hand as the other man's wife looked on in horror.

Each man then shot the other at close range. Both men were killed. Tragically, before the robber took his last breath, he shot the man's wife — killing her also.

If you're an untrained or irresponsible gun owner, you may be more dangerous to yourself than a potential criminal. Most firearm accidents are attributed to ignorance and carelessness. Safe gun handling is your responsibility, and safety must always be your number one priority.

To ensure the safe use of any firearm, always follow these four general safety rules:
1. Always assume a firearm is loaded.
2. Always point a firearm in a safe direction.
3. Never point a gun at anything you don't intend to hit.
4. Never put your finger on the trigger until you are ready to shoot.

Gun ownership also carries tremendous social responsibilities for athletes. The laws concerning firearm usage are not something you are going to learn overnight. Using a firearm for self-defense is legally complex. Consider, for example, the fact that it is not always justified to use a gun against an intruder in your home during a home invasion.

This fact is hard to believe or accept, but it's true. A gun places you in the position of judge, jury, and executioner — all in a matter of seconds. Athletes must be committed in taking on that responsibility and protecting yourself and your families, as well as accepting the consequences should something go terribly wrong.

Unless you have specialized training and are licensed, high school, college, and pro athletes are no more qualified to use a gun because you've got one than you are to conduct a Beethoven 9th Symphony — *The Ode to Joy* — just because you own the sheet music. You must fully understand the inherent risks involved.

If you violate public laws regarding weapons, like for possession of an unlicensed gun — you're not only subject to being suspended or kicked off your team and banned from playing the sport you love, you will also be subject to criminal prosecution — and bye-bye athletic career — *hello orange prison jump suit.*

It's called — "Finality of Reality™," and vice-versa.

Scenarios

You're an athlete. It's Saturday night. You take your wife or girlfriend out to a nice dinner and an evening out. The outing promises to be a lot of fun. The food and conversation was great, and as you leave the restaurant your thoughts are on the rest of the night's activities. You both go outside onto the sidewalk for a stroll together. A short distance down the street, you approach an inset doorway. You observe three men standing partially inside the doorway. As you walk by the men, one steps out onto the sidewalk, blocking your pathway.

The apparent leader has a gun in his hand, and you suspect the other two bad guys may be carrying as well. At this point, there are two possible scenarios that could happen in this situation.

Which of the following scenarios would you choose to be involved in?

First Scenario

One of the bad guys grabs your wife or girlfriend and forces her into the doorway while you are held at gunpoint. You make a decision not to fight back, and you know you're not carrying a gun on you. The third bad guy strikes you from behind with a weapon and you fall to the sidewalk. Both remaining attackers repeatedly kick you in the head and body, and you pass out.

Later, you awaken to find your lady beaten, your wallet, jewelry, and her purse and jewelry gone. Both of you need non life-threatening medical attention.

You're both injured — but alive.

Second Scenario

The leader of the bad guys steps up to within four feet in front of you while pointing a pistol in your face. You raise your hands into a surrender position. Suddenly, and in self-defense of yourself and your wife/girlfriend, you begin to throw punches toward the attacker.

The attacker pulls free of your grip and points his gun in your direction again. You then pull out your gun. The two of you wrestle for what seems like hours to gain control of each others weapon. The other two men stand and watch, waiting to see what happens next, while keeping your wife/girlfriend at bay.

Finally, you gain control. Your leading hand lands on top of the bad guy's gun, and with a rotating twist, you turn the gun straight back up the gunman's wrist with the muzzle of his gun pointed outside and away from you. You take control and now have possession of his gun. You strike the man in the face with your free hand and also give him a knee to the ribs. You grab the gunman and turn him around and use him as a shield, then use yours and his gun to disarm the other two attackers. The main attacker breaks free from you, and all three attackers flee on foot. Your lady uses her cell phone to call 9-1-1.

Shaken, neither of you are hurt.

Each scenario is over within a matter of a minute or two.

Which scenario would you most likely choose?

Expert psychologists say an athlete would be more likely to choose the *second scenario*. Why? Because of the nature of your competitive DNA, an athlete would be more likely to physically defend himself, or use his gun, when faced with a potentially violent situation. It's a risk you take. Any type of struggle with a robber when guns are involved could cost you your life and those you love.

Is it worth it? Only you can answer that question.

Consider the option in the second scenario. If you're carrying a gun, keep it in its holster. Your first option would be to give the robber what he wants. Take out your wallet. Take off your jewelry. Instruct your wife/girlfriend to give up her purse and jewelry. Let the robber know you're cooperating and that you don't want any trouble and will not attempt to fight back.

The robber expects you to do exactly as you're told under these intense situations, and he may be shocked into indecision if you do the unexpected. That indecision allows you time to get away as fast as you can. You could throw each of your belongings one way — and run the other way! Most likely, the attackers are going to want your *STUFF* — not you.

And, ladies, if you're wearing heels — kick 'em off and run!

What's Your MVP?

An athlete's MVP can have two meanings. One is, your Most Valuable Purpose™ in life. Two, your Most Valuable Passion™ in life. They could have the same meaning to you — or be different.

Success as an athlete comes from being excellent at what you do. Your sport rewards and awards you for excellent performance. Excellence is a continual journey, not a final destination. You never really settle there. You can never really relax. Your sport is always changing, and what constitutes as excellence today will be different tomorrow, and different next year and the year after.

How do you define your MVP if you don't already have it?

1. By standing, day-by-day, in the conscious presence of God, the One from whom your MVP is derived.
2. To do what you can, moment by moment, step-by-step, to make this world a better place, by following the guidance of God's spirit within you and around you.
3. Striving to exercise your talents as an athlete and human being, which you came to this Earth to use.
4. Putting yourself in the right positive places or settings, and giving yourself the opportunity to make good choices within those positive places or settings.
5. Finding your purpose for which God most needs to have you strive toward in the world.

Athletes are special. You arrive with a hopeful purpose to somehow SERVE your fellow man and woman. You are blessed with tremendous opportunities and given unique talents that, when leveraged, will be HOW you serve your fellow man and woman. Your talents provide the vehicle through which you express and share your gifts with others.

Please think carefully before you decide to buy, carry, or use a gun, as this may severely diminish your MVP.

Could You Survive an Attack?

Nothing replaces good tactical training. It is a proven fact that when you find yourself in a potentially lethal confrontation, you will do what you have practiced — just like in a game. If you have not practiced proper procedures and tactics, you stand a greater chance of losing any confrontation — just like in a game.

If you own a gun, going out to a range and shooting is good and, no doubt, will improve your shooting ability, but this will not keep you alive if you encounter one or more bad guys wanting to take your stuff, and maybe even your life. While pinpoint accuracy is desirable, it is not your most important asset in a gunfight.

Sudden trauma to the body's vital organs causes shock, and shock causes a quick end to any confrontation.

Athletes practice hard between games, but it's nothing like the experience of real live game speed.

The distance at which a gun attack may occur is very short. Experts say most attacks happen at arm's length or, at the greatest distance, only about the length of a car. Whatever might go down, it will be up close, down and dirty, and almost always comes as a complete surprise.

Police officers informed me they need to be very accurate out to about fifty or sixty yards — a half of a city block. In some cases, where a sniper or suspect is armed with a rifle or other long-range weapons, officers may be required to shoot at even more extreme distances. The trouble athletes may find themselves in usually comes from very close range.

A robber or attacker is more likely to assault you by suddenly appearing from nowhere, or while crashing through the door or window of your home during a home invasion. Police say 95% of the confrontations involving regular civilians occur at three to five feet — nose to nose and toes to toes. At this distance you will not have time to even aim your weapon if you're carrying one.

In reality, you are going to have to react from whatever position you happen to be in at the time. Attacks do not come when you are expecting them. You may be attacked while you have your hands full of groceries, preoccupied with talking or texting on your cell phone or Blackberry, listening to music on your iPod, or doing something else. You may be looking away, or not paying attention to what's going on around you. You may even be in a sitting position in a restaurant or in your vehicle.

If someone pulls a gun on you — run! *DO NOT BE A STATIONARY TARGET.* Never stay out in the open. Find cover if possible. Duck behind cars, utility poles, or anything that will stop or slow incoming bullets if you are on the street.

At home, heavy bookcases, waterbeds, refrigerator doors, etc. are pretty fair cover. Ladies, when out and about with your athlete, consider carrying your valuables in a fanny pack. Cover the fanny pack with a loose fitting blouse, T-shirt or other type clothing. Consider carrying a "dummy" purse filled with crumpled up paper to use as a decoy.

Since November 2008, it's been reported that firearm sales in the United States have increased an estimated 50% over the same time frame between 2007 and 2008. Many of the people who account for the increased sales are first-time firearm buyers. That should make you uneasy. Unfortunately, many of the first time buyers, including athletes, are not properly educated and trained on basic firearm principles before they bring a gun into their home or carry one in a public place, and this is when trouble may find you.

70 Gun Safety Tips

1. Make no mistake about this one — the best self-defense tip of all time for athletes — is *not* being at that location in the first place.
2. Consider other safety measures as opposed to carrying a gun in public, like hiring extra security personnel.
3. Do not put yourself in situations or places where you might be forced to use your handgun, if you carry one. The smartest, bravest, and most intelligent thing you can do is to think ahead and prevent as many bad situations as possible from happening. Common sense plays a large role in gun safety.
4. *NEVER* enter a nightclub, bar, gentleman's club, house party, restaurant, airport, or any other building or function carrying a loaded weapon.
5. *NEVER* mix alcohol or drugs with handling a weapon.
6. Abide by the laws. You should be familiar with all local, state, and federal laws regarding the safe storage and transportation of your firearm.

7. Stress and anxiety is an athlete's worst enemy in life threatening situations because it distorts time perception and clouds judgment. Adrenaline levels skyrocket to points that negatively impact the ability to effectively control a firearm. The amount of force necessary to squeeze the trigger of a gun can be misjudged — an incident responsible for countless accidental gun discharges. Learning to control stress and your emotions is a key factor in surviving a life threatening situation.
8. Fatigue, drowsiness, and guns don't mix.
9. Be careful about what comes out of your mouth at a club, bar, or party. Your words to others may be perceived as offensive, rude, and disrespectful to them. Think before you speak. If someone is rude or disrespectful toward you with their words — just walk away, mouth closed, and live to see another day.
10. These days, many people have their own issues in dealing with life's ups and downs. At a club, bar, or party, it can make a person argumentative and aggressive. Avoid people who seem agitated in any way. Even a casual glance at someone can set them off and into — PO'd Mode™.
11. Don't make the mistake of thinking that ANYBODY fights "fair" anymore. Those days are over in today's society. Expect the bad guys to come with multiple attackers, weapons, or possibly both. If something breaks out, let your trained security people handle it and call the police.
12. If you own a gun, store it unloaded and locked up. Lock it out of a child's reach.
13. Keep trigger locks on your guns for extra prevention, or disassemble your gun completely when not in use.
14. *Never* pass a firearm to another person — or accept a firearm from another person.
15. Before handling any firearm, understand how it operates. Not every gun is designed the same way.
16. *Never* rely on any mechanical device for safety.
17. Remember, a gun's mechanical safety device is never 100% foolproof.
18. Think before you shoot. Once you pull that trigger, you can't take back the shot you've just fired!
19. *Never* joke around or engage in horseplay while handling or using firearms.
20. *Never* attempt to handle a weapon if your emotions are frayed.

21. Don't sleep with a loaded firearm in your bedroom if you sleepwalk, sleep restlessly, or have other sleep problems.
22. If you see unsafe behavior any time when firearms are being handled or used, speak up and take action to correct it immediately.
23. If you don't know how to open the cylinder or inspect the chamber(s) to insure the firearm is empty, don't touch it. Seek assistance from a trained or experienced person who does.
24. Your dresser drawer or nightstand is never a good place to keep your firearm. The bad guys will look there first in the event of a burglary or home invasion.
25. There are an estimated 600,000 firearms stolen each year in the U.S. as a result of burglary. These stolen guns often end up in the hands of criminals. Make sure you know where your gun came from.
26. Go to firearm training in your area. Your local or state police departments may offer free courses given to the public by highly trained officers.
27. Let your league and agent know if you're carrying. Let them help you find ways to further educate yourself about the gun you own, and the specific laws pertaining to it.
28. Before you buy a gun, ask yourself this question: *"Am I comfortable with handguns?"* Not every athlete will be better off with a gun. In some cases, athletes can be more dangerous than their would-be attackers. If you're uncomfortable around firearms, don't buy or handle one.
29. Take as many licensing, safety and gun instruction courses as possible.
30. If you carry a gun, use a holster. It's better to be safe than tragically sorry.
31. Keep firearms away from your children. But, if they're old enough, consider allowing them to accompany you to the firing range, where they can see exactly what it will do. You should also instruct them to never touch it, or any other firearm, and to immediately tell an adult if they find one at a friend's house. The better educated your children are about firearms, the less likely they will be to let curiosity get the best of them.
32. If your children are still curious — as many kids can be — enroll them in safety courses designed for their age groups. Their curiosity will be satisfied, and everybody will stay safe. For you, make sure that all licensing and paperwork, including applicable registration, is in order at all times. Some paperwork must be

renewed, so keep on top of it. The last thing you want is to be caught carrying an unlicensed firearm that you thought was legal — and it's not.

33. Don't use your firearm if you have just taken any medications which may impair, even slightly, your mental or physical ability.
34. *Never* carry your gun inside your pants pocket. Items like your keys, cell phone, and coins can accidentally come in contact with the trigger and discharge the gun.
35. Know when a gun should be used in self-defense, and when not.
36. Keeping a gun in your home carries multiple risks. People are 21 times more likely to be killed by someone they know than a stranger breaking into the house. Half of gun murders are over arguments or romantic triangles. Many are caused by family or intimate acquaintances, not by strangers or non-intimate acquaintances.
37. The image of an unknown criminal breaking into your house is a frightening one for athletes who fear home invasion. Many feel it justifies keeping a gun in the home. But, to gun control advocates, a gun in the home means that a family fight or a night of drinking is more likely to turn deadly. It's a fine line you must carefully consider — and the consequences that may come with those decisions.
38. You must protect yourself and all others against injury or death from misuse of a firearm. If you feel you're not able to do this on a consistent basis — don't purchase or carry a firearm.
39. Accidents are the result of violating the rules of safe gun handling and common sense.
40. Safety must be the prime consideration of any athlete who owns or handles firearms.
41. When at home, talk to family members on a regular basis about gun safety. Game plan and talk about scenarios, and what you would do if an intruder broke into your home. Designate safe areas in the home where family members will go and meet later if there's ever trouble.
42. Never carry or store a firearm with the hammer or striker in the cocked position.
43. Do not allow a firearm to be used by individuals who do not know how to use it.
44. Ensure all accessories, such as holsters and grips, are compatible with the firearm, and that the accessories do not interfere with safe operation. Use the correct accessories for your particular weapon.

45. Know how to carry a weapon. How you carry a gun is generally more important than the kind of gun you carry. In most self-defense situations, if you can't access your gun cleanly and instantly, you may as well not have it.
46. In terms of quick, easy access, a waist holster is generally a good way to carry a handgun. An inside-the-pants waist holster will provide better security of the weapon and reduce improper handling accidents, like the one mentioned earlier in this chapter involving the former New York Giants wide receiver.
47. Inside-the-pants holsters fit inside the pants waistband, against your body. They are attached by loops through which your belt passes, or by a clip that grips your pants waistband and/or belt.
48. An outside-the-pants holster fits completely outside your pants. They are attached by means of loops or slots through which your belt passes, or by a "paddle" system. However, these are exposed, and may cause concern for you and others around you unless you're wearing a long jacket or coat. They also may be illegal in some states.
49. What's your true level of experience with firearms in general, and the particular gun you're considering, in particular?
50. Handguns are known to be the most difficult firearms to shoot well.
51. If a fight breaks out in a club or bar, and someone pulls out a gun — leave immediately. Leave before all the drunks and brawlers start swinging chairs, bottles, glasses and punches. A "free-for-all" usually starts with just two protagonists. Innocent bystanders often get injured or killed. Don't let this be you!
52. *NEVER* attempt to mediate an argument between a man and a woman at a club, bar, or party. Both will usually stop arguing or fighting with each other and turn on you — the common enemy. If you fear for a woman's safety, call the police, and let the experts handle things.
53. If someone pulls a gun on you, run if you can, in a zigzag pattern, which makes you a moving target and more difficult to hit. There is no shame in avoiding a fight. In fact, running away is smart.
54. As an athlete, have the attitude that you are part of the solution in the prevention of senseless gun violence in this country — not part of the problem.

55. It's one thing to be confident, but if you carry a gun and don't have the skills to actually back up that confidence in a potentially violent situation, it's useless, and there could be a tragic result.
56. If or when you are confronted by someone who has a gun, don't try to reason with him or her peaceably. Crazy people can't be reasoned with.
57. If someone pulls a weapon on you, stay calm and think as the situation develops. As soon as the adrenaline kicks in, everything will seem to happen in slow motion. If you're calm and don't panic, your mind will process thoughts so rapidly that it will seem like you have hours to make a decision about how to react.
58. There are a lot of self-defense myths out there. There are three big ones that seem to trick athletes time and time again. In hopes of exposing these myths, let's look at a couple of them.
59. **Myth #1:** There is only one ultimate self-defense style. This is not true. Every athlete's experience with violence or a crime against them is different. The truth is, a lot of things come into play. What's the level of the PO'd Points (POPS™) of your attacker? Have you been drinking? Have they been drinking? All these things, and more, come into play when you are determining the best self-defense method for you.
60. **Myth #2:** Athletes already know everything there is to know about guns, and how to react to a potentially dangerous or violent situation while at a club, bar, or party. Unless you've already been there — you really truly don't know how you would react. You must consistently study and practice the complete POPS™ safety system before, during, and after clubbing in order to prepare yourself for the worst.
61. The truth is, the most effective self-defense weapon is your mind and your attitude — sprinkled with some good ole' common sense.
62. Today's world is full of insecurity and more dangerous for athletes than ever before. Every added piece of information about how to be smart in self-defense means an improvement in dealing with a potential disaster.
63. Some athletes who were victims of an attack confessed to having ignored their intuition prior to the attack. Don't fear that you might appear as if you're overreacting or paranoid.

64. Staying on guard and being aware is an excellent way for athletes to stay safe. Activities of the day take you to different places at different times. Wherever you are, be aware. Always think in terms of safety and prevention.
65. Remain proactive. Consistently talk about safety with your teammates, coaches, and your league. Go out of your way to share your wisdom and knowledge with young athletes on your team, in your league, college, university, or at your high school.
66. Just because octagon and cage fighting events you see on TV have rules and referees, athletes know it's not the same in the streets.
67. If you sense there might be a problem with someone before they try to put their hands on you in an attempted assault — call 9-1-1. And if you are in any way injured, immediately go to the hospital. Do not attempt to cover it up. Do the right thing and report it.
68. Share any concerns or questions you have about guns. We can all become a part of the solution toward gun violence. Remember the old term — *"It takes a village..."*
69. Continue to educate yourself and others about guns and gun safety.
70. When you're finished reading this book, read it again. Take it with you to away games, refer to it often, and use it as a reference guide.

Who's Carrying Guns?

According to recent Crime Gun Trace Reports, the *Bureau of Alcohol, Tobacco and Firearms* (ATF) reported the following data about individuals possessing crime guns. A crime gun is any firearm that is illegally possessed, used in a crime, or suspected to have been used in a crime.

An abandoned firearm may also be categorized as a crime gun if it is suspected it was used in a crime, or illegally possessed.

- Juveniles (ages 17 and under) were associated with more than 10% of recovered crime guns.
- Youth (ages 18-24) were associated with slightly more than 47% of crime guns.
- Adults (ages 25 and older) accounted for nearly 43% of recovered crime guns.

If you have children and/or teens at home, explain to them that we all have strong emotions like anger and fear, but that these feelings can be expressed in ways other than using weapons. Demonstrate healthy ways to express anger and disagreement. Support your children and teens when they have used positive means of resolving conflict. Talk to them about the differences between violence in entertainment media, and violence in real life.

Watch television and movies with your children and teens to help them understand that what they see is not real. Find out what kinds of music they listen to, and what music videos they've seen lately. Explain that, in reality, guns can kill or cause long-term disabilities.

Inform your children and teens that most handguns have very little trigger resistance — that a gun can easily be fired by a three-year-old. Parents must know that, under these conditions, the potential for tragedy is overwhelming.

If you keep a gun in your home to defend your family, it makes no sense if that same gun puts your family member or visitors to your home at risk. If you choose to keep a firearm for home security, your objective should be to create a situation in which the firearm is readily available to YOU or other adults, yet inaccessible or inoperative to others.

No professional or college athlete should carry a gun if they are not mature enough to walk away from a verbal confrontation that might lead to them using their firearm.

"Our strong recommendation to players is that they should not own guns, and our policy prohibits all NFL employees from possessing guns or other weapons on NFL facilities or while on NFL business," said league spokesman Brian McCarthy in a publicly released statement to the media in early 2009.

One NBA agent said, "I don't see any negative in athletes learning more about safety." The agent estimated that up to half of the 14 NBA players he represents have guns, and have, at times, suggested they seek out training on how to safely use and store them. "I certainly don't think you can get enough training in that respect," he told a reporter.

The complexity regarding this issue is this — some athletes want to carry a gun for protection — as is their Second Amendment right — but their teams and leagues would rather you don't.

Whatever choice you make, choose *responsibility* either way.

Play Hard. Do Good. Live Smart.™

Chapter 4
DRUGS

Supplements, Diuretics and PEDs

"We can never solve our significant problems from the same level of thinking we were at when we created the problems."
– Albert Einstein

A Bitter Pill

Note: The following general outline of commonly used drugs and supplements is by no means exhaustive. For a complete rundown on the status of all sports-related substances, refer ***often*** to your team and league supplement and drug information guides, as they evolve.

As an athlete, you understand that there are two important facts about drugs and supplements in sports:

- There is a never-ending athletic quest for the competitive edge.
- The supplement industry is a multi-billion dollar enterprise.

High school and professional athletes choosing to take any type of supplement need to be as well-informed as possible about what you are taking. College athletes should know that the NCAA closely regulates the use of drugs and dietary supplements, and ban the use of many.

When athletes thinks about the word "Drugs," illegal street drugs, like marijuana, cocaine, and narcotics come to mind. These days, some athletes are finding themselves in trouble more often due to banned supplements than street drugs.

Before we delve further into supplements, let's briefly cover marijuana and cocaine, what they are and what they do to your body.

ATHLETE CAREER KILLERS

Marijuana has become a popular recreational substance choice for a good number of athletes.

Marijuana contains cannabinoids, the psychoactive chemicals in the cannabis plant, and ingestion is easily detected in an athlete's urine sample. Athletes should check the rules of your sporting organization in relation to marijuana and other cannabinoids, as they are classified as prohibited substances.

According to doctors, immediate side effects of cannabinoids may include impairment of balance and coordination, loss of concentration, increase in heart rate, dry mouth, increased appetite, drowsiness, hallucinations, and reduced ability to perform complex tasks, such as driving. Longer-term use of marijuana may result in loss of motivation and decreased concentration, impaired memory, learning abilities, and respiratory diseases, such as lung and throat cancer, and chronic bronchitis.

Cocaine is a powerfully addictive stimulant drug. The powdered form of cocaine is either snorted or injected. Crack is cocaine that comes in a rock crystal which is heated and smoked. The term "crack" refers to the crackling sound produced by the rock as it is heated. Many cocaine users report that they seek, but fail to achieve the same experience as they had with their first use.

Some users will increase their dose in an attempt to intensify and prolong the effect. But doctors say this can also increase the risk of adverse psychological or physiological effects. The risks of usage results in increased body temperature, heart rate, and blood pressure, headaches, abdominal pain and nausea, decreased appetite resulting in malnutrition, irritability, restlessness, anxiety, paranoia, paranoid psychosis, a loss of touch with reality, auditory hallucinations, and addiction or dependence.

Cocaine may also result in loss of smell, nosebleeds, and a chronically runny nose from snorting.

It could also increase risk of HIV and other diseases, respiratory arrest (stopped breathing), and heart attack or stroke, which may cause sudden death.

Cocaine and alcohol combined has been documented to dramatically increase the risk of sudden death.

Marijuana and cocaine are still illegal substances in this country. If you're caught with them, not only will it taint your reputation and good name — you risk losing your athletic career.

DAVID L. BROWN

Know What You Put Into Your Body

"I never learn anything talking. I only learn things when I ask questions."
– Lou Holtz

You *MUST KNOW* exactly what you're putting into your body! You, and ONLY you, are 100% responsible for what you take. In other words — *TAKE AT YOUR OWN RISK*! Burdens and standards of proof are in the hands of the individual athlete. If you don't know what's in a substance you may take — *ASK* someone who does.

For your own health and success in sports, it's strongly encouraged that you, as athletes, avoid the use of supplements altogether, or, at the very least, be extremely careful about what you choose to take.

Athletes must be explicitly advised and constantly reminded that supplements, unlike food and drugs, do not need Food and Drug Administration (FDA) approval before they are placed on the market. Products with misleading labels, or making false claims are not uncommon.

Inadvertent ingestion of a banned substance will not excuse a positive test result for an athlete.

Make sure when you leave the trainer's room, doctor's office, pharmacist's counter, or nutrition store, you understand exactly what you'll be taking and what it contains. When in doubt — don't.

"Asking questions provokes thought, which inspires open communication, which leads to a better understanding, which leads to change, which leads to solutions for athletes."
– David L. Brown

Eight tips for athletes:

1. Again...ask questions!
2. Read the ingredients thoroughly.
3. Read the label entirely.
4. Go to your team doctor or trainer.
5. Go to your league, player's association, or athletic director.
6. Know WHY you're taking it and for what.

7. If you don't feel comfortable contacting your league or the NCAA regarding diuretic and supplement verification, consult with an independent doctor or your player associations.
8. Pro and college organizations and leagues provide a list of banned substances athletes should avoid taking. **Make sure you read the list on a consistent basis.** They're there to protect your health and safety, and the integrity of the game you play.

Some supplements contain a banned diuretic. If you take a supplement or diuretic without fully knowing its contents, then are tested positive, you're looking at an automatic suspension, possible legal hassles, and a long dark cloud hanging over your athletic career.

Bumetanide, which can be used as a masking agent for steroids, has been found in some supplements, though it is not on the label. Often, ingredients in a supplement, diuretic, or PED, are NOT listed on the label. Read the label, but don't believe everything you read regarding ingredients on the label! You must be aware that the content of supplements may not match what is listed on the label of the bottle.

If you test positive for a banned stimulant, diuretic or water pill, this constitutes a positive test. Teams and leagues strongly suggest that athletes NOT take products that claim to "burn fat," or "lower weight," and other similar claims.

Ask an expert on your team or in your league to verify that what you're taking is legal.

Bumetanide is a potent diuretic for an athlete who might become dehydrated. An athlete would be taking a diuretic without knowing it. That could lead to serious health considerations. That could also lead, doctors say, to electrolyte abnormalities, cardiovascular collapse, cardiac arrhythmia, heart attack, stroke, and death.

What Are Diuretics?

Diuretics are a class of blood pressure medications. Commonly known as "water pills," they help the kidneys quickly process water and electrolytes, which reduces water weight in the body. There are many different types of diuretics which work in different areas of the kidneys, or are better at processing different minerals and water.

The most common types of diuretics available today are:
- Thiazide
- Loop diuretics

- Potassium-sparing diuretics
- Combination diuretics.

Thiazide Diuretics

Thiazide diuretics are generally recommended to help those with high blood pressure. They help block sodium and water from being reabsorbed into the body by forcing them into the urine. They may help increase blood flow by loosening the muscles in blood vessel walls.

Examples of Thiazide diuretics include:
- Indapamide
- Metolazone
- Chlorthalidone

Loop Diuretics

Loop diuretics work by stopping the body from reabsorbing chloride and reducing sodium in the blood stream. They may also reduce other essential electrolytes, like calcium and potassium, which may create an irregular heart rate.

Examples of Loop diuretics include:
- Bumetanide
- Furosemide
- Torsemide

Potassium-sparing Diuretics

Potassium-sparing diuretics are the weakest diuretic medications, but do not compromise potassium levels. They mainly help block sodium and water from being reabsorbed into the bloodstream. Because this type of diuretic is a weaker alternative, it is usually used in conjunction with another type.

Examples of potassium sparing diuretics include:
- Amiloride
- Spironolactone
- Triamterene

Combination Diuretics

Combination diuretics are exactly what they imply: a combination of diuretic medications. These are usually weaker than Thiazide or Loop diuretics, and are used in conjunction with potassium-sparing diuretics. This spares essential electrolytes while blocking and eliminating other minerals.

Examples of combination diuretics include:
- Amiloride and hydrochlorothiazide
- Spironolactone and hydrochlorothiazide
- Triamterene and hydrochlorothiazide

Why Athletes Might Buy These:
- Helps reduce water weight.
- Helps reduce water, chloride, and sodium in the body.
- Reduces risk of death from congestive heart failure and stroke.
- Costs less than most blood pressure medications.
- Has many clinical studies to prove effectiveness.

Why Athletes Won't Buy Them:
- May eliminate essential electrolytes like potassium.
- May cause an irregular heart rate.
- May increase risk of developing diabetes.

The implementation of *Good Manufacturing Processes* (GMP) in the United States has led to improved quality control, which helps to make it more difficult for contaminated dietary supplements to reach the market.

Supplement Tips

Before you intake — investigate™

1. Relatively little research is available on most supplements.
2. Long-term effects are mostly unknown for the majority of supplements.
3. Label claims on products can be vague, and hint at claims that are unsubstantiated.

4. Supplements with a USP (United States Pharmacopeia) seal on the label can provide for better content, which means what the label says is in the product, actually is. However, the USP seal does NOT mean that label claims are tested or true.
5. Natural is not synonymous with safe when it comes to supplements.
6. Stop taking any supplement if you experience side effects.
7. Consult with your team trainer, primary health care provider, your league, your player's association, or your NCAA substance committee about the safety of using supplements regarding drug interactions or effects on any medical conditions.
8. Ask your team registered dietitian about any dietary supplement, and what is known about its effects and side effects.
9. You should be aware that any product that claims to restore, correct or modify the body's physiological functions should be licensed as a medicine, according to current legislation. Licensed medicines can be identified by looking for a product license number on the label, which will look like this: *PL0242/0028*. (The numbers will change with each product.)
10. Supplements will not contain a product license (PL) number, as they're not licensed medicines.
11. The risk that supplements may contain prohibited substances are often not listed on the label.
12. How do you know if you need to take vitamin and mineral supplementation for your health? Ask questions!
13. For athletes consuming a normal, varied and balanced diet that meets their energy requirements, there is no evidence that vitamin and mineral supplementation is necessary to enhance health. In fact, recent studies suggest excessive ingestion of vitamins and minerals may be dangerous to your health. There are some practical situations in which qualified medical practitioners, accredited sports dietitians, and registered nutritionists may recommend specific vitamins or minerals for certain individuals. (For example, if iron levels are low.)
14. However, these should be taken with a qualified expert's advice, and only used as directed or prescribed.
15. Although some substances found in supplements are not on the list of prohibited substances and methods, this assessment can only be made of the substances actually listed on the label of the product.

16. Do your due diligence. Manufacturers are often aware of the competitiveness of sports and the continual striving to achieve. Many market their products by relying on personal endorsements by well-known sports personalities or anecdotal evidence, neither of which may be based on scientific studies or reliable evidence.
17. Can you get your supplements tested to make sure they are safe to take? Again, ask questions.
18. Supplement use by athletes presents many challenges. We need to respect the athlete's desire to optimize performance, and balance this with the need to protect your health.
19. Supplements are available so readily and hold significant appeal because of the promise of quick results with little effort. We need to ask the questions: what do you take, how much, and how often?
20. The ultimate goal is to help you strive, thrive, and stay alive.

Why Do Athletes Take Supplements?

Supplements and certain drugs have a variety of uses among athletes. A large number of preparations exist to treat legitimate medical conditions. Many of these substances have performance-enhancing benefits, especially when used in quantities above therapeutic doses. Athletes can receive therapeutic exemptions in the event they require treatment with such supplements and drugs.

Performance-enhancing drugs (PEDs) include those that produce direct ergogenic benefits, and also those that can produce benefits such as hastened recovery from injury, or allow an athlete to train or compete while injured. Sport is a business. Athletes now have to be the best to satisfy themselves, their team and teammates, fans, sponsors, and the mass media, among others.

You are expected to be a role model, and maintain good moral conduct and behavior on and off the field and court. The consequences of failing to do so can be huge, and can take a toll on your professional and personal life.

Athletes may simply desire to be able to consistently perform at their peak level. However, performance can be hindered as a result of uncontrollable situations, such as injury.

A range of drugs have been developed to allow athletes to recover more quickly, or to be able to return to competition while still injured, so that you do not have to face the social, financial and emotional consequences of being unable to perform.

An additional concern is the health-risk some athletes place themselves in by abusing performance-enhancing substances.

Such risks may manifest as short-term temporary problems or long-term health problems, reversible and/or irreversible, and in the worst case scenario — death. The fact that athletes are willing to risk their lives in the pursuit of victory has raised a large number of issues, and is one of the key factors in the development of anti doping codes, and a key reason behind the implementation of league-wide drug testing.

Drug and supplement use to improve performance, and used to return to competition after injury can be problematic for athletes if not taken correctly and legally. Although there are a range of legal treatments that can be, and are often used to reduce rehabilitation time, many of these, if abused, can also be detrimental to your health and ability to perform at a high level. This also supports the assertion that if drug use can be harmful to your health — testing is a means of discouraging adverse behavior.

Athletes are currently subject to a number of strict guidelines in order to ensure a relatively level playing field for all competitors, thus giving all athletes an opportunity to succeed to the best of your *natural abilitie*s. However, as long as capitalism in modern society plays a role in sports, the incentives to perform will most likely be enough to encourage some athletes to go beyond legal boundaries to improve their performance by taking, unknowingly or not, banned substances, which may be harmful to you and your sport.

Supplements to Build Muscle

Protein Powders

You may believe protein bars, powders and shakes are linked to muscle mass. This is a misconception. The key to building muscle is weight training (lifting weights), not consuming excessive protein. Certainly, if you want to build muscle you need adequate protein. However, the required amount is easily consumed through customary foods, such as milk, eggs, meats, fish, beans, soy and nuts.

There are a number of athletes who choose vegan and vegetarian diets. Vegetarian athletes who fail to consume adequate beans, tofu or other plant proteins may benefit from protein supplements. For these individuals, taking a protein supplement is better than not consuming enough protein.

Creatine

Popular among strength athletes and individuals who perform repeated bursts of brief, explosive exercise like in football, basketball, and hockey, creatine is reputed to enhance recovery from one stint of exercise to the next. Creatine helps to stimulate muscle growth, thus creating more strength and body mass. However, not all athletes respond to creatine in the same manner. Some athletes have little or no response. Athletes who consume creatine should know larger than recommended doses are unnecessary.

The use of creatine should be discouraged in high school athletics.

It is better for high school athletes to simply train hard and wisely, and implement an optimized sports diet, like eating a substantial breakfast and lunch to fuel yourself for a strenuous afternoon workout to reach performance goals. Creatine occurs naturally in your body. It helps to supply energy to the muscular and nervous systems. It provides short bursts of energy. Two grams of creatine are manufactured from your liver daily, and you can also get more creatine if you eat foods high in protein.

But using creatine on a daily basis comes with some side effects:
- Muscle cramps
- Nausea
- Stomach cramps
- Vomiting
- Diarrhea

Nutritionists and dietitians say abusing creatine by taking more than the recommended dosage can lead to kidney and liver failure, or heart disease.

Supplements for Endurance

Caffeine

Touted to enhance endurance and the ability to work harder with less effort, caffeine is popular among endurance athletes and individuals who want a pre-exercise energy boost. Like most ergogenic aids, caffeine's effects vary from athlete to athlete. If you rarely drink coffee, and then consume it, you may end up with the jitters. As with any dietary experiment, consume caffeine during training so there will be no surprises on game day.

Ephedra/Ma Huang

Ephedra (also called ma huang) is a stimulant banned by professional sports organizations and the NCAA. Ephedra is commonly contained in decongestants, cold medications, diet pills and Ripped Fuel — a popular supplement used to lose weight and enhance energy. Ephedra is a central nervous system stimulant and, therefore, accelerates heart rate and blood pressure, among other effects. While you may feel the "boost," you may also feel the hypertensive crisis or stroke, as individual tolerances to ephedra compounds vary.

Studies on the ephedra potency of supplement products available in the United States have reported that inaccurate and unreliable labeling is occurring. Some products contain more ephedra than stated on the label, while some contain less or none. Self-medicating with such a potentially dangerous and unpredictable substance is not recommended.

For more information on the effects of ephedra, visit the Centers for Disease Control and Prevention (www.cdc.gov) to view the number of medical problems and deaths associated with ephedra.

In general, you should be wary of products containing ephedra — and do your due diligence.

Popular Supplements

Ergogenic sports supplements come in many different forms. They're packaged to grab your attention with catchy phrases and vibrant colors. You can get them in pill, capsule, or powder form. They're available mostly over the counter, and some sports medicine doctors also distribute them to athletes.

But, are these sports supplements really safe?

Unlike prescription drugs, sports supplements are not regulated by the FDA (Food and Drug Administration). Therefore, there are no clinical studies to draw on. There is currently no verification of the effectiveness or hidden dangers of these sports supplements. Supplements may contain steroids, and include ephedra, creatine and androstenedione.

If you are caught taking these performance enhancing drugs you could face lengthy league suspensions.

Stimulants

Stimulants are used to propel an athlete through his training period or his sport. Stimulants can reduce fatigue, but will also bring with them bouts of aggressive behavior. Stimulants stimulate your central nervous system. Dexedrine and Benzedrine are common stimulants used by some athletes.

Overusing stimulants can cause addiction and long term problems, including:

- Heart problems
- Weight loss
- Hypertension
- Hallucinations
- Convulsions
- Brain hemorrhage
- Heart attack

Fat Burners

Ephedra-based products now lead the pack in negative publicity because recent studies show that ephedra-based products like fat burners, can lead to heart disease, strokes, and even death. These drugs are not regulated by the FDA prior to their release. The FDA will, after the drugs show an unfavorable or dangerous propensity, pull them off the market and claim they are now "dangerous, even deadly."

The rationale about supplements and fat burners is threefold.

Some substances pose a significant health risk, some deliver an unfair advantage, and some are banned by law to begin with. How can athletes train effectively and achieve peak performance without the use of sports supplements? Accepting the reality that supplements do play a critical role in improving strength and performance of athletes, you simply have to be smart about it and ask questions — consistently.

More about Diuretics

Diuretics increase the amount of urine produced by the body.

In common form, coffee and tea are considered diuretics because they leech the body of sodium, potassium, calcium and other vitamins and minerals. In medicinal form, diuretics are used to treat patients suffering from kidney dysfunction. Some athletes may use diuretics to assist them to fall within the required weight categories in certain sports, like football. They may also be used by some athletes to dilute their urine to avoid detection of anabolic agents.

Pharmaceutical diuretics should be avoided. Athletes using them may risk dehydration. This can also cause dizziness, headaches, nausea, loss of coordination and balance, cramps, and kidney and heart failure. Diuretics can cause weight loss in the short term because of fluid loss, but they do not help with long-term loss of body fat.

Clenbuterol is a banned substance because of its stimulant and anabolic effects. Because its main action is to relax muscle in the airways, Clenbuterol has been used in medicine as a treatment for asthma and chronic respiratory problems. Side effects are common, and a major problem with its use. They include increased heart rate, palpitations, tremor, insomnia, and possibly a rise in blood pressure and an increase in anxiety.

EPO (erythropoietin) is a recent addition to many banned substances lists. EPO is naturally occurring in the body, released by the kidneys to promote red blood cell production in the bone marrow. In injectable artificial form, this peptide hormone accelerates red cell production and thus enhances aerobic and endurance activity in athletes. Recombinant EPO, artificial, has a legitimate use in the treatment of anemia in patients with kidney disease, HIV, and some cancers.

Uncontrolled, it carries a risk of thrombosis and has been implicated in a number of deaths.

Cortisone, corticosteroids or glucocorticosteroids may be banned or limited in certain circumstances in the *NFL*, *NCAA*, and *Major League Baseball*, among others. *The World Anti-Doping Agency* (WADA) prohibits the use of some forms of corticosteroids during competition, yet other forms are allowed, but only when used *out of competition*. When ingested orally or injected in the bloodstream, they can have anabolic effects. While mainly used to reduce inflammation, cortisone is commonly administered in treating asthma, hay fever and arthritis.

Athletes are required to seek permission from their governing sports authority before use.

Tribulus, also known as Tribestan or Triboxin, is classed as a plant steroid compound extracted from herbs, seeds and plants. Pseudoephedrine, which appears in some everyday pharmaceuticals, is classed as a stimulant, and may incur a doping violation when present in the urine sample.

Products such as Sudafed, Demazin, Logicin and Actifed also contain pseudoephedrine. Some athletes may use stimulants such as pseudoephedrine in an attempt to increase alertness, reduce tiredness, and increase their competitiveness and aggressiveness on game day. This can cause problems with heat regulation, faster breathing, problems with coordination and balance, dehydration, weight loss, and hand tremors. Other side effects may include increased heart rate, palpitations and irregularities, insomnia, increased blood pressure, and sweating.

Energy Boosters

Energy boosters, fat burners, muscle gainers, and workout recovery enhancers make up the main categories here.

Most supplements marketed as energy boosters claim to either provide quick energy or delay the onset of fatigue, or both. Those which contain carbohydrates as the key ingredient will provide energy and delay fatigue when consumed as part of an overall healthy training regiment.

Sports drinks, bars, and powders are quick and easy ways for an athlete to supplement the carbohydrate from real food in their diets or during a workout. They are not substitutes for food, nor do they repair a poor diet.

Two energy bars and a bottle of sport drink are not breakfast and lunch.

A bowl of cereal, a piece of fruit, some crackers or pretzels can provide a better, more nutritional carbohydrate snack before a workout. Carbohydrate containing sports drinks are appropriate hydration vehicles for those exercising for over an hour at a time, or during tough resistance training to keep up important blood glucose levels.

Drink versions generally give their "boost" feeling because they contain some form of caffeine combination (caffeine, guarana or Brazilian cocoa, mate', gotu kola, green tea) and some carbohydrate. Caffeine amounts are generally not included on the label, and vary. While some studies have reported increased exercise time to exhaustion with small amounts of caffeine, there is no increased benefit seen with increasing amounts. Pill forms of these "energy boosters" also contain plant-based stimulants, sometimes more than one.

Ephedra, or ma huang, is a herbal stimulant contained in some of these supplements. More recently, ephedra is under closer government scrutiny due to reports of harm and deaths potentially associated with its use.

Other supplements marketed as "energy boosters" include ginseng, bee pollen, Co-enzyme Q-10, and pyruvate. Research on the effects of each of these on exercise performance has currently yielded no benefits. Ginseng may interfere with some medications and alter blood clotting. Taking herbs and other supplements in combination with medications is unwise without first consulting your team trainer, your league, or your primary health care provider.

Muscle Builders

Muscle-building supplements are a hot market for manufacturers. Retail supplement stores carry a large variety of products to entice athletes looking to get big and powerful.

Protein Powders

Protein powders are available in a variety of flavors, and from various sources like milk or soy, to be whirled in the blender into a mega-drink. It takes extra protein to build new muscle. High-protein foods contain other important nutrition not always found in a supplement. To build new muscle, athletes need more calories; better to get all that from real food. Current research proving the superiority of supplemental protein over food sources for muscle gains is sparse.

Amino Acids

The body uses amino acids as the building block for protein, including muscle.

The essential amino acids are ones the body can't make on its own and an outside source is required. Both plant and animal sources of proteins contain an abundance of essential amino acids, and most people get enough through their regular diet. Research on amino acids focuses on purported stimulation of growth hormone and improved recovery from intense workouts.

Results are mixed. In athletes who follow a healthy training diet, little effect can be found for the amino acid glutamine, touted for preserving glycogen, a stored carbohydrate. Amino acids, arginine and ornithine are marketed as stimulators of growth hormone, but claims are said to be unsubstantiated.

Small amounts of aminos are turning up in energy drinks. For example, an athlete may buy larger amounts in powder and pill form. Manufacturers list amino acid amounts in milligrams, and it may look impressive.

Closer due diligence reveals 1,000 milligrams of an amino is only 1 gram of protein. So, that glass of milk had 8,400 milligrams of amino acids!

Prohormones

Androstenedione and dehydroepiandrosterone (DHEA) are called prohormones because they are metabolic precursors to the male hormone testosterone. Androstenedione, or "andro" claims to build muscle because of a supposed ability to increase testosterone production. It has become increasingly popular due to celebrity athlete endorsement. Research on androstenedione has not turned up positive results for its muscle building ability.

In a study published in the *Journal of the American Medical Association*, athletes who took "andro" for 8 weeks and weight-lifted had no more improvement in muscle mass than those who weight-lifted only. Additionally, those on "andro" experienced a drop in HDL (good) cholesterol and an increase in estradiol, a female hormone.

Androstenedione also can cause an athlete to test positive for steroid use because of contaminants in mislabeled products and metabolite production.

Like many supplements, long-term effects and safety of using prohormones are unknown. Again — do your thorough due diligence! I have spoken to athletes who are taking a variety of supplements and can't tell me what any of them are. Or, if they can tell me what they are, they're not sure why they're taking them, how much they are taking, or what the potential side effects and long-term consequences may be.

If you are going to take a dietary supplement, do some research, understand what it's supposed to do, and know the recommended dose.

Here's a helpful short glossary of other supplements:

Multivitamin and Mineral

For athletes who are eating a sound, balanced diet, a multivitamin and mineral will act as "insurance." It is not necessary to have high doses of any vitamin or mineral.

Meal Replacement Powder

These may be adequate for convenience alone; however, you should not live off them. They are widely adopted by many athletes, especially those who struggle to find the time to prepare food in a healthy manner. They combine high protein levels with moderate levels of carbohydrates for energy and are typically low in fat. They also offer a full complement of vitamins and minerals.

Remember, meal replacement powders cannot provide the same benefit as whole foods, so you should not replace all of them. When making a meal replacement powder, add some frozen fruit as a way to get more fruit in your diet.

Meal Replacement Bar

Similar to meal replacement powders, these are also adequate for convenience. These are great for your locker or car, so there is always something available to eat.

High School Athletes and Supplements

The wide-ranging findings of recent studies show there is little consensus about the prevalence of supplement use by high school athletes. It has been reported that supplement use by high school athletes tends to be lower than that of college and professional athletes.

What Supplements Aren't

Again, products classified as dietary supplements are currently not required to meet any FDA standards. There are no current regulations that guarantee the safety or purity of products sold as a supplement.

Therefore, supplements are NOT:
- Required to meet the same safety requirements as over the counter or prescription drugs, or food ingredients.
- Held to specific manufacturing standards.

- Guaranteed to meet product potency or purity ratings.
- Required to prove the effectiveness of any health claim they make.
- Required to meet safety or efficacy testing prior to going to the market. The FDA is prohibited from removing a product from the market unless it can prove that the product will cause a medical problem. Most health risks of supplements are discovered after the product is on the market. Supplements that are pulled from the market are usually linked to a reported serious health risk or death that is tied to the use of the product.

Ergogenic Aids and Performance Enhancing Substances

Erogenic aids consist of substances, drugs, procedures, and even devices that are intended to improve athletic performance. Some of these substances are naturally occurring, easily available, and completely legal, while others are manufactured, illegal, or banned by many sporting organizations.

Anabolic Steroids

"Steroids never helps anybody do anything better long-term.
All steroids can do for you is kill you — and kill you the long, slow, hard way."
– David L. Brown

We all basically know what steroids are.

It's been in the news, with predominantly more headlines in *Major League Baseball* than any other sport. We all have seen and read about the ugly stories. We know the tremendous amount of media attention steroids get. Just the mention of the word and heads turn in interest to hear about the next athlete who's been caught using them.

Examples of anabolic steroids are androstenedione, boldenone, decadurabolin (nandrolone), dehydroepiandrosterone (DHEA), stanozolol and testosterone. Known side effects could result in jaundice and liver damage, acne, heart problems, euphoria, improved self-esteem, mood swings, depression, paranoia and aggression. Effects specific to male athletes may include the development of breast tissue, infertility, and baldness.

Effects specific to female athletes may include an increase in facial and body hair, menstrual problems, permanent deepening of the voice, and fetal damage.

Anabolic-androgenic steroids — or human growth hormone (HGH), are the synthetic derivatives of the naturally occurring male anabolic hormone testosterone.

Both anabolic and androgenic have origins from the Greek: anabolic, meaning "to build," and androgenic, meaning "masculinizing." The hormone's anabolic effect helps the body retain dietary protein, which aids in the development of muscles. Athletes may want to take them to increase muscle mass and strength.

How are steroids taken?

Steroids can be taken orally or injected. Those injected are broken down into additional categories; those that are long lasting, and those that last a shorter time. In recent years, their use shifted to the latter category — shorter lasting, water-soluble injections.

Injectable steroids aren't free of side effects either. There is no free ride with steroids.

There is a price to be paid with either choice. Anabolic steroids are designed to mimic the bodybuilding traits of testosterone. Anabolic steroids do not improve agility, skill or cardiovascular capacity.

What are the health hazards of anabolic steroids?

The side effects may be many, even with prescribed doses. Some side effects are visible to the naked eye, and some are internal. Some are physical, others are psychological. Doctors say with unsupervised steroid use, "mega dosing," or "stacking" (using a combination of different steroids), the effects can be irreversible or undetected until it's too late. Also, if anabolic steroids are injected, transmitting or contracting HIV and Hepatitis B through shared needles is a real concern.

All steroid-based hormones have one unique characteristic — their dangers may not manifest themselves for months, years, or even decades. Therefore, long after you gave them up you may develop side effects.

Physical side effects

Although anabolic steroids are derived from a male sex hormone, taking them may actually result in experiencing a "feminization" effect in male athletes, along with a decrease in normal male sexual function.

Some possible effects include:
- Reduced sperm count
- Impotence
- Development of breasts

- Shrinking of the testicles
- Difficulty or pain while urinating

Female athletes often experience a "masculinization" effect from anabolic steroids, including the following:
- Facial hair growth
- Deepened voice
- Breast reduction
- Menstrual cycle changes

With continued use of anabolic steroids, both sexes can experience the following effects, which range from the unsightly to life endangering.
They may include:
- Acne
- Bloated appearance
- Rapid weight gain
- Clotting disorders
- Liver damage
- Premature heart attacks and strokes
- Elevated cholesterol levels
- Weakened tendons

Nandrolone is a steroid derived from testosterone, and is prohibited as an anabolic agent. Many nandrolone positive tests have occurred in recent years, mostly due to ingesting norandrostenedione, an anabolic steroid widely marketed as a nutritional supplement on the internet. Norandrostenedione, in turn, is then broken down in the liver to nortestosterone, which is also known as nandrolone.

While it may have some legitimate medical uses, such as the treatment of burns, malnutrition and osteoporosis, nandrolone has the same potential side effects as anabolic steroids, including psychological and physical effects, such as jaundice, permanent liver damage, liver tumors, diabetes, acne (face and back), heart problems, high cholesterol levels, HIV infection through sharing needles, depression, mood swings, violent or aggressive behavior, and paranoia.

Androstenedione, although a naturally occurring substance that assists in the body's production of testosterone, is banned as a steroid with anabolic and androgenic properties. Possible side effects include liver damage, development of breast tissue in men, menstrual disturbances, hair loss, deepened voice, acne and infertility in female athletes.

Glutamine promotes growth hormone production. Athletes using products that contain glutamine as an ingredient may be advised to seek a written guarantee regarding the supplement's purity from the manufacturer.

Steroid dangers to adolescent athletes

Anabolic steroids can halt growth prematurely in adolescent athletes.

Doctors say steroids close the growth centers in a teen's bones. Once the growth plates are closed, they cannot reopen, so adolescents that take too many steroids may end up shorter than they should have been.

Behavioral side effects

Anabolic steroids can cause severe mood swings. An athlete may go from bouts of depression or extreme irritability to feelings of invincibility and outright aggression, commonly called "roid rage." This is a dangerous state beyond mere assertiveness.

Are anabolic steroids addictive?

Recent evidence suggests that long-time steroid users and steroid abusers may experience the classic characteristics of addiction, including cravings, difficulty in stopping steroid use, and withdrawal symptoms.

Addiction is normally an extreme of dependency, which may be psychological, if not physical. It has been documented when regular steroid users stop taking the drug they get withdrawal pains, and if they start up again the pain goes away.

Bottom line — any type of steroid you may take WILL NOT make you an *instant* super-athlete. Long-term, steroids will NOT help you become stronger, faster, or have better coordination. If you play baseball from the high school level and above, steroids WILL NOT help with your eyesight. They're NOT going to help you hit the ball. They may help you hit the ball a little farther, but you know that would be cheating yourself, the fans, and the game.

More education about supplements

- Dietary supplements do not "speed up" a young athlete's growth and development.
- Eventual maturity and athletic ability do not depend on how early a child begins adolescence.
- There is no scientific evidence that mega-doses of supplements improve athletic performance, give athletes a competitive advantage, or compensate for a lack of training or natural athletic ability.

Supplement dangers

- The short and long-term impact of dietary supplements, like vitamin/mineral supplements, ergogenic aids, and herbs, on young, growing bodies is virtually unknown at this writing.
- Unlike prescription drugs, the FDA does not regulate dietary supplements for safety, effectiveness, potency, or purity.
- Large doses of vitamins and minerals can actually be dangerous, and growing children and adolescents are at greater risk of experiencing adverse effects.

Supplements encourage bad eating habits

- Giving teen athletes supplements can encourage bad eating habits by leading them to incorrectly assume that, since their morning pills supposedly provide them with all the nutrients they need, they are free to eat candy and drink soda instead of cereal and milk.
- Supplement use can lead a teen athlete to erroneously associate improved performance with supplements they may be taking, instead of attributing his progress to training, hard work, and a balanced diet.
- This type of false reinforcement may also lead a teen athlete to try other types of supplements and substances (such as drugs and steroids), creating a snowball effect with potentially disastrous consequences.

The key for any young athlete, as for all athletes, is to consume a wide variety of foods from the *Food Guide Pyramid* to obtain the many different nutrients the body requires for optimal growth, development and performance. They can't be found in any one food or supplement.

Remember, a healthy well-balanced diet is best.

To help a young athlete resist any pressure to take supplements, we should:
- Emphasize how regular foods promote muscle growth and optimal performance.
- Reinforce our young athlete's confidence in eating "ordinary" foods.
- Help him keep a record of what he eats, when and how hard he trains, and improvements in his performance, which will both allow him to attribute improved athletic performance to good dietary and training habits instead of a pill or powder, and empower teen athletes to exert control over his athletic performance, as well as all areas of his life.

Drug interactions

Reading the label every time you use a non-prescription or prescription drug, and taking the time to learn about drug interactions may be critical to your health and athletic career. You can reduce the risk of potentially harmful drug interactions and side effects with a little bit of knowledge and common sense.

Drug interactions fall into three broad categories:
1. Drug-to-drug interactions occur when two or more drugs react with each other. This drug-drug interaction may cause you to experience an unexpected side effect. For example, mixing a drug you take to help you sleep (a sedative) and a drug you take for allergies (an antihistamine) can slow your reactions and make driving a car or operating machinery dangerous.
2. Drug-food/beverage interactions result from drugs reacting with foods or beverages. For example, mixing alcohol with some drugs may cause you to feel tired or slow your reactions.
3. Drug-condition interactions may occur when an existing medical condition makes certain drugs potentially harmful. For example, if you have high blood pressure, you could experience an unwanted reaction if you take a nasal decongestant.

Prescription Pain Killers

Prescription drugs are now easier to get than street drugs. They are also often sold on the street like other illegal drugs. You may think that prescription drugs are safer and less addictive than street drugs.

Think again!

Some high school, college and professional athletes may be abusing prescription and over the counter drugs. These include painkillers, such as those drugs prescribed after surgery, like antidepressants, sleeping pills or anti anxiety drugs and stimulants. Because these drugs are so readily available in our general society, athletes on all levels are finding easy access to them.

What are the dangers?

A single large dose of prescription or over the counter painkillers or depressants can cause breathing difficulty that can lead to death. Stimulant abuse can lead to hostility or paranoia, or the potential for heart system failure or fatal seizures.

Even in small doses, depressants and painkillers have subtle effects on motor skills, judgment, and ability to learn. The abuse of over the counter cough and cold remedies can cause blurred vision, nausea, vomiting, dizziness, coma, and even death. Many young teen athletes report mixing prescription drugs, over the counter drugs, and alcohol. Using these drugs in combination can cause respiratory failure and death.

Which drugs are most abused?

The most commonly used prescription drugs fall into three classes:
1. Opioids
    - Examples: oxycodone (OxyContin), hydrocodone (Vicodin), and meperidine (Demerol).
    - Medical uses: Opioids are used to treat pain or relieve coughs or diarrhea.
    - *How they work:* Opioids attach to opioid receptors in the central nervous system, the brain and the spinal cord, preventing the brain from receiving pain messages.

2. Central nervous system (CNS) depressants
   - Examples: pentobarbital sodium (Nembutal), diazepam (Valium), and alprazolam (Xanax).
   - Medical uses: CNS depressants are used to treat anxiety, tension, panic attacks, and sleep disorders.
   - *How they work:* Central Nervous System depressants slow down brain activity. The result is a drowsy or calming effect.
3. Stimulants
   - Examples: methylphenidate (Ritalin) and amphetamine/dextroamphetamine (Adderall).
   - *How they work:* Stimulants increase brain activity, resulting in greater alertness, attention, and energy.

Over the counter drugs

You may mistakenly think that prescription drugs are more powerful because you need a prescription for them. However, it's possible to abuse or become addicted to over the counter medications also.

For example, dextromethorphan (DXM) is found in some retail cough medicines. When someone takes the number of teaspoons or tablets that are recommended, everything is fine. But high doses can cause problems with the senses, like vision and hearing, and can lead to confusion, stomach pain, numbness, and even hallucinations.

What are the dangers of abusing medications?

Using prescription drugs for the wrong reasons has serious risks for your health. This risk is higher when prescription drugs like opioids are taken with other substances like alcohol, antihistamines, and central nervous system depressants.

CNS (central nervous system) depressants also have risks. Abruptly stopping or reducing them too quickly can lead to seizures. Taking CNS depressants with other medications, such as prescription painkillers, some over the counter cold and allergy medications, or alcohol can slow a your heartbeat and breathing -- even kill you.

Abusing stimulants may cause heart failure or seizures. These risks are increased when stimulants are mixed with other medicines, even retail products like certain cold medicines. Taking too much of a stimulant can lead a person to develop a dangerously high body temperature or an irregular heartbeat. Taking several high doses over a short period of time may make a drug abuser aggressive or paranoid.

Although stimulant abuse might not lead to physical dependence and withdrawal, the feelings these drugs may give an athlete can cause you to use the drugs more and more often so they become a habit that's hard to break.

The dangers of prescription drug abuse can be made even worse if you don't take the drug correctly.

Because there can be many variations of the same medication, the dose of medication and how long it stays in the body can vary. An athlete who doesn't have a prescription might not really know which one he or she has. The most common result of prescription drug abuse is addiction.

Athletes who abuse medications can become addicted just as easily as if they were taking street drugs.

The reason many drugs must be prescribed by a doctor is because many of them ARE addictive.

Additionally, the likelihood that you may commit a crime, be a victim of a crime, or have an accident, is higher when you are abusing drugs — no matter whether those drugs are medications or street drugs.

How do you know if you're addicted?

Many different signs can point to drug addiction. The most obvious is feeling the need to have a particular drug or substance. Changes in mood, weight, or interests are other signs of drug addiction.

If you think you, a teammate, family member, loved one, or a friend may be addicted to prescription drugs, talk to your team doctor or trainer. They can help you get the help you need. It's especially important for an athlete who is going through withdrawal from a CNS depressant to speak with their team doctor or seek other team or league medical treatment.

Withdrawal can be dangerous when it's not monitored.

If you have become addicted to prescription drugs, there are several kinds of treatment, depending on individual needs and the type of drug used.

According to doctors, the two main categories of drug addiction treatment are behavioral and pharmacological. Behavioral treatments teach people how to function without drugs, like handling cravings, avoiding drugs and situations that could lead to drug use, and preventing and handling relapses.

Pharmacological treatments involve giving patients a special type of medication to help them overcome withdrawal symptoms and drug cravings.

Tips for taking prescription medication

What if your team doctor prescribed a medication for you and you're worried about becoming addicted? Ask questions! If you're taking the medicine the way your team doctor told you to, you should be fine.

Doctors know how much medication to prescribe so that it's just enough for you. In the correct amount, the drug will relieve your symptoms without making you addicted.

If your team doctor prescribes a pain medication, stimulant, or CNS depressant, follow the directions exactly.

Here are some other ways to protect yourself:

- Keep all doctor appointments. Your doctor will want you to visit often so he or she can monitor how well the medication is working for you and adjust the dose or change the medication as needed. Some medications must be stopped or changed after a period of time so that you don't become addicted.
- Make a note of the effects the drug has on your body and emotions, especially in the first few days, as your body gets used to it, and tell your team doctor about them.
- Keep any information your pharmacist gives you about any drugs or activities you should steer clear of while taking your prescription. Reread the instructions often to remind yourself of what you should avoid. Ask questions if you don't understand what you're taking! If the information is too long or complicated, ask your team doctor to give you a thorough breakdown.
- Don't increase or decrease the dose of your medication on your own without checking with your team doctor first -- no matter how you're feeling.

Also, make sure your team doctor and team trainer are both on the same page. Your team trainer should know what the doctor has prescribed for you.

Your team doctor should also know if your trainer is supplying you with any drugs, supplements, stimulants, or other substances.

Never take someone else's prescription. And don't allow a teammate, family member, or friend to use yours.

Not only are you putting that person at risk, but you could suffer as well. Pharmacists won't refill a prescription if a medication has been used up before it should be. And if you're found giving medication to someone else, it's considered a crime, and you could find yourself in court and later — jail.

High school, college and professional athletes must work more diligently to learn about, investigate, and seek out answers to what ingredients are contained in the substances they may take.

I encourage athletes to become "private investigators" in regard to supplements, diuretics, drugs, prescription drugs, vitamins, nutritional drinks and powders, or any PEDs.

Ask questions often, and continue to learn everything you can about what you put into your body — BEFORE you do so.

You must allow your body to perform *naturally*. Anything less could jeopardize your athletic career and your life.

So, "bow up" and be a role model and an ambassador in your sport by leading by example.

World Anti-Doping Agency Update
September 22, 2010

LONDON - Associated Press: The *World Anti-Doping Agency* (WADA) has widened the net on performance-enhancing drugs by creating a new class of banned substances that include drugs sold on the black market before approval by the pharmaceutical industry.

At a meeting in Montreal last weekend, WADA's executive committee approved a new banned list for 2011 that will take effect on Jan. 1.

The most significant change is the addition of a new section on "non-approved substances," a move to combat cheating with drugs that are still under clinical development by medical companies.

"The intention is to look at things that are on the black market before they've been launched by the pharmaceutical industry," WADA director general David Howman told The Associated Press in a telephone interview.

"While substances are in the research and development stage, sometimes they do get out there."

"We just want to make sure that there is some way that they can be covered because we are alert to the fact that they're picked up."

Also on the new non-approved list are veterinary substances that have been used for medicinal purposes in humans in the past. Although they have since been discontinued, WADA says the drugs can still be obtained illegally for performance enhancement.

WADA also loosened the classification of Methylexanemine to the "specified stimulant" list, which covers drugs that are more susceptible to inadvertent use and can carry reduced penalties.

WADA said Methylexanemine was sold as a medicine until the early 1970s and has now reappeared in some nutritional supplements and cooking oils.

What does it all mean? More so than ever, the onus is on YOU to know what you put into your body!

Off-topic note: More and more, athletes have been finding themselves in embarrassing situations due to postings on social web mediums like Facebook, MySpace, and Twitter.

Tip: Be careful what you post on these social media sites!

Think twice before you tweet.™

Do not post improper photos or write derogatory things in poor judgment that will come back to haunt you later on any social media site, and embarrass not only you, but your family, your team, coaches, your professional league, your college or university, or the *NCAA*, resulting in you being reprimanded, suspended or kicked off your team.

Play Hard. Do Good. Live Clean.™

Chapter 5
DOMESTIC VIOLENCE

"Violence against women, or thoughts of violence against women is never acceptable. Likewise — women should not put their hands on a man. Unless either situation is in regard to self-defense, there should always be a simple, clear policy formed and adhered to for both genders by these two words — ZERO TOLERANCE."
– David L. Brown

In 1987, October was first observed as National Domestic Violence Awareness Month.

In 1989 the U.S. Congress passed Public Law 101-112 designating October of that year as National Domestic Violence Awareness Month.

Let us all take the time to remember those women and men who have been, or still are, victims of domestic violence.

The NFL personal conduct policy explicitly states, "It is not enough simply to avoid being found guilty of a crime. Instead, as an employee of the NFL or a member club, you are held to a higher standard and expected to conduct yourself in a way that is responsible, promotes the values upon which the League is based, and is lawful."

First-offenders of the personal conduct policy generally do not receive discipline until the legal process plays out. But Commissioner Roger Goodell has been strict in dealing with repeat offenders.

As an athlete, you must have the ability to separate and understand the difference between domestic violence and self-defense.

Here are two *generic* examples of each (there are a multitude of circumstances that can influence the "how, what, why, where and when" of domestic violence).

The following two *basic* instances are by no means exhaustive in the details leading up to incidents of each scenario. Neither do they suggest an entire scope of real-life scenarios that can and do play out in a sometimes volatile relationship, leading to domestic violence.

Every victim's circumstances are different.

Scenario #1

If a woman pulls a gun on you, or a knife, and there's a struggle — you certainly have the right to physically defend yourself! At this moment, you must forget about the gender of the person attacking you and do everything in your power to protect yourself.

Don't stand there thinking, "Oh, I can't fight her — she's a woman." Well, it's either fight her, or get shot, or stabbed. Which would you choose? Of course, if you can get control of her gun or knife, and then physically detain her until the police arrive, then do that. That's self-defense.

Scenario #2

You're out to dinner with your wife or girlfriend and an argument starts and lasts throughout the entire dinner. When you finish dinner and get into your car, the argument escalates. You allow your emotions to get the best of you and in the heat of the moment — you lean over and punch or back hand your lady in the mouth. Same thing if you're having dinner at home and an argument ensues. That's domestic violence.

Let's make one thing clear — the vast majority of men who batter women are NOT athletes. There is a clear and strong personal conduct policy in the *NFL, NBA, Major League Baseball,* and the *NHL*.

So, when there is a headline story in the news about an athlete being accused of domestic violence or abuse, it gets major attention.

Athletes don't make up the totality of males in the general society. Still, domestic violence in sports by male athletes is an issue that needs to be addressed.

Overall, domestic violence is tough to gauge because incidents often go unreported.

Sometimes a wife or girlfriend will keep quiet about abuse because of an athlete's "celebrity status." Other times, a victim of domestic violence will speak up immediately also because of an athlete's "celebrity status." It can go both ways.

Even when there is a police report, charges often are dropped. Many times, a woman will call the police in the heat of the moment, and then back down when it comes to pressing charges.

What's the solution?

I believe high schools, colleges and universities, and the pro leagues should create and organize workshops for athletes, to educate them from a young age about domestic violence and abuse.

Talking about it is the first step toward prevention.

What is Domestic Violence?

It's all about **power and control.**

Domestic violence is the establishment of control and fear in a relationship through physical, sexual, emotional, psychological and/or financial abuse.

Both men and women are capable of misusing power and perpetrating violence.

Male victims are often just as afraid to call the police. More resources for female victims exist, however, because women overwhelmingly suffer the most severe consequences (medical, legal, social, and financial) and therefore require the most intensive interventions.

Many women choose to stay in abusive relationships because they do not want their relationship to end…just the violence. Women often remain in, or return to, abusive relationships because their partners threaten to harm them and their loved ones if they attempt to leave.

Commonly, women choose to leave when they become convinced that their life is at risk, or that their children are in danger.

Domestic violence is not just a "family matter." The violence will not stop until men and women come together with a common attitude of non-tolerance. Some may argue that there will *never* be a common attitude of non-tolerance between genders. I disagree.

We must speak out for those who may not feel safe speaking up, and our children must learn through our words and example that violence is never justified.

It's not just about you — the athlete. It's mainly about you — the man, the husband, the father. It's about your life.

Zero Tolerance

"An injustice to one man, woman or child threatens justice to all people equally."
– Dean Tong

Education regarding domestic violence is just as important to the assailant as it is the victim. The courts and law enforcement must continually understand their responsibility to keep women and children safe.

Education and enforcement efforts on guns have been ramped up around the country. Getting the information out to court clerks, judges and battered women will continue to strengthen the system.

The truth is, not all victims know about all their options. If a woman is given all of her options, all of the time, and we can get the criminal justice system involved in enforcing restraining orders at the level they should be, it may help a great deal.

Under current federal law, people subject to protective orders due to domestic violence and abuse are not supposed to own or purchase firearms.

Advocates say that law has been rarely enforced. In some states, such as California, abusers who are subject to a restraining order may not legally own, buy, or possess any firearm during the terms of the order under state law.

In other states, such as Maine, a woman seeking a protection-from-abuse order would need to specifically address weapons in her complaint and ask the court to remove them.

Prevention and Solution

The best self-defense for athletes from being charged with domestic violence and abuse is prevention.

Not getting into a confrontation is the best way to survive one. This may sound obvious, but this advice is often ignored. Most random attacks against women by athletes could have been avoided.

ATHLETE CAREER KILLERS

Athletes Who Abuse Their Wives and/or Girlfriends

Reflection of Society?

A tremendous problem that faces the athletic community today is the occurrence of violent crimes against women.

Domestic violence is not the principle cause of injury to women in America.

Each year there are numerous reported incidences of assault, rape, and domestic violence committed by high school, college and professional athletes. One may question whether male athletes are any different from the rest of society.

It's possible that it's just a reflection of society. However, data shows that athletes have been involved in a disproportionately high number of assaults involving members of the opposite sex.

This is for sure — there's a great deal of pressure being an athlete, especially a professional athlete. Everything about your life, on and off the field and court, is on the line every year.

This can cause mental, emotional, and physical anguish for you. But that's certainly no excuse to commit domestic violence.

Some athletes come from violent backgrounds. Some come from dysfunctional families and were raised in poverty. These athletes were exposed to family violence and overrun neighborhoods at an early age.

Some do not develop adequate social skills, which can lead to problems relating to other people later in life. Often, athletes have been conditioned since childhood that women are less respectful than men are.

At an early age boys begin hearing many verbal comments that reflect negatively on women. These negative stereotypes are reinforced in society throughout their lives. Therefore, some male athletes tend to lack respect and sensitivity for women.

A related problem is that victims may think society will not believe them, that their celebrity, role model, athlete, husband or boyfriend would never become violent off the field and court, especially toward women.

Another solution is to teach children that women should be respected and that they're equal in status to men. Workshops at the high school and college level, and various other programs, could be organized that would be effective in fighting the negative conditioning that occurs at such an early age.

A group called *Mentors in Violence Prevention Project* is a workshop that already exists in several colleges around the country.

This program informs athletes and non-athletes about the problem, and then suggests ways to decrease the number of incidents.

This would increase the number of informed people actively fighting violence against women -- and that's a good thing.

Popular male and female athletes can also go into the classrooms and talk to the freshmen, proclaiming how "uncool" violence against women is. These freshmen would be enlightened as to the frequency that these crimes occur, how to prevent them, the cost of violence to the assailant, and prevention strategies.

The punishment for the athlete found to be guilty would be expulsion from the team. If a felony is committed by a pro athlete, then he should be suspended indefinitely from his league without pay.

These days, all college and professional teams conduct a screening procedure (due diligence) that checks the athlete's background. This enables teams, leagues, and colleges to be aware if any criminal or suspicious behavior has occurred over the course of an athletes' life.

I strongly encourage wives and girlfriends of high school, college and professional athletes to step forward and report *legitimate* domestic abuse and violence.

This is a serious issue — one that is not meant to be used by women to falsely accuse athletes or anyone else — which also does happen.

Important Studies

Multiple university studies have shown repeatedly that male athletes are at greater risk of violent behavior than non-athletes, and that they are more likely to be aggressive with dating partners and more accepting of hostility toward women.

The studies also probed the relationship between athletes and violence against women, and their sense of entitlement and being "above the law." Studies show dominant attitudes toward women established even before many athletes reached high school.

Tips Toward Prevention

The following is the best tip and technique I have created for athletes to live by when it comes to allowing your emotions to get the best of you — and regretting it later.

If you're in the midst of an argument with your wife or girlfriend, I don't care if she's one inch from your nose, screaming and cursing at you, I want you to do this — NOW. Put your hands behind your back and interlock your fingers, tightly. Take two lengthy steps backward to create some distance. While still facing her, find the nearest door — *and leave!*

Why do I want you to interlock your fingers tightly? So that you can practice self-restraint and not be tempted to put your hands on her or anybody else.

Why do I want you to put your hands behind your back? *Because if you don't do it then — you'll wind up doing it later anyway — when the police show up and take you to jail in handcuffs.*

Of course, if you feel she may assault you with a weapon, or attempt to, then by all means protect yourself.

And ladies, it's not funny when a woman hits a man either. In fact, it's also domestic violence!

Arguments and conflict are undeniable parts of society. An argument used to be an intelligent debate, but these days it seems to have turned into a boxing, stabbing, or shooting match. Is there any way to avoid arguments, having the different beliefs and viewpoints each gender has?

If you have a firm grip on your own actions, then you have a good chance of avoiding an argument before it starts.

The following tips, advice, and suggestions will show you how you can avoid arguments, or at least attempt to avoid them.

These tips mean nothing without *self-control*.

Self-control is vital if you want to learn how to avoid arguments.

1. Listen and be genuine. Why do people argue? Because they want to get a point across. But, do arguments ever accomplish that goal? It's not an argument you want, but an intelligent and real conversation. Having two people yell at each other because they think the other does not understand their point of view leads to nowhere. You must give up any notion of pride that you have. Pride usually tends to do more harm than good. Hear the other person out, and never interrupt while that person is talking, even if you completely disagree with her. This takes self-control. But if you want to avoid arguments, you have to push your ego aside. Remember — you have two ears and only one mouth for a reason.

2. Don't take the bait — avoid being aggressive. You should never respond to inflammatory words and phrases. It's best to let it go. At the end of the day, inflammatory or not, they're just words. If you believe in your viewpoint, and you have good and credible evidence to back it up, then you have nothing to fear. There is no need to purposefully be inflammatory. A heated argument goes two ways; it only continues if you keep feeding the fire. Controlling your anger and looking at the other person's argument logically rather than emotionally is a good step toward avoiding arguments.
3. Be humble. ***Kick any arrogance, sense of entitlement, power, control, and status to the curb!*** Humans are egocentric by nature. No one is always right, and that includes you, me, and everyone else. If you always believe that your way is the right way, with no room for alternative ways or a different interpretation, then you're just setting yourself up for a heated argument. Being humble is one of the vital parts of learning how to avoid an argument. Don't take yourself too seriously. Stay open to new ideas and viewpoints.
4. Empathy. Try your best to put yourself in the other person's shoes. You never know what you might discover. If you view the argument through her eyes, it might even start to make more sense. *Always seek to understand before trying to be understood.* This applies to any potential situation for an argument, whether it's a teammate, coach, friend, wife, girlfriend, or whoever. If you still think that they're wrong, then explain why in a non-derogatory manner. Being condescending is no way to avoid an argument.
5. Unconditional respect. You can't always convince people of your side of the story. No matter what you think of other people and their views, you must always show respect. If you give respect, you usually get it. Even if they can't be swayed, respect the faith they have in their beliefs and let the issue go. At least everyone can walk away relatively unscathed. You can't win every battle, and arguments shouldn't be battles to begin with. Strive to be the better person and show respect no matter how things turn out.
6. Do not retaliate. Unless you feel your life may be in danger, if a woman slaps you, kicks or hits you — DO NOT retaliate. Walk away by using my above-mentioned technique. It really works! If you don't, the percentages suggest that you'll be the one the police take to jail.

7. Educate yourself on the causes, effects, and prevalence of athletes and violence by getting involved thorough research, routine assessments and workshops offered by your team, league, or other sports organization.
8. Try to diffuse tension by discussing the problem and apologizing for anything you might have done to add to it.
9. Control your impulse to become physical by thinking of the consequences of your actions before you do anything you will regret. *One poor choice and your athletic career could very well be over.*
10. Stay as calm as possible. Don't escalate the argument. Try to convince the other person that arguing is simply not the way to go. If necessary, agree with the person if you know you're wrong.
11. Avoid the moral high ground when attempting to defuse the situation. Avoid words that could inflame the other person.
12. In a truly volatile situation, forget about your ego. Sometimes pride is a hard thing to swallow. Think of your loved ones and swallow your pride to stay alive.
13. When having a discussion that could potentially escalate, keep your hands in a defensible, yet non- aggressive position. Both palms pressed together in a "prayer position" is best, and non-threatening. Keep them near your face at all times.
14. Remember that walking away is always an alternative and nothing to be ashamed of. Always face the person as you walk away. If the other person is angry, they might attack you from behind.
15. If you are in a car, lock the doors and refuse to escalate the problem. Better — drive away if you possibly can.
16. Develop an open communication style with your partner. Set aside time to share your thoughts and feelings. This can prevent feelings from being repressed, leading to arguments later.
17. Keep a sense of humor. Sometimes arguments can be avoided by not taking things too seriously. Decide if the issue is even worth arguing about. Oftentimes it's not.
18. Allow your partner to express themselves about things they dislike without being defensive or feeling the need to prove them wrong. Arguments can often be avoided by letting your partner blow off steam.
19. Be sympathetic to her feelings, and understand that when she expresses something it doesn't mean it's a personal attack on you.

20. Try to talk about and resolve all issues beforehand so that arguments don't become a recurring theme. Many relationship experts advise never to go to bed angry at your partner.
21. Clear your mind of all distractions and concentrate on information that you don't already have. Nod your head occasionally to affirm that you are listening.
22. Avoid adding fuel to the fire. Eliminate making statements such as, "I'm sorry, but what you're saying makes absolutely no sense at all." Or, "If you would just calm down for a minute, maybe I could explain…" Statements like these only intensify the core of frustration or anger. Instead, go *"old school."* Bite your tongue when you find yourself tempted to say anything that may be perceived to be condescending.
23. When talking to your wife or girlfriend, lovingly refer to her by her first name. Then, immediately ask for clarification. People instinctively respond from a slightly calmer emotional state when they hear their own names. Then, speak with composure.
24. Avoid name calling.
25. Learn to accept each other for the way you are.
26. Learn to compromise.
27. Consider the benefits of not arguing.
28. Don't argue in front of children, family, or friends.
29. If you're wrong, admit it and apologize.
30. Don't take things personally.
31. Don't automatically believe what a third party may say about your partner. Seek an explanation directly from your partner if you have concerns. If in doubt, check it out.
32. Be positive that situations will be resolved amicably.
33. Start all conversations with something positive.
34. Seek to make a positive connection before starting a discussion.
35. Agree to disagree.
36. Don't be afraid to laugh. Life is full of funny things, and sometimes we make silly mistakes that may lead to an ugly argument, but could have been avoided by simply laughing.
37. Give yourself a time out — really.
38. Choose your words carefully.

39. Control your emotions.
40. Show compassion, empathy, support, and trust.
41. Avoid being judgmental.
42. When you feel things may escalate, learn to break conversational patterns that lead to an old argument rearing its ugly head. Take evasive action and change the subject as smoothly as you can. This will buy time until you are both prepared to talk in a calm, constructive way.
43. Be gentle. Try to control the tone of your voice, the look on your face, and your body language when you're talking. If you speak with a gentle tone, arguments are less likely to start or escalate.
44. Develop a solid relationship with your wife or girlfriend by keeping lines of communication open. Building trust and giving each other the benefit of the doubt goes a long way.
45. Keep your disagreements strictly between the parties involved rather than discussing them in the open.
46. Is someone hurting? Realize that the other person may be hurt in some way, but it may be expressed through anger, tears, or insults. By arguing, they may actually be reaching out for help, support, or simply to be acknowledged.
47. Hormones and illness. Consider how a woman's gender may be playing a role in the argument. Perhaps a woman's monthly cycle is causing her to be overly emotional. Maybe one person has been ill and is really striking out at others just because they don't feel well.
48. Forgive. Once the situation has been resolved, forgive one another and then let it go. Try not to bring the situation up again.
49. Humans are creatures of habit. That's right, she may want you to remember to put the toilet seat down, but many instances of leaving it up have made this a hard habit to break for you. Loving patience is a virtue, so apologize and reassure her you'll try to remember next time.
50. Everyone needs some alone time. You may want to tinker around in the garage, and she may need some time with her laptop. No matter how you choose to spend alone time, you definitely need some. So make sure you aren't pressing each other to spend every free minute together.
51. In today's society it's easy not to be dedicated and loyal to your spouse. There are a lot of temptations that could take your loyalty away from her, and her loy-

alty away from you. It could be another woman in your case, another man in her case, or the demands that come with being a professional athlete, among other things. Although most men and women now are career oriented, you both have to arrive at some point and ask yourself what is more important — the family or the career? When it comes to temptation with another man (her), or woman (you), is it worth it to put your marriage or relationship at risk? Not to mention putting your safety at risk?

52. Accept her weaknesses, and she should accept yours. If you love her, it comes with a complete package. You love her, not only for her strengths, but you also have to embrace her weaknesses. We're all human — we make mistakes. The most important thing is that you have the tolerance to accept those mistakes and you're beside her to deal with those mistakes. If you have the patience and understanding that she needs, and vice-versa, then you have the chance of success in your relationship without the threat of domestic violence.

53. Don't taunt your mate. Avoid the temptation to do or say things that you know irritate your mate. This includes teasing, ridicule, and gestures that send your mate into total frustration and anger. Avoid body language "comments," ranging from rolling your eyes to a sarcastic smirk on your face.

54. If it appears you're going down that familiar trail of bickering, ambush the conversation by jumping in with a comment on a more pleasant topic.

55. Keep to your agreements. If you say you will pick up your dirty laundry, then do it. Failing to come through on even small agreements can escalate into something bigger. Making agreements and not keeping them, minor or major, can set the stage for constant arguing, which could lead to domestic violence.

56. It takes two to tango. If you refuse to play the bickering game when your mate starts in, she will have to look elsewhere to direct her jabs.

57. Forget about being right, and focus on being happy.

58. Forget the "tit for tat" game.

59. If it's not a deal-breaker — let it go.

60. Find another outlet for venting, like calling and talking to a friend or family member.

61. Understand that arguments are a part of relationships. There is no way to avoid them. It is impossible to see eye to eye on every topic and discussion.

62. Teach and educate others about domestic violence. Be an advocate against it. This can be most effective by educating young people to help them understand that violence is never an acceptable behavior from either gender.
63. Promote domestic violence awareness. When people become aware of the statistics and effects domestic violence has on lives and communities, it keeps the issue alive and important.
64. Speak out against domestic violence. Talking about the seriousness of domestic violence amongst teammates, coaches, friends, family and other community members also helps to keep the importance out there.
65. Take a stand against entertainment, music and jokes that might trivialize domestic violence. Also, stand up against comments that may blame the victim.
66. Organize fund raisers to support the local efforts behind domestic violence prevention and awareness. The better funded the programs are, the more reach they can have to those who need it most.
67. Encourage your community to establish centers for domestic violence, if they don't already have them. Those who are being domestically abused will go get help when they know that it's readily available.
68. Support local laws and legislation aimed at supporting and protecting against domestic violence. When stricter laws and legislation are in play, abusers tend to think twice, while those who have been abused feel more secure with turning to law enforcement for help.
69. Demand that local social service workers and law enforcement are properly trained in domestic violence. For many years, women who were domestically abused refrained from reporting it or seeking out help because they were often re-victimized by those same people and systems that were supposed to help them.
70. Volunteer with domestic violence organizations. Many of these programs that are aimed at assisting domestic abuse victims are poorly funded and can use all the help they can get. In addition, it can be a positive way to give back to the community while reaching out and touching the life of someone in need. Remember -- *Play Hard. Do Good.*™
71. Support the development of aftercare programs aimed at assisting the psychological needs of families and individuals who lived through domestic violence and abuse.

72. Report suspicions of domestic violence to the proper authorities. Domestic violence is still a very secret crime, and it often sits silently within any given home in any given neighborhood. Sometimes, it takes that one person to make the call and report the suspicion to help someone out of a situation they may not be able to get out of on their own.
73. Promote respect and dignity for all people, regardless of their gender, class, race, nationality, sexual orientation or physical ability. Make a serious effort to better understand issues of *power and control* and the significant role they play as main causes of domestic violence. We must all work against oppression and violence.
74. Each one of us can do more — and this chapter shows you how.

Argument Triggers

Here are the most common subjects spouses and couples argue over, along with peacekeeping tips for dealing with them effectively.

Money

Money doesn't always top the argument list, but it's close. Husbands and wives disagree on how much to save, how much to spend, and even who gets to make the decisions about spending.

> **Tip:** Regardless of your budget, decide on a set amount of money for each spouse to be able to use without accountability. That way, whether it's $1,000 per month or $5,000 per month, you can each know that you have this amount to spend on whatever you deem necessary, or just for fun.

Division of Labor

Dishes, laundry, lawn care, cleaning…these chores only begin the list of all the responsibilities required to maintain a household.

And when two people live together, they will most likely experience some amount of conflict over who should be taking care of which responsibility, whether you have a housekeeper or not.

Often, you will each be taking care of much more than the other person realizes, possibly resulting in feelings of under-appreciation and even resentment.

> **Tip**: I know, you probably have a housekeeper, but for one week, each of you should keep track of everything you do around the house. Then sit down together and assess what you're both doing. Based on this, set up a chore list that feels fair to each of you. Depending on how much time you are both working outside the home on your careers, "fair" may not necessarily mean a 50-50 split. Work on acknowledging and thanking each other when you notice that chores have been completed.

Sex

It's not always the case, but the frequency, or infrequency, of sex is often the driving force behind many marital conflicts. Other arguments may also arise over differing amounts of desire for, or enjoyment of sex.

Tip: Although a large portion of the marital conflict surrounding sex would be solved if the wife or girlfriend initiated sex on a somewhat regular basis, it obviously wouldn't solve all the problems. I'm not saying that it's her responsibility, just that if she took the initiative more often, not only would she have more say in terms of frequency and schedule, but she might also have to deal with fewer complaints from her husband.

Suspected Infidelity/adultery

> **Tip:** Don't play that game! Refer to the upcoming chapter in this book, *Infidelity*.

Annoying Habits

Some annoying habits are so common that they've become cliché. But no matter how innocent or unique a person's habits may be, they can really drive you crazy!

> Tip: Let it go! There are too many other important issues to converse about in a relationship or a marriage. *Don't sweat the little stuff!*

Kids

Out of all the issues on this list, this may be the one that can get the most emotional. Parents care so much about how best to raise their kids that sharing responsibilities in this area can cause big-time conflict. Dads and moms will often argue about how permissive or strict to be, when and how to discipline, how best to protect and challenge their kids, and all kinds of other issues.

> **Tip:** Realize that Dads and Moms parent differently. It's okay if parents approach things differently from time to time. Decide which values and principles are most important, and then commit to responding from a united front. And, when you do disagree on how to handle a situation, discuss it out of the children's earshot, and make sure your kids realize that you're working together as a team. Or, if your kids know that you two disagree on how to handle a matter, discuss it with them and offer them a model of how two mature adults communicate and negotiate when they don't agree.

Remember, the best parents are — **BOTH** parents!

Texting – Love and War

How to diffuse and avoid potential arguments via text message, instant message, Blackberry, etc.

7 Things Athletes Must Know Before They Hit "Send."

1. When will you see the person next?
2. Why are you sending the message?
3. Where might the person be when they receive the message?
4. Who else might see or receive the message?
5. What else could you do instead of e-mailing or texting the message?
6. How would you react if you received the message you are planning to send?
7. Think before you send.

Texting Do's and Don'ts

Send your loved one a text message…
1. When you're thinking of her, a sweet note like, I miss you, I love you, be safe, always puts a smile on someone's face and could make her day.
2. When you have a feeling that she may not wish to talk because she is on a tight, hectic schedule, like working night and day to meet a deadline, preparing for an important presentation, etc., she may not have time to take a phone call and chat with you at length. However, a text conveys the message that you care about her and support her career. Most important, she will be thankful that you're understanding and reasonable.
3. Sometimes when someone is feeling down, kind words can magically uplift them and create positive energy and inspirations. Send an encouraging and uplifting text and put a smile on her face.
4. Text her when you have something fun, interesting or meaningful to share. It can be something that you see, hear, eat, drink, buy, or experience while spending time by yourself, with your own friends, or family. This is the art of being away from your sweetheart, yet feeling connected to her.
5. Text her when you have the urge to apologize to her for any hurtful behaviors or mistakes, and she is NOT by your side at that moment.
6. Text her when you feel like flirting. Some sweet, casual flirting is very sexy, and can even spice up a relationship if done correctly. Sometimes, a surprise or two makes our lives more exciting!
7. Text her when you are feeling affectionate and she isn't there with you. A text that says "Big Hug" or "Smile," or during an away game, "A goodnight kiss for you" warms her heart and is incredibly romantic.

When texting your loved one…

1. Do not use acronyms, symbols, or secret codes in your texting unless you are certain that your sweetheart knows exactly what they mean.
2. Do not use texting to deliver news that may cause misunderstanding or confusion. If for example, you unfortunately have some bad news to break, please call

her. At least then you would be able to prepare her mentally and emotionally before breaking the news, and it slightly reduces the shock.

3. Do not send a text to cancel a date or appointment to meet somewhere. That's insulting and disrespectful to her, unless you're in a formal, professional meeting and it's the last option.
4. Do not ask "life-changing" questions via text messaging, when you intend to bring your relationship to a higher level. For example: "Will you go out with me on a date?" "Will you be my girlfriend?" "Will you marry me?" If you're crazy about her, head over heels in love with her, or believe that she's "the one," she deserves to hear those words and feelings from you personally.
5. Do not use texting to manipulate or control her. Just because you both are dating or in a committed relationship doesn't mean you have the right to dominate or control her, and vice-versa. Give each other some space, and respect each others privacy. It's impossible for her to enjoy life and time away from you, or even just to focus on her own life and career if you keep sending her messages every other minute. Be mature and reasonable.
6. Privacy. Nearly a quarter of all married couples admit to snooping on each others emails and text messages, according to a new 2008 report by Oxford University.
7. Do not end a romantic relationship via a text message, like when breaking up with her or divorcing her. This is NEVER acceptable or appropriate, under any circumstances or at any given time.

Text Fighting

Imagine you're sitting at home, your significant other is out, and you suddenly receive a text message on your mobile device. You read: "I am breaking up with you, I don't love you anymore."

You then reply: "What...what did I do to deserve this?"

Hours later you both are still texting with short angry, hurtful messages. This has become a common ineffective avenue of fighting. These are ineffective methods of conflict resolution and will surely escalate in person, possibly causing domestic violence to later occur.

It has been reported that the majority of communication is through body language and tone of voice, not what is said.

A recent study concluded 55% of other people's reactions to you are based on your facial expression, 38% are based on your tone of voice, and only 7% of reactions are from the words actually being said.

Communication is more than words.

Addressing relationship problems through text messaging relies only on the 7% of what is being said, which requires the other 93% to be "guessed." Text fighting is usually a road to disaster, and doesn't help resolve conflict.

Next time you catch yourself picking up your phone to text fight, write down your thoughts. Address the issue in person to avoid guessing the tone of voice and body language.

The good thing about text messaging is that it can be a very effective mechanism to send short word messages, like, "I am running late. Pick up the kids at five p.m." Or "Give me a call when you're done."

It should never be relied upon to solve conflicts.

On the flip side, text messaging stalking is becoming widespread. One person is angry and hurt with the other, and texting is used to stonewall and/or attack the significant other.

A barrage of "Why are you ignoring me?" verbal attacks or expletives may soon follow. This sometimes escalates to physical violence when both parties eventually meet in person.

Simple questions without intonations can sound like an innocent question or comment. However, there is no insurance that the other person will interpret the message as it was intended. It could sound like a demand or accusation to check up on a person, like *"WHAT ARE YOU DOING?"*

This could be interpreted as yelling. If the two people are not getting along, that simple question could be interpreted in many different ways, and too often it is the worse case scenario that rules the mind.

Assumptions and misinterpretations are commonplace without the benefit of verbal and nonverbal cues.

When two parties argue face to face, they see each others body language, intonations, and can better know how their words are affecting the other.

The couple can ask each other for clarification in real human time in front of each other. The tone of the words and remarks are more clearly communicated, thus preventing the imagination of the other to determine the tone in text messaging.

Each person takes personal responsibility for what they say to each other in person, because they are saying it in actual real time with their words, body language and voice. There is less left to the imagination, hence less misunderstanding and misinterpretation, which often escalates conflict and fallout.

For many couples in new relationships, texting is used as a means of courting, and is felt to be romantic, interpreted as a means of flirting, showing interest, and signaling to each other that they are being thought of, and touching base.

The problem is that when people use text messaging to communicate emotional intimacy and/or to avoid emotional intimacy, the consequence too often results in unresolved hurt feelings and anger.

Text messaging is too often used to avoid the face to face communication of difficult topics.

Remember, direct one to one contact with your loved one is what attracted you in the first place.

Don't sell your relationship short by text message, instant message or e-mail wars.

The Other Side of Domestic Violence

I must be honest with what I'm about to say.

Unfortunately, there are women out there who *purposely* attempt to push an athlete's buttons to send him over the edge toward domestic abuse and violence in the hope of securing a financial settlement, to embarrass an athlete, gain an upper-hand in a child custody battle, or slander his name in the media.

It happens — probably more frequently than some would like to believe.

> *"Not every woman you meet will turn out to be "sugar and spice and all things nice."*
> – David L. Brown

It has been reported that false allegations of domestic and sexual abuse in society have become so commonplace that they now threaten the integrity of the American legal system.

The bad thing about that is, false domestic violence and sexual abuse allegations hurt the *real victims* and distort the efforts of other wives and girlfriends of athletes who have legitimate reasons for filing charges.

It is estimated that false allegations of domestic violence and abuse by women cost taxpayers $20 billion a year, according to *Equal Justice Foundation*.

Sometimes false allegations of domestic violence by married women are used as a means to cover their adultery.

The advantages for an adulterous wife to make such an accusation are clear. They get the house, the kids, the car, the bank accounts, and virtually anything else they want with basically no questions asked since due process is historically initially in her favor.

The athlete husband is often presumed guilty in the minds of public opinion until he can prove his innocence. In this instance, the unintended consequence of harsh domestic violence laws is that they may provide a perfect initial cover for adulteresses.

Some athlete husbands may become violent upon learning of their wife's infidelity. But it appears such men are a tiny fraction, only about 1% of the husbands who are falsely accused of domestic violence by adulterous wives.

10 Tips After a False Allegation

1. If you truly know you have done nothing wrong, call your attorney immediately. You must protect yourself.
2. Inform your team and league of the allegations.
3. Call your agent, who may offer you other resources.
4. Based on the advice of your attorney, make a public statement and declare your innocence. Don't wait to do this!
5. Do not attempt to contact the other person yourself.
6. Do not take this false allegation for granted.
7. The onus of truth will be yours to prove.
8. Know that public perception is a powerful entity.
9. A close-knit support system of family, teammates, and close friends is essential.
10. If you've done nothing wrong — know that you can and will prevail, and clear your good name.

Now, if you know you're guilty, and you made a poor choice and a mistake in judgment — admit it — accept your punishment — let the chips fall where they may, and try to move forward as best you can.

It's a good possibility, at that point, your athletic career will be severely damaged or ended by this one senseless choice.

Teams don't want athletes who have been convicted of domestic violence and abuse. That's just the way it is — and should be.

Many women, contemplating divorce, or feeling that the relationship is slipping away and not wanting to give up the lifestyle they've been accustomed to living as an athlete's wife or girlfriend, file false allegations of domestic violence or sexual abuse against their partner as a matter of tactical advantage in a divorce case.

Some women simply don't like rejection. If a woman makes advances toward an athlete and he respectfully declines, this could cause a woman to potentially claim false allegations of domestic or sexual abuse.

Likewise, some athletes don't like rejection either. If an athlete makes advances toward a woman and she respectfully declines, this could cause him to have an attitude of *entitlement, power and control,* potentially later committing a crime of sexual abuse, assault or rape.

Women Who Commit Abuse and Violence

Women are doing virtually everything these days that men are. They work as doctors, lawyers, entrepreneurs, scientists, fly helicopters in combat, and ride horses in the Kentucky Derby, among other careers.

When it comes to nonreciprocal violence between intimate partners, women are more often the perpetrators.

A study of intimate partner violence conducted by scientists at the Centers for Disease Control and Prevention (CDC), and published in the *Journal of Public Health*, found that regarding perpetration of violence based on the general population, more women than men (25% versus 11%) were responsible for false allegations of domestic or sexual abuse.

The study found that 71% of the instigators in nonreciprocal partner violence — were women.

False accusations are said to be increasing, although there is disagreement as to the frequency and nature of false claims.

Professionals agree that false accusations are most likely to occur in the environment of vindictive and angry divorce and custody battles.

In another study of more than 400 cases, in which expert consultation was provided involving sexual abuse in the past six years, 40% were divorce and custody cases. The report also concluded that 77% of divorce linked sex abuse cases coming to the Human Sexuality Program at the University of Minnesota, turned out to be *"hoax"* cases.

This is based upon the opinion reached by the system upon the individual cases.

Sports and its athletes are oftentimes a reflection of society as a whole. Accusations of sexual and domestic abuse often occur in a bitter and acrimonious divorce or relationship, at all stages of the process.

For married athletes who have children, a *Gardner* study noted that an accusation of sexual abuse by a woman is a powerful weapon in a divorce and custody case. The study describes *"parental alienation syndrome"* (PAS).

Parental alienation syndrome is a disorder that arises primarily in the context of child-custody disputes. It results from the combination of a programming *(brainwashing)* parent's endoctrinations, mostly the mother, and the child's own contributions to the vilification of the target parent, mostly the father.

(Excerpted from Gardner, R.A. (1998). *The Parental Alienation Syndrome*, Second Edition, Cresskill, NJ: Creative Therapeutics, Inc.)

Basically, this means that through verbal and non-verbal thoughts, actions and mannerisms, a child is emotionally abused *(brainwashed)* into thinking the other parent is the enemy. This ranges from bad-mouthing the other parent in front of the children, to withholding visits, to prearranging the activities for the children that *purposely* interferes with the other parent's plans during visits, according to the *Gardner* study.

One parent may believe they are only hurting the other parent; when in truth, it's the *children* she or he are hurting. The children then — are the victims.

A *Ross and Blush* study describes three personality patterns they have observed in falsely accusing women, and specific details of each one.

The first is the histrionic personality. This individual appears anxious, concerned, and nervous, and presents herself as victimized by her estranged spouse, boyfriend, or loved one.

She describes herself as manipulated, coerced, and physically or psychologically abused by this spouse, and perceives her child as now in danger of victimization from him.

The justified vindicator is a variation of the histrionic personality. This person initially offers an intellectually organized, assertive, and justified agenda armed with many facts, figures, and opinions supporting her evidence.

She presents herself as justifiably outraged and concerned by the behavior of her spouse. However, when clarification is sought concerning the details, she becomes hostile, resistant, and passive-aggressive.

She will argue, and counter even carefully-framed questions, is likely to discontinue contact with the evaluator who challenges her statements, and may threaten to sue or make ethical complaints.

The borderline personality, by virtue of a basic propensity and the stress of the divorce, functions in a highly dysfunctional way, and may lose contact with reality. This person may be most readily identified by peculiar and bizarre descriptions of events in her history.

If you're an athlete who has truly found the woman of your dreams for all the right reasons, and the relationship has survived the test of time — hold on to each other and don't let go!

Treat each other with love and respect, and thank God each day for how blessed you both are.

Not every athlete is so fortunate.

On Campus

Some within the athletics community are quick to blame the media for hyping the occurrences of athlete violence against women.

They assert that men, in general, commit violent acts against women at the same rate. But the media focuses on athletes more because of their status and popularity.

It is understandable that the first step high schools, colleges, and universities have taken in the effort to combat student-athlete violence against women is to enact, and more rigidly enforce, sexual harassment and assault policies.

Under pressure from groups outside the athletics department, as well as concern for possible legal liability for student-athlete violence, many high schools, colleges and universities have attempted to confront the issue and hold student-athletes accountable for their behavior.

They are to be commended for taking this initial step.

However, merely stating a policy in a code of conduct for student-athletes does not guarantee an educational environment free from physical and sexual violence.

It is highly doubtful that each student-athlete will take the time to actually read an entire code of conduct policy. With the demands placed on student-athletes, reading a sexual harassment and assault policy within a code of conduct falls rather low on the list of priorities.

Even if the policy is highlighted or mentioned, the effect it will have in deterring violent conduct is arguable, unless the policy is adhered to and stressed by teams, coaches and athletics department.

It must be remembered that violence against women, especially domestic violence, is a socially learned behavior that has been conditioned within many student-athletes for years as socially acceptable behavior, most of which starts at a young age.

We cannot expect student-athletes to suppress violent behavior against women simply because they are told it is wrong and will not be tolerated. We have to dig a little deeper.

Instead of focusing solely on reactive policies, the athletics community should also be discussing what steps need to be taken to ensure that most, if not all, student-athletes never commit violent acts against women in the present and future.

Policy alone is not a deterrent to violence. Consistent open communication and effective education are the keys.

A study of programs and manuals aimed either at the athletics or general population, suggests that there are three basic components that athletic departments can implement to prevent violence against women on campus and in the community:

1. Create an awareness campaign that does not avoid the issue, but fosters communication and dialogue for discussing violence against women.
2. Educate student-athletes, coaches and athletics administrators of the issue of violence against women, along with its impact on the entire community and families.
3. Promote healthy relationships through student-athletes, coaches and athletics administrators modeling the proper respect for women.

Before there can be any active solution to ending violence against women by male student-athletes, we must first make the issue a common topic of discussion.

We are all responsible for the continued growth and maturity of our student-athletes as men, not just athletes. We must be open to discuss and confront violence against women. If the athletics community will not openly talk about the issue, the acquiescence to this behavior will continue.

Talking about the problem is a start.

The most important step an athletics department can take to prevent violence by student-athletes against women and change behavior, is to provide examples of athletes, coaches, and administrators who are involved in healthy, non-abusive relationships.

Good role models in the sports community are essential to preventing domestic violence by student-athletes.

Coaches are the most influential people in a student-athlete's life. Coaches define the appropriate standards of behavior that are required, and set the value systems for their student-athletes.

Therefore, appropriately modeled behavior by coaches is crucial to any program. The same goes for parents of student-athletes.

Athletes have provided more than enough domestic violence headlines for the sports pages. It's time the trend is reversed. Sexual harassment and assault policies are important first steps, but attention should also be focused on ending the violence before it starts.

It is all our responsibility to student-athletes, to society, and to the women who have been disrespected and ignored by our communities for far too long.

Knowledge is power. And that's the purpose of this book.

Play Hard. Do Good. Prevent Domestic Violence.™

Chapter 6
INFIDELITY

Don't Play That Game!

"One of the greatest perceived perks for college and professional athletes is the availability of women. One of the greatest pitfalls awaiting athletes has always been — the availability of women."
– David L. Brown

Infidelity and adultery are games you should never play.

This chapter will show you how to choose the right woman in your life, and how to avoid the sometimes tragic pitfalls of playing Russian-roulette with your social life and athletic career.

Availability of Women

"If you have a wife, you don't need a girlfriend.
If you have a girlfriend — one is enough."
– Romeo Crennel, NFL Defensive Coordinator

Sometimes what you do socially can put you at tremendous risk, personally and athletically.

If you don't believe that, just ask the *world's most famous golfer* about his recent admitted infidelity. He no doubt today still faces the consequences from the choices he made that will continue to impact his personal life and golf career.

If you're a married athlete, it's not the "attraction" that gets you into trouble, it's the "action" part of the word that will put you in the headlines for all the wrong reasons.

Your thoughts are yours alone, but when you put them into action due to a possible sense of "entitlement" because you're an athlete, that's when trouble can start.

I want to help you focus on searching for and finding the right woman of your dreams... from the start, so that you can *RESIST* and avoid the many temptations that can lead to infidelity and adultery, and the negative consequences that follow.

I'll give you tools you can apply in your daily life *right now*, to make you a better person and athlete when "Ms. Right" does come along.

I also want to make this clear: infidelity and adultery amongst males are NOT an athlete thing...they are a MAN thing!

Given that, the truth is, for professional athletes, infidelity and adultery are often a part of the lifestyle, albeit one that is routinely overlooked or ignored by those who idolize their competitive achievements, not to mention usually left unreported — until you get caught.

Then, if you're a high profile athlete, the media frenzy kicks in full force!

My advice to athletes, young and older — seek independent women who are grounded. Seek women who possess the ways and means of taking care of themselves, with or without you.

Find a woman as close to your current status, financial and otherwise, as possible.

You will *NEVER* find the woman of your dreams at a nightclub, bar, late night party, gentleman's club, or in a restaurant.

Seek a woman who is mature, emotionally grounded, and spiritual. Understand that a nineteen or twenty-year old young woman will generally not be at the maturity level to handle your status as a public figure, a high profile athlete, or a professional athlete making millions of dollars a year. It's just too much for many young women to grasp.

When her and your fantasy begin to diminish and things go sour, as they often do, that's when your life and career could be in danger.

This type of behavior, by both men and women, is not openly advertised, but widely accepted. It's been said that the difference between a person who cheats and one who doesn't is one who puts themselves in a position to cheat.

Staying faithful to your wife or girlfriend becomes a lot more difficult when beautiful women are throwing themselves at you. And, most times, an athlete's mentality may be, "We're on the road. Who's going to know?"

You are aware of how the opposite sex presents themselves to you, and why those who pursue athletes make the extra effort to get noticed. The dominant dynamic of sex in sports can generally be described this way — where there are athletes, there are many women.

But that doesn't mean it's simple, good or right.

"There are a number of women who are lining up to meet you," one professional athlete who plays in New York told a reporter. "You have access to a lot more women. They know what restaurants you're going to go to, what clubs you're going to go to.

And they make themselves presentable, walk in your line of sight so you can see them. It's calculated," he said. "There are women out there who are sizing up which guys they think they can hook up with, or get their claws into."

In essence, sports and sex are inextricably intertwined. With so many women, there are endless possibilities. That includes bad ones — which may lead to poor choices.

"If you're not married before you come into this lifestyle, it's probably best if you wait until the middle or end of your career," the New York athlete continued telling the reporter. "Because that allows you to be a young man and enjoy whatever perks that come with it."

In 2001, Steven Ortiz of the University of Oregon presented his findings after interviewing 47 wives of professional athletes. The study concluded that there is a "fast-food-sex mentality" among professional athletes.

It also found that how the wives dealt with adultery depended on their motivations for marriage," Ortiz said.

"Women who marry the 'athlete' more than the 'man' tend to be more accepting of their husbands' affairs," he said.

Ortiz interviewed the wives over a four-year period, whose husbands were athletes from the four major team sports — football, basketball, baseball and hockey.

Ortiz also said many pro athletes' desire to commit adultery stems from the preferential treatment they've received most of their lives. "I call this the spoiled athlete syndrome," he said. "Part of the syndrome has to do with the idea that they are above any responsibility for their actions off the field." He labeled it as a "culture of adultery."

Ortiz specializes in marital relationships of professional athletes. More on the Ortiz study later.

This is not a new phenomenon.

Today, the role of the sports wife is no different, and often no less difficult. The results, too, are no less messy.

One common strategy a married athlete may use is to have multiple cell phones, with the bills sent somewhere other than to their home to conduct extramarital communication.

Again, don't play that game. In the end, it's just not worth it and, eventually, you will get caught.

Choose a Woman Wisely

Choose your woman and bed partner wisely. What's your lady like when she's sad, angry, happy, disappointed, irritated, or calm?

You must strive to see how she reacts in each of these circumstances before you make a commitment to her. How long should that take?

At least one year. You can't possibly know someone well in a few months. Let time be your best friend when it comes to a potential relationship.

To meet the right woman — you must first become the right man.

16 Tips on Finding the Right Woman

1. *Be your best you.* If you want to find and have a healthy relationship with Ms. Right, first make sure you have a healthy relationship with yourself. If you have any leftover baggage from past relationships, you don't want to drop them in the lap of Ms. Right. Take care of yourself — body, mind, and soul, so that you feel confident in who you are when you meet women you're interested in — for the right reasons.

2. *Educate yourself about women.* What most men *don't know* about women has filled many books! You might have had enough dating experiences to make you feel that you know "everything about women," but you could be wrong. Knowing about the feminine nature is very important. Learn about the differences between the genders. Read and research various studies conducted on the mysterious nature of the opposite sex.

3. *Write down what you're looking for.* It can be hard for you, as an athlete, to find the right woman if you don't know what you're looking for. Make a list of character traits and values you seek in a woman. Think about coming up with a list of questions to ask her over a period of a few months. Write down which behaviors, characteristics, or values would be deal-breakers for you. You might not be able to find someone who fits every single characteristic on your list, but if you write down what you're looking for, you might be able to find a woman who fits the most important attributes — and does not fit any of the deal-breaker criteria.

4. *Put yourself out there.* You are not going to meet Ms. Right sitting alone at home. You need to put yourself out there if you are going to meet the right woman.
5. *Search in the right places.* You won't find Ms. Right in the wrong places. For example, if you want a quiet lady who loves reading books, you likely won't find her at the bar, nightclub, or gentleman's club. If a one night stand is what you want, then those spots are ideal for you. However, if you want more from an encounter than sex, don't expect to find it in the club or bar, where the atmosphere is loose and casual. Alcohol often dominates actions and decisions. It's a recipe for disaster, and will only result in you waking up the next morning with a hangover and a handful of regrets. Women know that most men have an agenda when at a club, bar, or late night party — **SEX**. But know this — women also have agendas, hidden or otherwise. There are better women waiting to be found in much better places.
6. *Look before leaping.* Before you jump into a full-fledged relationship with a woman, be sure to take time to test the waters. Ask her about who she is, share about who you are, and subtly make your way through the list of questions you have compiled for any potential mate. If you stumble upon a deal breaker, don't be afraid to be tactful, yet up front about your decision, then move on. Any time spent with Ms. Not So Right could be keeping you from crossing paths with the woman who is truly meant for you.
7. *Be patient.* While you're out seeking Ms. Right, always instill in your mind that you need to be patient. You can't expect the right woman to appear out of nowhere. She will come into your life at the right place, in the right time. How to meet the right woman is all about patience.
8. *Think like Ms. Right.* If you're going to find Ms. Right, you must learn to think like Ms. Right. Where would she spend her time? If you want to find her, you'll need to begin spending time where she might be. If you're looking for a woman who's involved in social justice and activism, it would be logical to join some local social-action groups. If you want someone who cares deeply about academics, spend time teaching or taking classes in the off-season.
9. *Don't choose a woman based on immediate attraction.* While attraction is a prerequisite condition for any healthy relationship, some athletes may rely completely on physical attraction when it comes to choosing their partners. This is a mistake. Many attractive young women are good looking, funny, self-confident and expe-

rienced — but not necessarily trustful, reliable or ready for a meaningful relationship. Before spending your precious time, money, and emotional resources on a woman who has little to no potential to become your full time partner for life, it's imperative that you learn how to quickly analyze the relationship potential. Instead of judging a woman by her physical attributes alone, you want to know how to identify the warning signs of a future bad relationship before wasting your emotions on a woman who will leave you heartbroken and discouraged — or worse.

10. *Know your woman.* What are you really looking for? What does your dream girl look like? How does she dress? What is she interested in? How does she talk and behave? What are her character traits? Does she share your interests? What sort of qualities do you desire in her? Seek the answers to these questions and more, before, during, and after your search.

11. *Brush up on your social, verbal, and communication skills.* Women love great and stimulating conversation. Keep her wanting more by challenging her and your mind.

12. *Laugh, and laugh some more.* Women love a man who can make them genuinely laugh.

13. *Seek intelligent, attractive, professional, grounded, humble women* who can take care of themselves, and like it that way. Seek women who have their own money, and don't need a man to take care of them. This type of woman is clearly on solid ground. They are simply looking for the right man to share their lives with — and are NOT looking to be financially and emotionally rescued, or taken care of. This type of woman is looking for an equal partner in a relationship. They may seem hard to find — but they're out there!

14. *Let her be her own woman.* She took care of herself before she met you — and she can certainly take care of herself afterward! Respect her, don't smother her or try to control her, or invade her privacy. Likewise, seek a woman who will let you be your own man for the same reasons.

15. *Have a positive mental attitude.* Believe that you will find Ms. Right. If you're currently dating with the belief that you'll never find her, chances are you never will. Negative beliefs will reflect in your actions and words. The wrong attitude on your part may put off the very women you're trying to attract. Enhance your understanding about attracting the right woman into your life. Focus on your-

self. Pay attention to self-growth. Learn to be happy. Cheerful, optimistic, and humorous athletes attract hordes of charming women — the right charming women.

16. *Time reveals all things* — so take it slow and let time be your guide. If a woman has a hidden agenda — time will reveal it. If you have a hidden agenda with her, the same applies. Approach her with a genuine heart, and just be yourself. Time will tell you if she's the right one for you…or not.

The Mistress Mind

"Not every encounter with women will wind up being high and mighty and everything tidy."
– David L. Brown

You not only risk your athletic career when engaging in infidelity, and the trust of your fans, family, colleagues, sponsors, and the media — you also could be risking your life!

You may have heard about the following tragic story…

It's now official that the twenty-year-old girlfriend of a former NFL star quarterback shot him in his right temple while he was asleep, then fired three more shots at close range. She then sat on the couch next to his body and killed herself so that she would fall into his lap, according to Nashville, Tennessee police.

The former well-known QB was found dead with multiple gunshot wounds. The young woman was also found dead at the Nashville condo the athlete was reported to have shared with another person. The former all-pro quarterback took two bullets in the chest and two in the head. The young woman was found with a single shot to the head.

The incident was officially classified by police detectives as a murder-suicide.

The alleged troubled young woman ended a life that was coming undone as she got in trouble with the law, faced mounting bills, and saw a new relationship unraveling with a former high-profile pro football quarterback, who played for the Tennessee Titans and Baltimore Ravens during a thirteen-year NFL career before retiring in 2008.

Police believe that's why the woman killed the former athlete with a 9mm semi-automatic pistol while he slept, then turned the gun on herself in the early morning hours of July 4, 2009.

"We can't put ourselves in the minds of people who do these terrible, irrational acts, but there is evidence she was spinning out of control," a police chief told reporters.

The woman, a waitress, wasn't sure how to pay the bills for her upscale apartment and new SUV reportedly given to her as a gift from the athlete, which was found to be registered in both their names. She was arrested for DUI on July 2, 2009, with her famous boyfriend in the passenger seat just two days before she killed him and herself.

She reportedly suspected the athlete, who was still married, was involved in a second affair. The woman reportedly had told friends and relatives that she and the former pro quarterback were going to be together because he allegedly told her he was divorcing his wife.

They believe the former QB spent that Friday night bar-hopping before going to his condo where the young woman was waiting.

The former quarterback, age 36 when killed, left behind a wife and four sons. He is best known for taking the Titans to their only Super Bowl following the 1999 season.

Problems were mounting.

The woman was reported to be showing signs of falling apart, police learned from her friends and co-workers. On the previous Thursday before the shootings, and several hours after her DUI arrest, she was allegedly in the parking lot in the middle of her shift at a local restaurant buying a gun.

She reportedly purchased the gun for $100. Why do these things happen sometimes? Is it simply about love and sex? You know — you love your wife, but you have sex with your mistress. You love your wife, but you feel like a twenty-one-year-old again with your mistress.

Again...don't let this be you.

It's not a black or white thing.

It's not an athlete thing. It's a man thing that we haven't been able to shake since Eve gave Adam that apple.

May we all appreciate the life we have, knowing that it's not guaranteed or permanent — and can end in an instant.

Quiz for athletes: What's the one most important word in *"mistress"*?

Answer: **STRESS!** And who needs that — right?

Double Coverage

What's double coverage? It's having a wife *AND* a girlfriend.

Triple coverage is having a wife and two girlfriends. You will eventually lose playing that game!

Nobody likes a cheater, especially in the sporting world.

With media following you around day and night, you'll eventually get caught.

Wives Left Behind

Athletes' wives must cope with "adultery culture," according to Dr. Sherry Blake, a clinical psychologist practicing in the Atlanta area.

Her belief was in response to the 4th of July 2009, murder-suicide shooting of the former NFL quarterback mentioned previously. Dr. Blake told a reporter she calls infidelity amongst professional athletes "a wake-up call."

She said she expects most athletes eventually will forget about the tragic murder-suicide and return to their old habits.

"Many players have had extramarital affairs for years," said Blake.

She said she has counseled athletes and entertainers about the temptations of drugs, alcohol and women. Most pro teams and leagues have "player development programs designed to help with certain personal aspects of their lives, such as finances. But some programs don't deal enough with relationships or marriage," Dr. Blake said.

The pro leagues and the NCAA discuss with their athletes the potential risks in personal relationships. For example, each team offers life skill options that include programs for managing relationships and violence against women.

"Relationship management is a critical part of what we do in player development," NFL spokesman Greg Aiello wrote in a statement to the media.

Dr. Blake said pro athletes — particularly retirees — often seek women to validate "they still got it...although they may have the perfect setup at home."

Many wives of professional male athletes have to consider the possibility of their husbands' infidelity — particularly during a long season with numerous road trips. A study suggests that how they handle their fear and stress varies, and may depend on their motivation for marriage.

While media reports of sexual exploits of athletes aren't new, little had been written about how wives respond to adultery — and to the possibility of adultery — until the Steven Ortiz study was released in 2001.

What emerged from interviews with many athletes' wives were profiles of adaptation as wives developed coping strategies that often evolved over time. The wives who were interviewed also identified a category of wives who were drawn to marriage more for the glamour and money than for love or the relationship.

"It may be that women who marry the 'athlete' more than the 'man' may tend to be more accepting of their husband's affairs," Ortiz said. "Not only do they fear losing financial security and the affluent lifestyle, they often possess low self-esteem."

According to the study, women who married before their husbands became professional athletes — including most of the interviewed wives — did not tolerate long-term extramarital affairs, though many were forced to deal with their spouses' one-time only "one-night stand."

Ortiz also found a major difference between new wives and wives who had been married to an athlete for 10 to 15 years.

"The majority of the new wives truly didn't know what they were getting in for," Ortiz told a reporter, "and often they have to learn the ropes from the veteran wives. The wife of a baseball player who has been married and 'in the league' for fifteen years can be fairly hardened. She has seen or heard it all." And when she hears from her husband that he's had an affair, Ortiz said she has to make a decision to cope with it, or dissolve the marriage.

"Most wives will give the husband the benefit of the doubt," he pointed out, though they may use the incident to set ground rules afterward.

"One thing that I learned from the interviews is that these women are strong," Ortiz said. "If they don't know what the lifestyle is like, they quickly learn. And then they develop strategies to manage that ongoing stress."

The strategies vary in confronting the 'possibility' of marital infidelity, since the possibility is always there, though the infidelity may not be.

"Some of the wives use humor, while others may change the boundaries of trust in the relationship," Ortiz added. "Whatever strategies they rely on, they continue to manage the family life. Most of the wives are very strong, intelligent, and resilient. That's why the men married them in the first place."

Ortiz said some strategies for handling the stress of possible infidelity have negative consequences. He said some wives are in denial and don't want to talk about it. Others acknowledge the issue constantly, and may feel like they are pressuring their husbands for constant reassurance.

"Many wives of professional athletes engage in 'suspicion management,'" Ortiz continued. "It's all in their approach to the issue. Some wives look for signs that their husband has been unfaithful, others may deny the possibility by avoiding the issue completely."

They are different strategies of dealing with the same fears.

"Also, there are wives of professional athletes who actually condone infidelity in order to continue living the great lifestyle afforded them. From the research I've conducted and the information I have received from reliable sources, it appears there are wives who are clearly aware of affairs and choose to turn the other cheek," Ortiz candidly told a reporter.

The sex lives of professional athletes is an area that the management of most teams would like to ignore, and by and large, they do, Ortiz said. However, media scrutiny transcends privacy issues. Outsiders tend to view those incidents as the tip of an iceberg, and Ortiz says that depiction may be accurate.

There exists a culture of adultery, he said, that management and coaches usually ignore, that fellow players may often encourage, and with which the wives must contend.

"These men spend so much time together practicing, working, and traveling, that they bond very closely," Ortiz said. "I would argue that in certain ways, many of them are closer to their teammates than they are to their wives and families. Yet, it is the women who become the support system without which many men could not survive."

"I talked to one woman who learned on the radio that her husband had been traded to a team across the country. He didn't call her because he was trying to catch a plane to his new team. It is the wives, though, who must pack up the furniture, pull the kids out of school, sell the house and move the family. And this is very common in their world, as it is in other career-dominated marriages," Ortiz commented.

It has been reported by the media that on long road trips, some athletes have an extraordinary amount of downtime with which to entertain themselves, and those boundaries of "entertainment" are clearly quite wide.

Many experts suggest that it starts with harmless events like going to a club or a bar, but often escalates to bringing a girl back to the room to have sex with.

Another real issue is athletes having children out of wedlock.

Infidelity and adultery in sports are nothing new. It's unfortunate that such occurrences happen, especially with athletes coming into the professional ranks at younger ages, accompanied by large paychecks. It's often difficult for them to stay away from the temptation.

Due Diligence

Unfortunately, there are women out there who will purposely try to get pregnant by athletes, or make false statements of being pregnant — more often after the relationship goes sour.

This happened to a famous Dallas Maverick NBA all-star in the off-season, 2009.

The woman, then 38, who the athlete was engaged to at the time, had moved into his home and later claimed she was pregnant with the star's child. A private investigation into the woman's past, as part of a prenuptial agreement urged by the athlete's advisers, revealed outstanding arrest warrants for her in two states, and her reported use of more than 20 aliases.

She later received a five-year prison sentence for violating terms of her probation in Missouri from a decade-old forgery and felony theft case. It was also later determined that she was not pregnant with the athlete's child.

In order for an athlete to begin an investigation of a person, your purpose of the investigation must be clearly defined. As always, consult your attorney for the best, proper, and legal ways to get the answers you deserve about the woman in your life.

Even if it's "awkward," always do background research before making any commitments.

15 Background Search Tips

1. Think about why you want to investigate the person, and what type of information you're looking for. Are you curious about criminal background, previous relationships, work, family, or other issues in her life? Determining what you want to learn will place you on the right track.
2. Know that all investigations don't have to be secretive. Go straight to the source if you can. Tell her that you have a concern or curiosity, and ask her about it straight out. In a solid relationship, communication is the key. If you find your-

self uncomfortable talking to her, or feel reason to distrust her responses, then you should question the stability of your relationship with her.
3. Research and find reputable online background checking services. Many times, these searches are affordable and relatively easy to complete. As an added bonus, they are convenient, and can be done from any location as long as you have internet access. You can do this on your own, or have your attorney or agent assist you.
4. Hire a private investigator. A professional can sometimes work angles and draw more information than anyone else. An investigator can also use resources in your case that others may not be aware of or may not have access to. Better yet, a private investigator has done this before, which you may not have.
5. Use the information you receive to your benefit. If necessary, confront the woman in your life. Of course, if you learn anything serious or concerning, you should end the relationship immediately, for your own protection and hers.
6. Due diligence is a requirement. Everything you can possibly learn about a person is of prime importance. This also includes employment and education verification. This is another comprehensive background check available to you.
7. When you absolutely must know the facts about a person's history, an extensive profile report gathers all records and sources available. It includes: county and state criminal and civil records, real property ownership, liens, judgments, and any bankruptcies.
8. A complete background check and comprehensive profile report confirms a person's identity and provides the essential facts you need to know. This includes any eviction records and much more.
9. Your lawyer or private investigator will also conduct a search that will scrutinize county, state, national, and federal databases to determine whether she has an adverse driving record, and any DUIs and arrests.
10. A complete people identifier report and public records search will help you stay ahead of potential trouble by giving you information that provides pertinent background information about the person in question — including the use of fictitious names.
11. An asset search will inform you about a person's real property and assets, like land, homes, automobiles, boats, and aircraft.

12. A business background check, if you are considering a business relationship with her, will supply you with valuable information regarding professional licenses, tax liens, and previous judgments.
13. A current or previous rental screening search will help you determine previous addresses, landlords, roommates, civil court records and complaints.
14. Use common sense and intuition. Listen to the advice of your attorney, close friends, and family. Possessive women may treat you wonderfully at the start; however, it will not be long before they exhibit warning signs.
15. *Always think due diligence, first and foremost* — no matter what, no matter who, no matter where, no matter why, no matter when.

12 Ways Athletes Can Stay Safe, and Warning Signs

1. Avoid internet connections with women. Do not seek out or date women from the internet in any way, shape or form.
2. According to the American Social Health Organization, using statistics compiled from the Center for Disease Control (CDC), 65 million Americans have an incurable sexually transmitted disease and 15 million new infections occur each year. Most of these infections are Human Papillomavirus (HPV genital warts) and herpes. However, millions of Americans carry dangerous infections, including HIV/AIDS, gonorrhea, hepatitis B, chlamydia, and syphilis. You must protect yourself — and her, also. This is a very difficult subject for couples to discuss. However, if either of you has been sexually active, it's an important issue. STD (sexually transmitted disease) screening is an essential safeguard for all athletes, and a very good way for couples to demonstrate their concern for each other.
3. If you do experience fireworks and raging hormones, please keep in mind that it's often attributed to simple lust. Lust is fine if you and your partner recognize it for what it is. Be the one to show respect and self-control.
4. Lust will bring up spiritual, moral, legal, ethical, and health issues, which are difficult for couples to discuss, but far too important to ignore.
5. If a couple becomes intimate early in the relationship, sex will probably become the centerpiece. You will view each other primarily as sexual partners, and friendship may be pushed to the background. After the passion cools down, will you have any reason to stay together? Birth control methods are not foolproof.

Condoms can slip off or tear. Planned Parenthood reports an 8% per year pregnancy rate among women who are less than perfect in taking birth control pills according to directions. This is a mutual responsibility. Male athletes cannot assume that the woman will "take care of" this issue. You must also do your part.

6. Excessive jealousy, possessiveness, and controlling behavior. Your lady may demand an accounting for all the times you spend apart, always insist on where you go together, try to put limits on where you go and what you do when you are apart, or give you the third degree about any member of the opposite sex you may speak to.
7. If you notice drastic mood swings, excessive anger, alcohol and drug abuse, this is a major problem, and it is very unlikely that you can cure it for her.
8. Threats and physical abuse. Her shoves and slaps can quickly escalate into more serious behavior and domestic violence. Gentlemen, it's not uncommon for an abusive woman to attack you to the point that you must fight back to protect yourself. When the police show up, guess who usually goes to jail?
9. Blaming you or others for all of her problems. How can you have a successful relationship with a woman who does not take responsibility for her own actions, and vice-versa? If any of these behaviors occur repeatedly, end the relationship! Do not waste time or listen to promises of change — end the relationship — NOW!
10. Excessive criticism of your friends and family. This is an especially bad sign if your lady expects you to break ties with friends and family members.
11. A violation of trust. You suspect she's been cheating on you, or she suspects you've been cheating on her.
12. Read the situation critically. If she gets angry about your reasons for wanting to end the relationship, simply cut the lines of communication. If your most sincere efforts to guard her feelings are rewarded with hostility, then it only validates your sense that the relationship is not working for you any longer.

10 Ways to Respectfully and Safely Say Goodbye

1. Be sure you're prepared for anything she may say. Be sure this is what you really want. Be calm and respectful. If there is a way to salvage the relationship, tell her if that's what you both want, then discuss how to do that. If it's not what you want, stand your ground in a respectful way.

2. Talk to her in person, and talk honestly, but calmly. Communicate with her why you don't want to continue the relationship. Let her verbally know what you want. After all, she's not a mind reader.
3. Listen to her. Reply with any answers to her questions. Don't say, *"Can we just be friends?"* That will hurt her, and is disrespectful, if it's not something you genuinely want. Be open and honest, but compassionate. Don't give in if you truly no longer want a relationship with her.
4. However kind you may be, there is no way around the fact that this is going to hurt her feelings. All you can do is try to minimize the pain.
5. Try not to break up with her by phone, email, or text message, as this is disrespectful and may cause serious animosity on her part. Have the decency to do it privately and in person, if at all possible. If you believe there may be an altercation, by all means take another route to break things off. Consult your attorney or private investigator for more information and input.
6. Try to avoid placing blame for the breakup. Reflect carefully on the reasons for your decision to break up, and be prepared to justify them without blaming her.
7. Let the breakup be final. Don't keep going back and *"hooking up"* with her over and over again unless you really think there's something still there.
8. Don't lose focus if she starts crying. You can be sympathetic during the conversation, but don't let someone manipulate you with tears.
9. Put yourself in her place. Putting yourself in her shoes will give you insights to protect yourself from making another mistake in the future.
10. Let no one control you. You, and *you alone*, decide the direction you want your life to go. All relationships are volunteer situations. You're not required to continue any relationship you don't want to be in. Now, that doesn't give you a license to go out and use women for your own gain and then drop them, but it does give you permission to end a relationship that doesn't seem to be a give and take situation that is beneficial to both of you.

Also, tell your closest family members or friends of your decision to end the relationship. Don't wait for days or weeks to pass before you inform someone. Be sure to express that you would like to keep it confidential. I know, as an athlete your privacy is important, and you're right, but in this case, in this day and age, in our current society, you MUST let someone know as soon as possible about a likely breakup.

In the end it's for the best. Not being in a negative relationship any longer makes you a better person, and hopefully, her as well.

Sports and Character

By character, I mean moral excellence — a life characterized by prudence, fortitude, self-discipline, and humility in pursuit of what is good.

High character and moral conduct is not about being perfect. No one is. It's simply about making good choices and using good judgment.

University of Colorado sociologist Dr. Jay Coakley, in his book, *Sports in Society*, explains that we mistakenly believe that sports builds character for two reasons. First, Dr. Coakley states we wrongly assume that all athletes have the same experiences in all organized sports.

Secondly, he says we wrongly assume organized sports provide unique learning experiences that are not available from any other activities.

He goes on to say that school-age athletes are immersed in a world of adults who are masters at cheating, gambling, violence, serial adultery, lying, drunkenness, drug abuse, and misogyny. *"Bad company corrupts good character"* is such compelling ancient Greek wisdom that it is quoted in the Bible (1 Corinthians 15:33). By the time many young athletes become "professionals," they may have already adopted the dissolute values learned in the company of malformed adults, Dr. Coakley wrote.

The fact is, sports do not build character in young people, but virtuous adults do.

In one sense, youth sport is simply a medium for adult mentoring within the context of challenging situations. Character is bestowed — or not — from one generation to another.

Until adults in the world of sports are willing to commit their own lives to virtuous character, until they are willing to pair a valid desire to make money with an equally powerful concern for the true welfare of athletes, the cycle of the young "professional" athlete making poor choices and jeopardizing his life and career will continue.

In athletics, as elsewhere, we reap the moral character we sow.

A significant aspect of athletes being new pros coming in from college is protecting yourself now that you're on the big stage. Many athletes entering the pros are young, and often naïve. Many come from modest backgrounds. You're about to receive steady paychecks with lots of commas. That makes you targets.

Infidelity and adultery are real, and potentially deadly.

The life of a professional athlete's wife just brings that to light more, and once again gives the opportunity to bring to center stage a sin that every married person needs to deal with, not just athletes.

And don't forget about the real victims of infidelity and adultery — the *children* that may be left behind to pick up the pieces.

Play Hard. Do Good. Be Smart About It.™

PART TWO

Chapter 7
HOME INVASION

The Fear is Real!

"A danger foreseen is half avoided."
– Unknown

There have been more than a few home invasion headlines involving athletes over the years — some resulting in death.

For many of us, when we think of home invasion, we think of a stranger who targets an athlete's home, waits for him to leave, then breaks in and steals whatever he can get his hands on. From time to time, this does happen.

Home invasion can also occur when an athlete and/or family members are at home! The fear and feeling of being violated are real.

This chapter will provide you with many simple, practical tips you can immediately apply to keep you and your family safe.

These tools can help you NOW — and each and every day, to keep you and your family safe at home. They will also give you peace of mind when you're on the road at away games or other events.

*"The more difficult you make it to get into your home,
the less likely you are of being a home invasion victim."*
– David L. Brown

Could This Be You?

John and Michelle were spending a quiet evening relaxing at home, when they were suddenly taken by surprise by their front door crashing open and seeing two masked intruders coming into their living room, one brandishing a .57 Magnum.

Michelle was in the den, and through the doorway, saw another man with a shotgun. Without any regard for human life, one intruder shot John at point blank range. John quickly turned his back to the intruder, taking a bullet to the back of his right arm.

Witnessing this in horror, Michelle grabbed her loaded 9mm semi-automatic pistol from a desk drawer and fired five shots at the assailants.

A shot hit one gunman in the upper chest, the other gunman in the abdomen. Three other shots missed their intended targets.

As one of the intruders went down, he fired three return shots toward the wall Michelle was hiding behind. The bullets ripped through the wall, killing her.

One gunman died a few moments later, the other fled on foot and was later apprehended and taken to the hospital in serious condition.

John survived his ordeal, but lost his beloved wife, and the use of his right arm.

The story I just wrote is *fiction*.

The characters are not real. But the reality of this actually happening *IS* very real, and does happen often in our society and to our athletes. Michelle knew how to shoot a gun, but she didn't know how to safely protect herself by positioning her body behind a more stable barrier than a regular wall.

Bullets from all kinds of guns can penetrate through regular walls easily. How many sad stories have you heard about involving drive-by shootings where young children were killed inside their homes by bullets sprayed from cars of assailants?

Michelle may have survived being killed if she had known to use C & C — concealment and cover. What is concealment? Concealment is an armored-like protective barrier you can position yourself behind, like a reinforced wall, a reinforced doorway, or any piece of furniture or other object that is designed to stop incoming bullets, yet conceal you from a gunman's view.

What is cover? Cover is something you can get behind, like your refrigerator, your kitchen island, your desktop computer, your dresser in the bedroom, and your car, trees, and your home's brick walls (if you're outside).

Basic drywall and hollow core doors will not protect you from possibly being shot and killed by bullets fired at you.

Your means of survival may come down to placing a heavy and thick object between you and your assailant.

As in John and Michelle's unfortunate ordeal, you never know when an attack may occur. If an attacker gains entry into your home, you may have zero amount of time to retrieve a weapon and defend yourself.

If, for example, your weapon is in an upstairs bedroom, or some other distant location in your house, you may not have time to get to it.

If you have a registered and licensed gun in your home, you could have a chance at survival, but there are certainly no guarantees.

Make it a purposeful priority to seek training for yourself and your family members if you keep guns in your home. After all, you wouldn't trust your banker with a medical condition, your pastor with your investment portfolio, or your general healthcare provider with your marital or relationship matters.

The point is, find a professional to help you with your defensive in-home training.

Facts and Prevention

A home invasion occurs when criminals force their way into your home to commit a robbery or other crime.

Home invasion is unlike a burglary. Burglars traditionally strike during the day, when a home is unoccupied, and are likely to be deterred by alarm systems and strong locks, doors and windows. They often flee when confronted.

However, home invaders typically strike at night or on weekends when athletes or family are at home. They attack when alarm systems are likely to be mistakenly deactivated.

Their strategy is dependent upon taking control of your home.

Home invaders often target athletes because you tend to have more lavish homes to invade. They may select you as a target by the car you drive, or the jewelry you wear and sometimes may follow you home.

Many home invaders will first attempt to enter your home as a repair person, or attempt to gain a glimpse into your home by pretending to deliver a package. Some will just bust right through the front door, wearing masks to conceal their identity. These robbers typically work in groups and rely on their ability to overcome their victims when the opportunity is right.

The most common point of attack is your front door or garage. Home invaders will inevitably use extreme force to take control of your home and intimidate you and your loved ones.

This initial confrontation is often the most violent part of the home invasion and the point in which your family's safety is most at risk. After taking control — often subduing residents with duct tape, rope or handcuffs — home invaders bent on robbery will typically begin to search their victim's home for valuables. They will sometimes force victims to locate hidden items, open safes, and provide PIN numbers to ATM cards.

Other Basic Facts:

1. Police authorities estimate that 90% of all burglaries/home invasions are preventable.
2. In 17% of all crimes, domiciles were violated. In other words, you may have more than one residence, but you only have one domicile (your main, permanent, legal residence).
3. The average burglar will spend no more than two minutes trying to get into your home.

The New "Prevent Defense"

Fortify your home with solid core doors, strong locks, and security devices on windows. To strengthen locks, secure heavy-duty strike plates with at least four three-inch screws. Keep all doors and windows in your home and garage locked at all times when home or away.

Install a peephole, and use it before opening your door. Make sure your porch light is in a position to help you see people at your front door clearly.

Never open your door to strangers or solicitors, and never rely on a chain-latch. If a solicitor acts suspicious, call the police.

Keep window shades closed at night. Windows can give a criminal a lot of information about your home's vulnerability. If a home invader can't see into your home, he may not feel confident about storming in.

Never make it obvious that you're home alone. The fewer the occupants, the easier a home invader's job becomes. A single occupant may be the opportunity a home invader is looking for. Keep extra lights on. Use your television or radio to create the illusion that more people are in the house.

Hold frequent family meetings to discuss home security practices. Too often, the weakest part of a home security system are the habits of the occupants. If your family is educated about the risks and certain home security practices are followed, this will greatly reduce the risk of a home invasion.

Forgetting to set your alarm system before you go to bed at night could expose you and your family to tremendous risk. Speaking of alarm systems, make sure you install a remote alarm system, whereby the electricity to it does not depend on your regular home electrical grid. This way, if your electricity to the house is compromised in any way, your remote home alarm system will still alert police.

When going on vacation during the off-season, have a family member or close friend, someone you absolutely trust, stay in your home while you're gone. If that's not possible, have a neighbor, friend, or a family member keep an eye on your home, and stop by daily to take in the mail and any newspapers you have delivered. They should also do a daily walk around the house and check to make sure all windows and doors are secure.

There have been reports that athletes have gone away on vacation for a couple of weeks during the off season, only to come back and find their home broken into. Later, it was determined that their home was broken into only a couple days after they left.

If you don't have anyone available to check your home and take in your mail, you can have your mail held temporarily at your local post office until you return.

The New "Cover Two" Home Invasion Defense

If an intruder is able to get inside your home, here are some tools you can use to help protect you and your family.
1. Practice in-home drills, depicting every conceivable possibility that might happen.
2. Cooperate with the invader(s). This may help calm the criminals and reduce the likelihood of violence. No matter how discomforting it is to lose your valuables, *NEVER* risk your life to save your *STUFF!*
3. Avoid looking the intruder(s) in the eye. If a criminal feels you can identify him, he may react violently.

4. If you own a firearm, you may want to keep it hidden in your master bathroom. Statistics say victims of a home invasion are most often contained in the master bathroom.

5. Establish a secret code word or phrase with a friend or family member who regularly calls you on the telephone. Should this person call during a home invasion, you could claim that you're expecting an important phone call and that not answering would arouse suspicion. If the home invader lets you answer, you could use the code word or phrase to alert them to call 9-1-1. Don't make your secret code obvious to intruders that it is a secret code! Use common words or phrases.

For example, let's say your name is Mike. During a home invasion your buddy Greg calls. You tell the bad guy you are expecting a call and not answering the phone will raise suspicion in the caller. **You:** "Hello. Joseph, hi, how are you, bro?" **Caller:** "Joseph? Huh...who's Joseph? This is Greg, man. What's up with you, Mike?" **You:** "Yeah, my aunt Patti hasn't been feeling well lately and I was planning to stop by tomorrow and check in on her." The caller remembers that this is your secret phrase, and says, "Okay, tell aunt Patti I hope she's feeling better soon. Someone's at my door. I'll call you back later." The caller hangs up and dials 9-1-1.

But wait! Smart home invaders may request that you place that call on *"speakerphone"* so they can hear the entire conversation. Here's what you do: phone rings and you tell the bad guy you need to answer it. The smart bad guy says, "Put it on speakerphone, so I can hear both of you!" **You:** "Hello. Hi, Greg, how are you?" **Greg:** "Hey, Mike, what's up, man? Just wanted to call to say hi and see how Bobby's soccer game went last night." **You:** "Thanks for calling, Greg. Hang on, man. Let me put you on speakerphone real quick."

Speakerphone is your secret code word! Greg instantly recognizes the call as unusual behavior, pretends again that someone's at the door, says he'll call you back later, hangs up and dials 9-1-1. Greg knew you were in trouble because, one, you had previously informed him that if you ever have to place a personal call with him on speakerphone, that means you are in trouble! Two, how many people do you know place *personal calls* on speakerphone? Three, when was the last time you placed a personal call on speakerphone? It doesn't happen very often. Business calls, yes. Personal calls, not so much.

Additionally, when verbally addressing home invaders, respond to them as *"Yes, sir. No. sir."* If it's a female home invader (yes, there have been cases of females in a group of home invaders), refer to her as *"Yes, ma'am."*

When the invaders leave, make sure everyone meets at the predetermined emergency meeting place in your home.

6. Stay calm. Use your awareness and common sense to your advantage.
7. Don't stand still — move! If you happen to find yourself in a potential shootout with an intruder, ducking and dodging in different directions as you fire and when you're being fired at, makes you a moving — and much more difficult target to hit.
8. Police say a large majority of home invasion incidents will occur at three to four feet, or even less. Sometimes it may be in the grasp of your assailant.
9. If you find yourself in a close encounter with the attacker, if you can, lock onto them by tightly wrapping your arms around their arms in an "up close and personal" position, like athletes sometimes do in hockey fights. This will allow you to "tie up" your attacker, limiting him from extending his arms to shoot at you or physically assault you.
10. The "up close and personal" technique can be dangerous and potentially deadly. You must react quickly and not hesitate if you choose this option. Any hesitation will give the attacker time to raise his gun at you in a shooting position...and *Pop, Pop, Pop,* you could be dead. Your critical decision making process will have to be sharp at this moment.
11. If your attacker already has a weapon in hand, then you obviously don't want to lunge at him to establish an "up close" position. You must be able to draw your firearm from concealment, fire, and shoot your attacker before he shoots you or a family member.
12. Keep all cell phones in your house handy. Recharge them at night before you go to bed. Attackers wanting to break into your home may be smart enough to cut your land line phone beforehand. They may also attempt to disable any home alarm system from automatically calling the police. One thing they can't disable from outside is your cell phone.

As an athlete, you may have at some point wondered, "who's next." Am I being targeted? It's definitely something sports teams have to pay more attention to, and continue educating athletes to keep a watchful eye.

This chapter will help you do that.

Regardless of where you live, or how nice your community is, or whether or not it's a gated community — crime happens, whether you're in a big city or in a rural community. It can happen to anyone.

Be prepared, just in case.

75 Tips That Work

What Athletes CAN Do

1. Check your home for all possible entry points and any weaknesses they may have.
2. Check for overgrown shrubbery and trees; maintain clear lines of sight for your entrances and driveway. Trim shrubs to a height of three feet, and tree canopies up to eight feet. Eliminate hiding areas around entrances.
3. Check exterior lighting, including the back and sides of your home. Try to maintain uniform lighting to eliminate dark spots and shadows.
4. Check windows and door locks to make sure they are in working order. Install a wide-angle door viewer that permits you to look outside before opening the door.
5. Lock all doors, including the garage, and windows whenever possible, prior to leaving your residence, going to bed, or leaving on vacation.
6. Move and secure items that could be used to facilitate entry through ground floor windows. Make sure that casement windows cannot be pulled open to allow entry.
7. At night, close your drapes, blinds and window treatments as a deterrent. If bad guys can't see into your home, they may be reluctant to enter. You know your home's floor plan layout better than any intruder. Use this to your advantage.
8. Again, please don't forget to set your alarm before going to bed.
9. You may consider having a panic button installed near your bed, or use a wireless remote alarm key chain or pendant.

10. Have a cell phone near your bed. Consider keeping a secondary cell phone, always fully charged, in your master bathroom.
11. Leave an interior light on, or use a timer to turn the light on and off. Leave a radio or television on when out of the house.
12. Discontinue any deliveries while away on business or vacation. Arrange for family or friends to visit your home while you're away.
13. Prepare a videotape of your home's contents, and store it in a safe place.
14. Keep valuables out of the master bedroom. Store them in a fireproof safe, or a safe deposit box at your local bank.
15. Mark your property using an engraving tool for identification.
16. When approaching or leaving your home, look for suspicious persons or vehicles.
17. As a deterrent, vary your day-to-day routine. Someone targeting you will be more apt to act if they have the schedule of when and what time you come and go down pat.
18. Start a neighborhood watch.
19. If you discover evidence from the exterior that your home has been burglarized, *DO NOT ENTER. IMMEDIATELY CALL THE POLICE BY DIALING 9-1-1.*
20. Have a solid-core door for all entrance points.
21. Use a quality, heavy-duty deadbolt lock with a one-inch throw bolt.
22. Use a quality, heavy-duty, knob-in-lock set with a dead-latch mechanism.
23. Use a heavy-duty, four-screw, strike plate with three-inch screws to penetrate into a wooden door frame.
24. Use a secondary blocking device on all sliding glass doors. Use anti-lift devices such as through-the-door pins or upper track screws.
25. Use highly visible alarm and "beware of dog" decals, or neighborhood watch decals.
26. Secure all accessible windows with secondary blocking devices.
27. Make sure someone cannot reach through an open window to unlock a door or remove a blocking device.
28. Use anti-lift devices to prevent the window from being lifted out.
29. Secure windows at night and, if need be, leave only a slight opening for ventilation purposes.
30. Set your phone to speed dial 9-1-1.

31. Get to know your adjacent neighbors.
32. Agree to watch out for each others home.
33. Use motion sensor lights near or around key entry points.
34. Use good lighting along pathways and your driveway to and from main entry points.
35. Make sure any exterior lighting allows for 100-foot visibility.
36. Make sure your alarm system has an audible horn or bell to be effective.
37. Instruct your neighbors how to respond to your alarm should it become activated.
38. Ensure your alarm system is up to date and always fully functional. Have the company who initially installed the system periodically come out to check it for preventive future defects.
39. Identify your valuables by engraving objects with a set of numbers that only you would know. Make a list of the items and their numbers, and keep the list in a safe deposit box or somewhere in your home.
40. Take time to inventory, photograph and have an appraisal conducted on valuable items.
41. Photocopy the contents of your wallet and other important documents.
42. Do not keep the PINs for your credit cards or debit cards in the same place.
43. Patio doors are another entry way that need to be secured. Many athletes may not realize that some patio doors can be lifted up slightly and disengaged from their locking mechanism.
44. An easy way to secure a patio door is to put a pole in between the patio door end and the wall. Place the pole on the track where the patio door slides when opening up. This will prevent the door wall from being opened until the pole is removed. You can use an old broomstick handle, or even a board.
45. The same security tip above goes for your windows. Make sure they are locked and secured the same way.
46. Make sure your security alarm company knows which police department to contact for your jurisdiction.
47. Install deadbolt locks for all doors, not just in certain areas of your home.
48. Install outside lighting on motion detectors. That way the lights will go on when motion is detected. Many times they will detect small animals or some other ob-

ject. Just because they go on doesn't necessarily mean there is someone there. But having them go on is a good deterrent if someone was there.

49. Make sure you have some non-lethal self-defense weapons handy, such as pepper sprays and stun guns located in a few places around the house.
50. Install visible outside perimeter surveillance cameras. This is a huge deterrent for a potential intruder.
51. Install a sign in your yard that says *Beware of Owner*. This lets a potential intruder know where your mindset is in regard to protecting your home from an invasion.
52. Think like an intruder! Conduct a security check of your home to determine possible entry points and any weaknesses it may have. You need to think like an intruder, and what he would be looking for.
53. Don't keep large amounts of cash in your home! Athletes may be targeted by intruders if they suspect you have a large amount of cash and/or expensive jewelry in your house.
54. Realize that there is nothing in your house more important than you. There is nothing that can't be replaced — except you and your family.
55. Practice navigating around your home in the dark. For example, while in the dark, count the number of steps it takes to walk down or up the stairs from your master bedroom. Is it 16 steps, 20, 24? This will help you in the event of a home invasion where your electricity is compromised by an intruder.

    Also, consider navigating around your entire home in the dark at least once or twice a month! Shortly after nightfall, turn off all the lights and the TV. For half-an-hour walk around your house as you normally would – in the dark.

    Navigate around your living, family, dining rooms and kitchen in the dark. Be careful not to stub your toes, but if you do, it will only reinforce your senses about where things are located, and that's good. Most people will stub their big toe during this rehearsal, but I must tell you from personal experience, nothing hurts more than stubbing your *pinky toe*! Ouch!

    I have placed myself on the PUP list (an NFL term meaning *Physically Unable to Perform*) many times due to injuring my pinky toe in the dark on furniture, tables, corner walls, etc., while practicing navigating in the dark. My children seem to find this very amusing!

Ready for bed and need to brush your teeth? Brush them in the dark. Reach into your bathroom drawer or medicine cabinet, retrieve your toothbrush and toothpaste and brush your teeth in complete darkness. Now, beware, because if you store your toothbrush and toothpaste in your medicine cabinet, you can easily cause an avalanche in there! I know because I've done it myself!

In addition to brushing your teeth, combing your hair, washing your face and other bedtime rituals, *shave in the dark too*, just don't cut yourself.

In the unfortunate circumstance that you do become victim of a home invasion, you'll be skilled at navigating around your home if the electricity is compromised, or if you choose to turn all the lights off to make it difficult for the bad guys to see you. After practicing this technique a few times with the lights turned off, you'll be able to quickly dart around furniture, scamper under dining room tables, run up a 24-step flight of stairs – effortlessly, while your attacker is busy running into chairs, couches, and stumbling or falling down stairs.

The truth is, when it comes to the safety and security of yourself and your family, it's the little things that you do on a *consistent basis* that could save a life someday.

Do You Write Well In The Dark?

Could you write a legible distress letter in the dark, leaving clues for police if you were ever abducted in a home invasion?

Here's the key – PRACTICE!

Let's role play! I'm a bad guy and I invade your home. I have already shut down your electrical system and your home is dark, except for flash lights I brought with me. I intend to abduct you, your wife, or your children for ransom money.

But before I leave, I want to take a bit of time to sift through your valuable belongings (primarily in your master bedroom). I temporarily detain you in your master bathroom while I ransack your bedroom.

Frightened but unharmed, you remember that you have a note pad and pen hidden in the cupboard under the bathroom sink. Unbeknownst to me (*the bad guy*) you have been diligent in practicing writing in the dark.

With limited visibility and a glimmer of light from a full-moon outside the bathroom window (if you have one), you write a legible, detailed description of each home invader you have come in contact with. You write down their names if one of the other invaders mistakenly refers to the others by name or a nickname. You describe their face (scars, broad or thin nose, abnormally large ears, etc.), eye color, estimated height, weight, age, hair (long, short, straight, shaggy, thinning, bald), color, race, accent (southern, foreign, if any.), visible tattoos or body piercings, and if they walked with a limp or have an unusual gate.

If you do happen to have a window in your master bathroom, use it as an escape exit, even if it's on the second or third floor. If your bathroom window is not large enough for you to escape, try to get help by opening the window and waving at a passersby, whether driving or on foot. You can also use a towel or the shower curtain to flag someone down.

If you live on a private lot and there is generally little or no vehicle or foot traffic, look out of the window and see if you can spot any vehicles the invaders may have arrived in. If so, write down as much information about them and write in abbreviations!

For example, you look out the window and can make out two letters and one number from a license plate. You can also tell the color of the vehicle, make, model and estimated year.

Now, don't waste time writing in long-hand!

Instead of writing it like this:

> 2002 Pontiac Grand Prix, two-door, black. Partial license plate number JXT-9, with a sunroof and tinted windows. Has a dent in left back panel on drivers side and a spoiler on the back.

Abbreviate it like this:

> 02 Pont GP/2-dr/Blk/Lic. PL. JXT-9/SunR/Tnt. Win/dent-L pan-driv./spoil.

Believe me, police and detectives will easily put the pieces together.

Finished writing, you tuck the notes back under the bathroom sink cupboard but leave the door slightly open, only noticeable to you.

Shortly after, the home invader returns to the bathroom and abducts you.

When the police and detectives arrive later to investigate the crime scene, they find your notes hidden in the bathroom, under the sink, increasing your chances of being found – alive.

What's the key to your ultimate survival? *Just like in a game, the team that makes the most plays usually wins.* Be the smart and prepared family that make more plays than the bad guys.

56. Get slightly tinted windows whereby during daytime you can easily see out, but no one can easily see in. Do the same for your garage windows also.
57. Purchase window curtains and drapes that are double-lined, which won't allow anyone to see through them. Make sure you pull your window coverings closed when it's close to dawn, and especially at nightfall. You'd be surprised how many homeowners keep their window curtains, drapes and blinds wide open at night — for all the world to see inside your house.
58. Turn your blinds upward. When most people close their blinds, they normally turn the blinds downward. This is not the safest way to go. When turning them downward, a potential intruder can stand close to the window, look down and still see your movement in the immediate area. When your blinds are turned upward, if an intruder stands close to your window to look in, all they will see is the ceiling. For second story windows, you want to do the opposite and turn your blinds *downward*. Why? Because if you turn them upward, a person can still look up and see you clearly from the ground level. *Try this at home and see for yourself!*
59. Get the kind of windows that when someone approaches them during daytime, that person sees a reflection of themselves instead of inside your home.
60. Make sure you have something covering the small string holes of your blinds. If your blinds do not have window covering and you close them, either up or down, preferably up, an intruder standing close to your window can still see much of your movement through the tiny slits of the blind strings. The same rule applies for plantation or Levelor blinds.

    Quick true story: When I moved into my new home, it did not initially have blinds or window coverings. When I had a person come over to install my blinds, she told me that the blinds were all I needed and I wouldn't need any other covering. I knew this was not true, so after having the blinds installed, I walked outside onto my front porch. While standing close to the window, nearly pressing my forehead against it, and with the blinds fully closed, I could *STILL* see in full view, my living and dining rooms through those tiny string slits of the blinds!

So don't let anyone tell you all you need are blinds — you need double-lined drapes and curtains, too!

61. The same rule applies to plantation shutters and wood blinds. Basically, you would need to install both the proper blinds AND proper drapes and curtains for the best protection. If a home invader can't see into your home, he may not feel confident about storming in.
62. Vertical blinds. These may seem safe, but they are installed at a small distance away from the window or door. An intruder may be able to see your movement inside the house due to the gap at the "sides" of each window or door.
63. Make sure that there are no other convenient places close to the front or back door that an intruder might hide in and lie in wait for someone who might open the door coming in or out of the house.
64. Consider easy-to-release locking mechanisms that allow you, your family, and even small children to quickly unlock your windows in case you need to escape from the inside should there be a need for an immediate evacuation.
65. Make a list of all access points. Doors and windows are the obvious ones, but what about other access points such as:
    - Cellar
    - Regular basement
    - Walk-out basement
    - Garage
    - Roof
    - Dog and cat flaps
    - Large drains
    - Air ducts or vents

    Note: A walk-out basement features a doorway that leads directly to a ground level patio or backyard.
66. To implement these procedures effectively you must think like a criminal. Pretend you're looking for the easiest way inside your own home. Wander around your residential property, examine all the ways to get in that you can see — looking through the eyes of a burglar.
67. For each access point, examine each one closely to ascertain whether:
    - It is sturdy.
    - Are the hinges sound?

- Is the framework solid and securely embedded in the wall?
- If it's a sliding door, can you just pop it out of its tracking?
- Can you easily force it open?
- Would unscrewing a couple of screws from the outside let you remove it?
- Look for signs of rotted wood or crumbling concrete. Such signs of weakness are of great interest to would-be burglars.
- Check whether it closes properly and securely.
- Check whether there is a locking mechanism. If there's no lock, then install one. If there is, then make sure that it works properly and that you still have the keys. Once you have checked all the doors and windows and have them fitted with good quality locks, then be sure to use them.

68. Lock your doors, even when you are home. This includes the garage door, cellar door, basement door, attic door, etc.

69. Make sure everyone in your home knows *HOW* to operate the locks and *WHEN* to use them. All doors and windows must be locked when leaving your home, even ones above ground level.

70. *DO NOT* leave your house keys in obvious places, like under a stone, plant pot, or doormat. The bad guys have always been known to look there first. If someone in your household frequently forgets their keys or if you want an emergency key left somewhere, then find another system that doesn't leave you wide open. Security is a combination of physical devices and procedures. There's no point in having a lock if nobody uses it, or if an intruder can easily find the key.

71. Consider a fire resistant home security safe. Athletes and their families have personal valuables, cash and jewelry, sentimental items that are irreplaceable, computer data and documents, all of which need extra protection in the event of a home invasion, burglary or fire.

72. Make sure your home insurance policy is up to date in case you need to file a claim for stolen or damaged items.

73. If you live in a gated community or subdivision, keep the lines of communication with security personnel open. Let them know in advance of any plans you may have for extended time away from home that will last more than two weeks. Have them make a note of anything different or unusual about the exterior of your home while you're away. Instruct them to call the police if they notice anything suspicious. Also, if you notice a new security person on staff whom you

have never seen before, check with security management and confirm that person was actually hired, and when, along with their name. Don't be shy about asking management if they conducted a thorough background check on the individual. You won't be privy to that information, but at least you'll know a background search was conducted.

74. Avoid putting your name on your mailbox or house. Criminals may use your name to gain your trust.
75. Know who your family members are friends with. Know who your friends are friends with! Athletes lead busy lives, even in the off season. You may have many friends who might come over for a visit often, or from time to time. If they bring someone with them that you've never met or vaguely remember meeting, ask your family member or your friend about them in detail. Like, how they met them, where they're from, are they from out of town and staying with your friend or family member? How long have they known them? Ask your friends and family members to inform you of their friend's arrival BEFORE they come over, if you have never met them or have met them only once.

As hard as the community and law enforcement agencies try to keep athletes safe, the final responsibility of personal protection ultimately falls on you — the one living in your home. The best ways of securing your life and preventing home invasion are the simple ones that all athletes can commit to.

More about doors and locks: It won't do you any good to buy expensive dead-bolt and window locks if you put them on cheap front/back doors and windows!

What's the use? A bad guy will easily bypass that expensive lock and strike plate, and just kick the door in because you installed a cheap door onto a shabby door frame!

Same with window locks. An expensive window lock will do you no good if that cheap window has only one pane of easy to break glass.

> *Parking Lot Tidbit:* When you or mom are out with the kids and walking through a parking lot, be sure to train your children to watch for rear white automobile lights, indicating a vehicle is backing up. Many times young children and teens are preoccupied and distracted with other things and don't pay attention.

Some drivers will not be able to see you walking directly behind them when backing up. In any parking lot, especially when walking between two rows of parked cars on each side, like at a mall, teach the kids to listen for car engines and watch for white rear vehicle lights.

For toddlers, you can even create a game for it! Instruct them to count how many white lights they see before you get to the building entrance. The winner is rewarded with a big hug and a resounding round of applause from dad and mom for a job well done!

Car Safety

When leaving home to travel to the store, mall, golf course and other places, when you get into your vehicle, <u>LOCK THE DOORS FIRST</u>! In fact, before your **butt** hits the seat, the car doors should be in locked mode. Do this first and foremost – consistently. Do not get into your vehicle, put the seat belt on, put the key in the ignition, adjust your seat to get comfortable, adjust the rear view mirror, make a call on your cell phone, etc.

Lock the doors first, before you do anything else!

Why? Because those few precious moments you are preoccupied inside your unlocked vehicle is ample time for a criminal to walk or run up to your vehicle, open your unlocked door and assault you!

While in a store, mall, or even at home and preparing to leave, you want to reinforce to your toddler, young child, and teen, that you are leaving soon, and to enter the car quickly with no goofing around allowed.

If you're in a grocery store for example, remind them of this car safety policy and tell them clearly, what your and their expectations are.

Many moms and dads become so focused on making sure the baby or toddler is properly and securely strapped in the car seat or booster seat; as well they should be, but while doing so can leave themselves vulnerable to an attack, carjacking, or both.

The good news is that after strapping your child in his/her seat so many times, you probably can do it with your eyes closed!

Try this. Periodically and quickly look up from what you are doing, but thoroughly scan not only the immediate area but distances up to fifty feet away in a 360 degree motion, while at the same time still carefully tending to your child and strapping him or her in.

Use the same techniques career criminals use. If a bad guy is in the process of stealing a car on the street or breaking into a home during the day or night, he likely will often and quickly scan the immediate area to see if anyone has detected him.

Think like a criminal and protect yourself.

Even if you forget to lock the doors (I hope you won't), it's difficult for someone to drag you out of your car if you have your seat belt on. Also, the steering wheel serves as a barrier to a quick exit. However, a smart bad guy knows this and when opening your unlocked car door, will reach over and adjust the steering wheel lever, lifting the steering wheel up! This makes it easier for him to pull you out.

If a bad guy approaches your vehicle now, you were smart enough to remember to lock your doors first, so he won't be able to immediately attack you. But there's still work that you need to do to protect yourself.

Here's how. *Horn Sequence*™. Press down on your horn in an *unusual and long sequence,* in order to attract attention from a passersby, whether walking or driving. Do not press the horn in short sequences. Why? Because that sounds too much like a regular car alarm horn and will likely be ignored by others.

How many times have you gone shopping or for groceries, and you hear a car alarm horn go off in the parking lot? You will likely keep walking, while nonchalantly listening for the driver to shut it off as you continue on your merry way.

If someone is desperate to take your vehicle, assault you, or worse, breaking your window in the process, you should drive off as quickly as you can! Realize that your vehicle now becomes a weapon to your advantage and can be used to run over an attacker.

Tinted Windows: When I was a kid many years ago, nobody had tinted windows. Now it seems everyone has them! That can be good or bad, depending on how you use them to your advantage.

It's *good* because tinted windows afford you a degree of privacy, whereby no one can easily see inside. However, it's also *bad* because...no one can easily see inside your vehicle if you are being ASSAULTED! Now, those same convenient tinted windows become a privacy feature for the bad guy! That's why it's vitally important to lock your vehicle doors *FIRST AND FOREMOST* to prevent a bad guy from gaining access in the first place.

Walking Along Sidewalks

When walking down a sidewalk with your lady, for example, if a suspicious person is approaching you from the left side of the sidewalk, casually but firmly place your hand around her waist and guide her to your right side. This will allow you to use your body as a barrier and deterrent if a bad guy tries to get to her. *He'll have to go through you first!*

The same technique applies if the bad guy is fast approaching from the right side. Guide your lady to your left side.

When you're walking down sidewalks with your children, the same principles apply.

If a potential bad guy is approaching you straight on, keep your head up and make continual eye contact with him as you casually chat with your lady or kids. Squeeze their hand tightly to warn them of potential danger. Eye contact with a potential bad guy is a deterrent to possible harm, and will put him on alert that you are keenly aware of his presence.

If you or your lady are professionally trained and licensed to carry a firearm, that could be bad news for the bad guy – unless he's packin' too! Your best chance to survive a potential attack is to avoid using a firearm as long as possible.

If your life is threatened, you will have to make a choice when and how to use your weapon.

Do you simply show it to thwart an attack, then wait and see if the bad guy runs away or pulls his own gun? Or do you wait and see if he even has a weapon, then react accordingly?

These are tough choices, to be sure. Your own gun could wind up being used against you.

Inclement Weather

Don't let inclement weather knock you off your safety game plan!

When it rains, for example, people tend to walk much faster (or run) to get to their destination, whether carrying an umbrella or not.

The potential problem with that, in regard to your personal safety and security, is the faster you walk, the less you notice! Most people who carry umbrellas when it rains are so focused on getting *out of the rain* that they briefly lose focus on who and what's around them.

Try this experiment for yourself. The next time it rains where ever you are, watch how people respond to it. If they have an umbrella, watch how the umbrella is generally held as close to their head as possible, with their head and eyes fixed downward, as they hurriedly try to get to their destination without getting soaked.

Umbrellas not only cause blind spots and reduce your peripheral vision, when your head is down, you may not notice a bad guy about to step up on you! And if you have children with you, your short-term focus is even more reduced.

Also, watch people without umbrellas, who obviously didn't check the local weather forecast. These folks will use whatever they have to shield their head. They will use their hand, a newspaper, magazine, folder, anything!

It may surprise you, but those lucky folks who got caught in the rain without umbrellas are less likely to be a potential target! Why? Because they aren't carrying a large, dome-like object above their heads which greatly reduces vision in their immediate personal space.

When I get caught in the rain with my own children, with or without an umbrella, I teach them to... SLOW DOWN and keep their heads UP! Why would that make sense? Just like driving in heavy rain or snowfall, you'll naturally drive slower, because you understand if you drive fast, it could be a car accident waiting to happen. When you slow down – you become more cautious and aware. When you're cautious and aware – you tend to pay closer attention to the road during inclement weather.

Here's something bad guys don't want you to know: They LOVE lousy weather!

The worse the better! They know you'll likely be distracted by it and pay less attention to your surroundings – so don't lose focus!

Police are also aware of this strategy. A bad guy may likely attempt to rob a bank or a store during heavy rain or snowfall because he believes poor visibility and road conditions will slow down police response time when driving to the scene of the crime, thus affording him/her enough time to complete their dastardly deed.

Objects of Survival

In the event of a home invasion or attempted burglary, always have something easily and quickly accessible to use as a weapon. Note that I did not say, "Have a weapon accessible," which is not always practical or advisable. I mean, if someone surprises you at home, there should be something instantly accessible to aid in your defense.

It can be your league MVP trophy, a set of golf clubs, your bowling ball, a can of vegetables, your laptop or desktop computer monitor — anything.

Aim for the head with something with a point, like a knife or pen, for example. This is much more effective when targeting something soft on an attacker, like the throat, eyes, crotch, armpit, or belly. If you do strike at something hard, like the kneecap or shin, chances are the point will bounce off without doing any real damage.

During a home invasion, you can prepare against different threats by practicing how to quickly reach nearby objects, and how to use them effectively and safely. Unfortunately, during a confrontation situation, your imagination will not usually be fast enough to invent weapons out of these above type objects, so planned objects should also be carried. Always practice how to quickly and effectively use them.

For example, if I exploded into your home right now, at this very moment, suddenly and unexpectedly, what would be the first thing you would grab to protect yourself and your family from me and my crew assaulting you with a gun or other weapons?

To prevent home invasion, athletes must think ahead, and *"think safety"* often.

Everything that surrounds you, whether it be indoors — like lamps, chairs, bottles, kitchen utensils, heavy decor, small statues, etc., can all be used as weapons. Outdoors, you can use sand, stones, rocks, tree branches, and firewood to throw. Bricks can also be used. An assailant can be thrown against sharp pointed gates, railings and walls.

If you choose not to own a gun at home due to children or a legitimate disbelief in firearms, you still have options to protect yourself and your family.

Stun guns are probably the most popular personal security products around because they will temporarily disable your attacker for several minutes so you can get away. Stun guns have stored energy that is released into the attacker's muscles. This powerful energy causes the muscles to do a whole lot of work rapidly, thus depleting the attacker's blood sugar by converting it to lactic acid. This temporarily takes away the attacker's ability to function properly. The attacker may also lose his balance.

Keep in mind that even if you use a stun gun while the attacker is touching you, the current will not pass to your body. Stun guns come in various sizes and different degrees of voltage. There are mini stun guns that are easy to carry in your pocket or your lady's purse. Voltage ranges from 80,000 volts up to 800,000 volts! There are stun guns with alarms and lights, and even some that look like a baton that you can carry in a holster.

Some run on batteries, some have a built-in charger. There are also Tasers called Advanced Taser M-18s, which combine injury reducing benefits of traditional stun technology, with the stopping power of Electro-Muscular Disruption (EMD) technology. It has a higher instant incapacitation rate than a .9mm handgun.

Stun guns can be carried by members of your family, including teens, whether male or female; however, you should never allow small children to hold or play with a stun gun.

For teens in your household, try a cell phone stun gun. These look just like a real cell phone and can contain up to 150,000 volts. Cell phone stun guns provide an easy way to surprise an attacker and protect your family.

Dogs are also excellent home invasion deterrents. If you have one dog, consider getting another.

Dogs not only make for great protectors, they make for loyal, devoted friends as well, who will relentlessly bite an intruder to protect you and your family. *Hey, it's not just your house — it's your dog's house too!*

Home Invasion News Update:
Wednesday, July 21, 2010

It was reported that three men broke into the home of an NBA Charlotte Bobcats athlete.

The men locked his wife in a bathroom, making off with a gun and some luxury items, police said. His wife was not injured by the three masked gunmen, who entered the home in a gated community of two dozen million-dollar homes, as reported by media organizations.

The break-in happened while the athlete was in Texas for a basketball camp.

Charlotte-Mecklenburg police had made no arrests as of Friday, July 23, 2010. Officers reported the thieves took a 9mm pistol, a ruby-encrusted wristwatch, a Louis Vuitton wallet and other items.

The athlete is a shooting guard who helped lead the Bobcats to their first playoff appearance last spring. He has also played for the Indiana Pacers and Golden State Warriors.

Home invasion is a real and growing threat to athletes and their families in our society. You must not only protect yourself — you have to be *prepared* to protect yourself.

So what are you waiting for? Let's get busy. Let's prevent home invasion!

Play Hard. Do Good. Think Safety.™

Chapter 8
GAMBLING

All Bets Are Off!

Why do some pro athletes gamble? Why do other people associated with or directly involved with sports gamble?

Because they can generally bet with money they can afford to lose.

If you're an athlete, and you suspect you may have a gambling problem, or you know of a teammate, coach, friend, or family member who may have a gambling problem, this chapter is for you.

Gambling can become addictive for athletes.

Normally, when athletes gamble, they do so not to win money, but to satisfy a potentially crippling urge to take that chance or challenge. It satisfies their immediate urge for excitement.

Gambling is a big money making industry in our country. The gaming industry generates billions of dollars each year. People are spending more money on legal gambling, and quite a bit of it on illegal gambling, as well. Under U.S. federal law, gambling is legal in the United States. Each state is free to regulate or prohibit the practice.

Gambling has been legal in Nevada, for example, since 1931, forming the backbone of the state's economy. Las Vegas, not surprisingly, is perhaps the best known gambling destination in the world.

Types of Gambling

1. Casino games
2. Table games
3. Card games
4. Online gambling (internet)

5. Fixed-odds gambling: frequently occurs at many types of sporting events, and bookmakers offer fixed odds on a number of sports related outcomes.
6. Sports betting: Betting on team sports has become an important service industry in many countries, including the U.S. In addition to organized sports betting, both legal and illegal, there are many side-betting games played by casual groups of spectators, such as NCAA Basketball Tournament Bracket Pools, Super Bowl Squares, Fantasy Sports Leagues with monetary entry fees and winnings, and in-person spectator games.
7. Arbitrage betting: Arbitrage betting is a theoretically risk-free betting system in which every outcome of an event is bet upon so that a known profit will be made by the bettor upon completion of the event, regardless of the outcome. Arbitrage betting is a combination of the ancient art of arbitrage trading and gambling, which has been made possible by the large numbers of bookmakers in the marketplace, creating occasional opportunities for arbitrage.
8. Other types of betting: An athlete may also bet with another person that a statement is true or false, or that a specified event will happen (a "back bet") or will not happen (a "lay bet") within a specified time. This occurs, in particular, when two people have opposing, but strongly-held views on truth or events. Not only do the parties hope to gain from the bet, they also place the bet to demonstrate their certainty about the issue.

Some means of determining the issue at stake must exist. Sometimes the amount that is bet remains nominal, demonstrating the outcome as one of principle rather than of financial importance. Betting exchanges allow consumers, both back and lay bets, at odds of their choice. Similar in some ways to a stock exchange, a bettor may want to back a horse, for example, hoping it will win, or lay a horse, hoping it will lose, effectively acting as bookmaker.

The point is, an athlete with a gambling problem or addiction has to admit you have a problem before you can be helped. This is the first step on the road to recovery. You have to admit you're a compulsive gambler and recognize that you can't view gambling as just a game to have fun with anymore.

First, realize that gambling can be a soulless, ruthless beast! It doesn't care if you're a Hall of Fame athlete or sitting at the end of the bench. Just because you're a pro athlete and have a sizable contract worth millions of dollars, it doesn't mean you'll be a good gambler.

In fact, most athletes are lousy gamblers!

You must always remain *humble* and understand that today's big break in your athletic career could be tomorrow's major headline headache. There is also a valuable and important lesson to be learned about money management. If you, as an athlete, ignore the fundamentals of money management, you're begging for financial trouble down the road when it comes to gambling.

Gambling has become a mainstream staple in our country over the past decade, more so than at any other point in the last century. Between NFL and March Madness office pools, the explosion of poker on TV, the building of more casinos, the proliferation of state run lotteries, and even church bingo, it's hard to find anyone who isn't a participant either in or somehow directly exposed to some form of gambling.

In organized sports, gambling is looked upon as a "no-no" on every level, but especially in professional sports, given the need for athletes and leagues to maintain a high level of integrity. Whenever the taint of gambling exists in sport, it immediately calls into question the honesty of the competition. And that's not good for the "business" of sport, or the "character" of sport.

Legal gambling, which is technically acceptable for professional athletes, is also frowned upon by many, at least while athletes are still playing their sport. Just about every team locker room and clubhouse in the nation where gambling may exist has a sign on the wall explaining, in explicit detail, the rules against gambling, and the consequences and penalties for breaking those rules.

Teams are regularly subjected to a series of briefings by league security personnel about how gambling can creep into their lives and what athletes can do to prevent it.

> **Update:** In January, 2010, two NBA athletes with the Washington Wizards were suspended for the year by Commissioner David Stern as a result of possessing firearms in the locker room at the facility where his team plays home games. The incident occurred on December 21, 2009.

Commissioner Stern released this statement to the media:

> "The possession of firearms by an NBA player in an NBA arena is a matter of the utmost concern to us. The NBA has conducted a thorough investigation of events relating to this matter. It is not disputed that,

following an argument on the team's flight home from a game in Phoenix, both [athlete name] and [other athlete name] brought guns to the Verizon Center locker room and -- with other players and team personnel present or nearby -- displayed them to one another in a continuation of their dispute. The players engaged in this conduct despite a specific rule set forth in the collective bargaining agreement between the NBA and the Players Association prohibiting players from possessing a weapon at an NBA facility, and reminders of this prohibition given annually by the NBA to players both in writing and in person.

"The issue here is not about the legal ownership and possession of guns, either in one's home or elsewhere. It is about possession of guns in the NBA workplace, which will not be tolerated," Stern said.

"I have met separately with [athlete name] and with [other athlete name]. Both have expressed remorse for their actions and an understanding of the seriousness of their transgressions. Both have volunteered to engage in community service in order to turn the lessons they have learned into an educational message for others. I accept fully the sincerity of their expressions of regret and intent to create something positive from this incident.

"Nevertheless, there is no justification for their conduct. Accordingly, I am today converting [athlete name] indefinite suspension without pay to a suspension without pay for the remainder of the 2009-2010 season, and am also suspending [other athlete name] without pay, effective immediately, for the remainder of the 2009-2010 season."

The driving source of the actions between the two players and the consequences that resulted were from...**GAMBLING!**

The star player on the team later entered a guilty plea to a felony weapons possession charge after admitting to bringing four guns into the locker room following a *heated argument* with the other player during a card game on the team plane.

The other player involved in this incident was later released by the Wizards.

Sport is filled with stories of athletes who love to gamble and their unfortunate and financially devastating outcomes. A former NBA referee spent time in prison after a 2007 betting scandal.

A former All-Star NBA forward, who played 12 years in the league and had reportedly amassed more than $110 million in salary over that time span, is currently bankrupt, and is now facing trial for writing ten bad checks to casinos and reneging on his promise to repay nearly $1 million in gambling debts to three Las Vegas casinos.

He now faces the possibility of probation, or up to twelve years in prison if convicted.

For those who keep gambling in its proper perspective, it's a harmless hobby. Others develop serious problems. Perhaps the fierce competitive nature athletes and sport figures are born with that enable them to become professionals to begin with is what leads to their compulsive gambling habits.

Or maybe it's simply the huge salaries that most pro athletes receive these days and the urge to throw some of that money around. Whatever it is, there are countless stories of pros who simply couldn't resist that trip, or trap, to the casino or phone call to their bookie.

Not every athlete is a compulsive gambler, of course.

The overwhelming majority of players never let themselves lose perspective. Most of them simply love a good game, and an occasional legal bet makes it a little bit more fun — and that's that.

Is there potential for a little bit of harmless gambling to become a much larger problem? You bet (no pun intended), and that's the concern with athletes and other sports figures and gambling.

One famous Hall of Fame NBA player said this about gambling and money: "I understand it's a lot of money, but it is my money. Nobody has the right to tell me what to do with my money."

This narrow-minded perspective is invaluable because it's obvious he really doesn't care what anybody thinks about his gambling.

In other words, it's his money to lose, so everybody else just butt out!

That former athlete went on to say, "It's not a problem. If you're a drug addict or an alcoholic, those are problems. I gamble far too much money. As long as I can afford to do it, I don't think it's a problem."

Uh...okay. See you later in bankruptcy court.

ATHLETE CAREER KILLERS

Gambling addiction is a serious issue, with major consequences. It should not be trivialized like some meaningless fetish. At the college level, a 2009 NCAA study revealed that nearly 30% of all male athletes admitted wagering at least once in a year's time on college or pro sports, which is a violation of NCAA rules. A similar study conducted five years earlier showed a small percentage of all male athletes say they or a teammate agreed to participate in game-fixing.

The study also noted that a little less than 1% of the responding athletes in Division I football — 0.9% — and 0.6% of those in men's basketball, said they accepted money or some other reward for "playing poorly" in games. Between 1-2% of athletes in both sports said they knew of teammates who did.

Why take the risk? Is it really worth the gamble? I say no.

Here's an interesting list breaking down the process an athlete must go through in order to have a shot at the "big time" in just one sport — football — and the *reality* that comes with it in a given year:

- Play High School Football — 1,100,000 athletes
- Play College Football (5.9%) — 65,000 athletes
- Scouted by NFL Teams — 6,500 athletes
- Invited to the NFL Combine — 350 athletes
- Drafted by an NFL Team — 256 athletes
- College Free Agents — 590 athletes
- In an NFL Training Camp (0.07%) — 946 athletes
- Released before week #1 — 646 athletes
- Make an NFL Team (0.03%) — 300 athletes
- Play in the NFL 4+Seasons — 150 athletes
- Play in the NFL at age 30+ (0.003%) — 30 athletes

What's the message here? It's enough of a gamble just to have the opportunity to play professional sports. Why gamble that away?

The next time you get the urge to gamble or make a bet on a game or another sport, think twice — don't throw that dice.

*Statistics courtesy of *AtlantaFalcons.com*, 2009.

Education and Prevention

Athletes may be more vulnerable than the general population when it comes to gambling, simply because they have the financial means to do so.

Here are some common signs of a compulsive gambler:

1. High levels of energy
2. Unreasonable expectations of winning
3. Very competitive personalities
4. Distorted optimism
5. Bright, with high IQ's

Other Signs

1. Excessive phone bills to 900-number services or excessive use of internet.
2. An obsession with point spreads.
3. Unusual interest in obscure games.
4. Association with other sports bettors.
5. Shifting allegiances for/against the same team on different days.
6. Defensive when questioned about gambling behavior.
7. Debts, unpaid bills, financial troubles.
8. After losing, eager to bet again to get even or ahead.

Even the smallest of bets can cause much larger problems down the road.

For athletes who choose to gamble, there are general guidelines that can help you make it safer and reduce the risk that problems will occur.

1. Many athletes think of gambling in terms of *"winning,"* more so than a way to make money. Most professional athletes already have the money. Over time, they may wind up losing more of it than they win. The fact is, all forms of gambling have the same principle — the vast majority of people *lose* so that a very small minority of folks can have occasional big wins. That's just how the system works. An athlete with a gambling problem may hold the false expectation that he's the one who'll be the big winner. That belief only feeds the problem.
2. Athletes should never use money that they need for important things, like the mortgage, bills, and other more important, legitimate expenses.

3. Establish a hardcore money limit. Decide how much money you can afford to lose before you play. When you lose that amount of money, quit and go home! If you win, enjoy it, then quit and go home! Remember, winning won't happen most of the time.
4. Set a time limit. Decide how much time you should spend gambling, regardless of the amount of money you have. Just because you might have $50,000 on hand to gamble with, doesn't mean you have to gamble all night long until it's gone. When you reach your designated time limit, stop gambling and go home — win, lose, or break even.
5. If you lose money, never try to get it back by going over your limit. This usually leads to larger losses.
6. Don't gamble when you're highly emotional, excited or upset. It's hard to make good decisions about gambling if you're too excited or your emotions are running high. Stay calm and in control at all times. Know when to say *"enough is enough."*
7. Balance gambling with other activities. It's important to enjoy other hobbies so that gambling doesn't become too big a part of your life.
8. If you must gamble, keep it in proper perspective. See it more as an occasional hobby and a casual form of entertainment rather than a compulsive way to leisurely spend your valuable time. Yes, an athlete's time is *valuable* — spend it and your money wisely.
9. Athletes who gamble tend to bet big when they gain confidence. If you lose big, you may be inclined to bet even bigger and faster in order to recoup your losses. This could result in financial disaster for you. But, by knowing you have limits, you're less likely to put yourself at risk.
10. Never let gambling become bigger than your own life, your career, and your family.
11. Accept losing as part of the game — because it *will* happen, sometimes often.
12. Don't borrow money to gamble, or take out loans and use that money to gamble.
13. Don't let gambling interfere with the opportunities afforded you in being a college or professional athlete. The *opportunity* to play the game you love can quickly be taken away from you with one poor decision.
14. Don't gamble to win back losses. Never chase losses.
15. Don't use gambling as a way to cope with emotional or physical pain.
16. Know the warning signs of a gambling problem. Gambling addicts tend to hide their gambling from people. Some athletes may become so preoccupied with it

that they ignore family, teammates, friends, and their athletic career responsibilities. If you see any of those warning signs in yourself, reflect on what you're doing and *STOP* before you lose everything you've worked so hard to achieve.

17. Don't give in to overindulgence. Take only cash with you, and leave all your debit and credit cards at home so you won't be tempted to use them.
18. Seek professional counseling and financial consulting if you believe the problem is severe.
19. Get a reliable accountability partner. It could be your teammate, a family member, or a friend. Have him/her track your every move and be there to support you and keep you on the right path. Get a partner that you can call when you feel "the itch" so he or she can talk you through it.
20. Don't use gambling as an excuse for boredom, like when you're stuck in a hotel before away games. Find a more constructive hobby to participate in.

Many times, professional athletes believe that the money will keep pouring in for years to come. Even if you have success in the *NFL, NBA, Major League Baseball,* or the *NHL,* statistics say you're generally looking at a short career.

Many athlete careers extend into double-digit years, but that is certainly not common.

Everyone can't live like you. This is one of the hardest things for athletes to grasp because when they get fame and wealth, they want to do the things they weren't financially able to do before.

However, gambling usually results in you driving yourself down a dead end — and *broke* street.

Getting Help

Let's not be naïve. Many athletes and sports figures who may have gambling issues aren't likely to call their perspective league or team and say, "I've got a gambling problem and I need help."

Education and early detection can make a difference between financial life and death for athletes who have or will end up with a gambling addiction.

Gambling can be fun on a minor level, but the evidence is that it too often results in a major addiction. Compulsive gambling is an addiction just like alcoholism and chemical dependency.

All three diseases are recognized by the *American Psychiatric Association's* D.S.M. Yet, we treat compulsive gambling differently than the other two addictions.

Dangers of Student-athlete betting

1. Athletic and academic ineligibility
2. Crime
3. Relationship problems
4. Alcohol and substance abuse
5. Debt
6. Suicide

How Can Teams Get Help for Athletes?

1. Provide screening for athletes as part of a routine annual physical.
2. Has the athlete ever felt the need to bet more and more money?
3. Has he ever had to lie to people important to him about how much he gambles?
4. Add more rules to the personal conduct policies, specifically for illegal gambling activities.
5. Provide athletes with awareness education, including available help resources for gambling and other disorders.

The pride you feel as an athlete after playing the game you love should be enough to never want to leave your sport. Some athletes may become overconfident and think nothing could hurt them. Whether it's clubbing, alcohol, drugs, gambling, or infidelity, for example, if you let something take control of you, you're headed for a downward spiral.

Talk to a Teammate, Friend or Family Member

If you have a teammate, friend or family member with a gambling problem, it's only natural to want to help.

The individual, however, may not be ready or willing to admit that they have a problem, and may not want to talk about it. For this reason, it's important that you be prepared to intervene.

Before you approach the person, try to learn what you can about their gambling issues, including any warning signs and negative impacts you may have noticed.

There are tons of options in this country for help and recovery. If possible, talk privately to someone that you can trust about their gambling issues, like a coach, counselor, pastor, doctor, or a parent if it's a student-athlete.

You should not reveal who the person is, but you do need to talk about the issue, get some support, and generate a plan of action to help them if their gambling has gotten way out of hand. Try to gather indications of the negative impact of the person's gambling issues, such as missed bills, absenteeism from team meetings and practices, or deteriorating performance on the field or court.

Keep in mind, when you approach your teammate, friend, or family member, they will try to rationalize their actions or deny that they have a problem.

If you can, have contact information for local counseling services handy, in the event that he agrees he has a problem and wants to get help. The most important thing to remember is that you can't stop someone from gambling. They have to be willing to help themselves by making a dramatic change in their behavior.

Other Gambling Issues to Consider

1. *Get informed!* It's important for athletes to gather all the information they can about gambling issues before they approach someone who they think might have a problem.
2. *Don't hide the problem.* Often, teammates, friends and family of the person with a gambling problem think that they're helping them by making excuses for the individual, lending them money, enabling them, or covering up their behavior. In reality, all they're doing is feeding the problem. If you help feed it — it will grow. Teammates, friends and family should acknowledge the problem by identifying and naming it clearly -- Gambling Addiction. As a teammate, you can let him know that you're there for him and will support him in his efforts to get professional help, but you should leave the responsibility for gambling and its negative consequences to him and him alone.
3. *Choose the right moment to talk.* If the person with a gambling problem is expressing remorse or they've just finished a gambling episode, they may be more open to talking about the issue. If they are, and you're prepared to talk to them about

it, try to do so in a caring and understanding manner. Stay calm. Becoming angry or condemning makes matters worse. If the person tries to rationalize their actions, counter it with evidence to the contrary (e.g., the person has shown signs of a change in behavior or personality that you feel may be detrimental to themselves, their families, the team, and your league). Let them know that you're not attacking them as a person, but your focus is on their current behavior, actions, and the poor choices they may be making.

4. *Discuss the negative impacts.* Let the person with a gambling problem know how their decision making process is affecting others, including you. If the person agrees that they have a problem and are willing to seek help, give them a number to the problem gambling help line or a local gambling counseling agency. If the person is afraid to go on their own, consider offering to go with them for support and be prepared to follow through.

5. *Express feelings from an "I" point of view.* When discussing a friend or family member's gambling issues, try to express your feelings from an "I" point of view (e.g., "when you do this, I feel…"), as this will make the person feel less defensive and reduce the likelihood of arguments. If there is any chance of violent or abusive behavior, use caution to ensure the safety and well-being of everyone involved.

6. *Set fair, yet firm boundaries.* When talking to a teammate, family member, or friend about their gambling issues, try to reach an agreement regarding your expectations for future gambling behavior, like complete abstinence, better management of household finances, and other financial responsibilities.

7. *Be supportive.* Try to support the person with a gambling problem in making changes for the better. Recognize and acknowledge any positive steps they've made as they work through their problem, and give praise when they have successfully achieved their goals. Talk to them about how their recovery is progressing, ask how you can continue to help, and remember that quitting any compulsive behavior is a difficult and often long process.

8. *Take care of you, too!* Finding a safe place to discuss your own feelings and emotions can help you cope with your teammate's gambling problem. Even if they choose not to seek help for themselves, the support you get can still make things better for you.

9. *Remember that change takes time.* It takes hard work and commitment to change one's own behavior. It may take several attempts before the person is able to suc-

cessfully change their behavior and attitude toward gambling. Understand the potential for a relapse. This is when a person falls back into their old gambling patterns of behavior. This occurs when they may have difficulty coping with stress.

10. *Identify your triggers.* It's important to be able to identify triggers of stress, as it results in gambling. Learn coping strategies to help yourself deal with a teammate, family member or friend. It may mean avoiding gambling venues altogether, and other friends that gamble. It's possible to get back on track, knowing that it takes one day at a time for change to be successful.

Warning Signs

There are a variety of signs that may indicate you have a problem with gambling. The more signs you show, the greater the chance of a problem.

Some of these signs include:

1. Constantly thinking or talking about gambling.
2. Spending more time gambling than you used to.
3. Finding it difficult to control, stop, or cut down on gambling, or feeling irritable when trying to do so.
4. Feeling a sense of emptiness or loss when not gambling.
5. Gambling more in order to win back losses or get out of financial trouble.
6. Thinking that you can stop gambling on your own anytime you want.
7. Taking out second and third mortgages on your home, selling things, committing, or considering committing criminal acts in order to pay back huge gambling debts.
8. Having increased debt, unpaid bills, or other financial troubles because of your gambling.
9. Often gambling until all of your money is gone.
10. Needing to gamble with larger amounts of money or for longer periods of time in order to get the same feeling of excitement.
11. Experiencing extreme highs from gambling wins and extreme lows from gambling losses.
12. Gambling to escape personal problems or to relieve feelings of anxiety, stress, depression, anger, or other negative emotions.

13. Getting irritated more easily, or having less patience when dealing with normal, everyday activities.
14. Feeling guilty about gambling or what happens while gambling.
15. Getting criticized by others for your gambling.
16. Having arguments with family and friends about money and gambling.
17. Refusing to discuss gambling with others, or lying to cover it up.
18. Hiding bills, past due notices, winnings, or losses from your spouse or family member.
19. Gambling instead of attending family or other social functions.
20. Neglecting family or household responsibilities because of gambling.
21. Neglecting your athletic career because of gambling.
22. Neglecting personal needs (food, sleep, hygiene) because of gambling.
23. For athletes who might live with a teammate who has a gambling problem, another sign may include having money or valuables belonging to you that mysteriously disappear.

If you or someone you know might have a gambling problem…DON'T:
1. Lecture, accuse, preach, or get angry with them.
2. Act as though you're a better person.
3. Give deadlines or ultimatums unless you plan to follow through.
4. Gamble with the person.
5. Exclude the person from non-gambling related activities.
6. Expect an immediate recovery.
7. Lend money to, or bail out the person with a gambling problem.
8. Deny or make excuses for their behavior.
9. Fall for the "I can beat this thing on my own" excuse.
10. Or the "I'll do better next time" rationale.

Negative Impacts

Gambling problems can have a variety of negative impacts — on the athlete themselves, family and friends, teammates, their organization, and society as a whole.

Some of these impacts may include:

For the Individual Athlete

- Mental health problems, including bouts of depression, anxiety, increased stress, reduced self-worth, anger, suicidal thoughts, increased alcohol or drug use.
- Physical health problems like insomnia, headaches, back or neck pain, upset stomach.
- Self-care problems like poor nutrition, lack of sleep, and a reduction in personal hygiene.
- Social problems like arguments, strained relationships, alienation, separation, divorce, physical or mental abuse.
- Financial problems like inability to pay bills, increased debt, and bankruptcy.
- Legal problems such as arrests due to not being able to pay off a gambling debt, league problems like violating personal conduct policies, and indefinite suspensions.
- Team problems like absenteeism and decreased productivity on the field or court.

For Family Members

- Financial crisis, such as a huge financial burden often put on family members, sometimes leading to ongoing debt and property loss for them.
- Being manipulated into lending money to the person with a gambling problem.
- Lying to cover up, and making excuses for the gambler's behavior.
- Mental and emotional health problems such as high levels of anxiety, depression, sadness, anger, resentment, embarrassment, exhaustion and self-doubt.
- Physical health problems like insomnia, ulcers, digestive problems, headaches, neck and back pain and other stress-related health conditions.
- Self-esteem problems such as feelings of helplessness, being overwhelmed, insecurity, and even feeling as though you are responsible for their gambling problem.
- Relationship problems with spouses, children, teammates, and friends.
- Role imbalance, such as parents overprotecting their grown children.
- Verbal and physical abuse, which can lead to arguments, strained relationships, alienation, separation, divorce, loneliness and isolation.

- Poor self-care. Sometimes family members become so focused on the person with a gambling problem, they neglect themselves and their own needs.

For Friends

- Being manipulated into lending money to the person with a gambling problem.
- Lying, covering up, and making excuses for the gambler's behavior.
- Verbal and physical abuse that leads to arguments and strained relationships.
- Financial problems when money lent is often NOT repaid.
- Ignoring changes in behavior or attitude to avoid getting involved.

Common Myths about Gambling

Athletes may often hold false beliefs or myths about gambling that can lead to problems. Some of the more common ones are listed below:

Myth: If I keep gambling, my luck will change and I'll win back any money I've lost.

Reality: Each time you place a bet, the outcome is completely independent of the previous one. This means that the odds are no more in your favor on the twentieth bet than they were on the first bet. Over time, the more you risk — the more you lose.

Myth: I almost won — I must be due for a big win.

Reality: "Almost" winning does not mean a real win is around the corner. Future gambling outcomes are in no way influenced by previous outcomes.

Myth: If I play more than one poker game at a time, I'll increase my chances of winning.

Reality: You may win more often by playing two poker games at a time, but make no mistake about it, you'll also spend — and ultimately lose — more doing so too.

Myth: I have a special strategy that helps me win.

Reality: The outcome of most games of chance, particularly at the tables, is completely random. You can't influence it, regardless of what you do.

Myth: "I'm grown! I can handle it! Tomorrow will be better."

Reality: It takes time to change your gambling behavior. The problem didn't develop overnight — you won't be able to beat it overnight either.

Money Management

Tips for Controlling Gambling Debt

1. Take responsibility for your financial situation. Contact a credit counseling service, a bankruptcy trustee, and/or make a "proposal to the creditors" and pledge to repay a portion of your outstanding debt. This will not only help with your finances, it will help rebuild your self-esteem and credit score.
2. Don't try gambling as a way to solve your financial troubles.
3. Find another hobby, if necessary. This will occupy your free time and help keep you from looking for the "quick thrill" that gambling can cause. It may be tough, but in the long run will help with your financial situation and make you feel better.
4. Put someone else you trust in charge of your ATM or credit cards, at least for a period of time, or destroy them completely while you're getting help with gambling issues.
5. Protect your assets by transferring their titles to your spouse, or a family member you trust.

Limit the Amount of Cash You Have Access to By:

1. Having your wages from being a professional athlete automatically deposited into your bank account, if you're not doing this already.
2. Destroying ATM cards or personal checkbooks you don't need or often use.
3. Setting up bank accounts that require two signatures for withdrawals, rather than just your own.
4. Setting up daily cash withdrawal limits.
5. Paying bills electronically, not in cash.

ATHLETE CAREER KILLERS

For Family Members: Protecting an Athlete's Money

1. Keep track of all money that is spent and owed.
2. Protect assets. Consider changing bank accounts and other assets so that an athlete with a gambling problem can't access them. A financial adviser may be helpful with this process.
3. Negotiate controls for the management of family finances. Try to assume responsibility for his credit or ATM cards. Give him access to money for daily necessities only until the gambling issues improve.
4. Don't rescue him by offering money to help pay off debts. This will only allow the problem to continue.
5. Seek professional help for both financial advice and emotional support.

If you're a college or professional athlete holding this book in your hands right now, and you've made it this far in your athletic career, consider yourself *blessed*.

You've spent years working hard, sacrificing, training, improving your skills and fundamentals for the opportunity to continue to play the game you love.

Playing sports is a *privilege*, not a given — it can easily be taken away from you. Don't gamble all that away!

Remember, the only difference between where you are right now and where you'll be next year, at this same time — are the *choices* you make.™

Play Hard. Do Good. Don't Take a Gamble.™

Chapter 9
MONEY

"Athletes who often look invincible on the field and court are often financially vulnerable off it. Know that you CAN put your financial life back on track and recover from a major financial loss. For those athletes that have, I am proud of you — and you should be proud too."
– David L. Brown

Short Career Lifespan

You've worked hard to get to the professional level.

You earned that opportunity and the money that comes with it.

Now you must work even harder to keep it!

The average length of an NFL career is about three and a half seasons. The average length for NBA athletes is about five seasons. Athletes leave the game because of injury, making poor decisions off the field, self-induced retirement, or being cut by the team.

This also means that while you may make more money than most people, you are only making it for an average of three and a half years to five years. To make sure you are successful in the future, you must invest your money well and make plans for your next career when you can no longer play football, basketball, baseball or hockey.

It's about financial responsibility and accountability.

That's what this chapter is all about. A practical, easy to read and understand financial guide for all athletes, especially professional athletes. In this chapter, as does as each chapter, offers you a substantial and valuable amount of *"takeaways."*

In sports, a takeaway is when an athlete takes the ball away from the other team and runs with it!

So take away the many practical tips contained in this chapter — and run with them, to help you improve your long term financial standing!

The truth is — if you don't manage your money well during your playing and post-career, you will be left dealing with the consequences of not having enough money after retirement from the game.

The NBA Player's Association, for example, has continually recommended to athletes a financial firm that gives them free second opinions on their finances.

That's the easy part. Getting athletes to act is the big challenge!

Also, there's an issue with athletes having children out of wedlock. This is yet another expense, in addition to the cars, houses, expensive jewelry, lavish spending on entertainment, etc., that must be accounted for.

Child support, for example, is an expense that doesn't go away for at least 18 years. A professional athlete five years removed from the game with two to three (or more) monthly child support payments, can easily and quickly run out of money.

Consider this: In the United States, male life expectancy in 2010 is 75.6 years. So if you're a thirty-year-old professional athlete retiring this year, you potentially still have another forty-five years of life to live!

Do you really need to buy another car, house, more expensive jewelry, or have another woman on the side?

You're Wealthy — Now What?

There's a perfect storm of inexperience, ignorance, peer pressure, bad advice, and multimillion dollar contracts that make it difficult for a professional athlete to hold onto wealth long term.

You need smart financial advice just like everyone else — perhaps more so. The sad truth is, most of the time you don't get it, or you simply ignore it.

There are many people in the financial industry that will gladly profit from the ignorance of an athlete's new found wealth. And it's not just lousy advice that creates the problem. Athletes themselves are prone to making poor choices regarding their money, especially when they're young.

Some athletes, young and older, attempt to sustain and maintain a *"Rolls Royce"* lifestyle. If you choose the smart way to go and save your money now, you have a better chance of living comfortably for the rest of your life after retirement.

Recession or no recession, some *NFL, NBA, NHL,* and *Major League Baseball* athletes have a penchant for losing most or all of their money, regardless of how much they make.

Here's one indulgence I guarantee professional athletes will enjoy when their playing days are long over — hindsight. It's the old *"I wish I would've, could've, should've"* syndrome.

Another issue I see in speaking with many professional athletes is, the language in dealing with contracts, financial agreements, investments, attorneys, accountants, etc., sound foreign to you.

In many cases, athletes lack the time and desire to understand and monitor their investments. Some lose any interest in educating themselves about the various financial products on the market today and the legally binding complexities of a business deal.

Here's one answer to that problem — *Ask questions!*

Don't ever be afraid to question authority! If something doesn't sound right, feel right, or read right — ask questions, and don't stop asking until you feel comfortable with the answers.

It's all about due diligence and the desire to *educate yourself.*

Yes, due diligence and education are hard work, but it's hard work that will pay you a higher dividend in the future than that portfolio of stocks you own.

Did You Know? Athletes have a different set of financial challenges than, say, entertainers. Why? Because there is a far shorter "peak earnings period" in sports than in any other profession.

Entertainers, musicians, and rock bands, for example, can perform and earn a good living well into their senior citizen years! Are the *Rolling Stones* still touring? Sorry, I just can't see you actively playing professional sports at age 60!

Your money earned as a professional athlete is supposed to outlive your playing career. Be the athlete who can say, *"Yeah, I get it."* Strive to form a solid financial game plan around it today, before it's too late.

You must acquire some *financial savvy* about yourself.

Our current anemic economic condition also increases the anxiety in professional athletes, especially those closer to retirement or those who have recently retired. We've all heard the sad but true stories of former professional athletes selling their championship and Super Bowl rings, trophies, and other sports memorabilia as a disheartened and embarrassing last resort to shore up their depleted financial situation.

If you're a veteran professional athlete and you see a teammate, especially a young teammate, heading toward financial disaster, don't be afraid to speak up and speak out!

Impart some of your wisdom, and talk to them about your own experiences. If you have to, insist they partake in a financial "intervention."

We can no longer sit back and watch our athletes become ignorant of their own financial affairs, ignorant of the people who handle their money, and continue to watch their lives end in financial ruin.

According to the NFL Players Association, at least 78 players lost a total of more than $42 million between 1999 and 2002 because they trusted money to financial advisers with questionable backgrounds.

I can only imagine what those figures will be by the end of 2010! Even when athletes trust financiers of high reputation, things can still go terribly wrong.

No financial planner, adviser, consultant, broker, wealth or fund manager is perfect — they make mistakes too, which can cripple your financial well-being for life.

You love playing sports with your teammates and other athletes in your league. It's a tremendous bonding experience — a true brethren. But please avoid stock tips, business investment tips, or hedge fund tips from teammates, other athletes, coaches, or former athletes. It's not that they're bad people; in most cases they're not.

It's just that, a person who manages money must have a certain "skill set" that is legal, licensed, and registered with the SEC (*Securities and Exchange Commission*), which is required by law of any investment advisory firm with at least $25 million in assets under management.

Giving or receiving stock market tips or financial advice to a teammate is the easiest and quickest way to lose a good friend! Most people don't understand, nor have the patience for the high-low, up-down reality known as the stock market. Stock market values increase, decrease, or remain relatively flat. Resist the temptation when someone asks for advice. Instead, give them the business card of your trusted, licensed financial planner and leave it at that.

Also, keep an eye out for the dreaded and financially disastrous **Ponzi scheme**! What's a Ponzi scheme? In short, it's a fraudulent investment operation that pays returns to investors from their own money, or money paid by subsequent investors rather than from any actual profit earned.

Be careful purchasing real estate as investment property. In today's economy, especially in real estate, anything you bought in the last two years is likely upside down, meaning its value has significantly depreciated and is currently not worth what you initially paid for it.

I GUARANTEE THIS — when you become a professional athlete, new people you've never met will beat a path to your door. Just make sure the door is locked!

People, including family members and friends you haven't seen or heard from in years, will want you to loan them money, help them find a job, invest in a business deal, or try to get you to hire them to work for you in some capacity.

Countless women will want to date you, marry you, have your children, and a host of other things. Be bold, have courage, and never be afraid to say — NO!

Agents and advisers will want to schmooze with you and your family members. Be careful! Individuals break the rules, but unfortunately, it's the colleges and universities that pay the price.

Quick quiz: What's two of the worst things that can happen to an athlete financially? Answer — divorce and business deals gone bad!

Matters of the Heart

As a professional athlete, you absolutely must wisely choose the right woman to marry. Most don't consider the financial consequences of divorce until it's too late.

Athletes should be concerned about being involved in unjust lawsuits and/or divorce proceedings. There is a reported high divorce rate of 60%-80% for professional athletes. That's astounding!

In many divorce proceedings, athletes may lose half of their net worth. But timing is key. Some divorces occur in retirement, when an athlete's peak earnings period is long over, and making a comparable salary to that of their playing days is virtually impossible. There is a tremendous lifestyle change when athletes retire from the game. This can also be brought on by *infidelity* — and you certainly don't want to risk playing that game!

Given the pressures of being a professional athlete, one should consider the benefits of a prenuptial agreement before tying the knot. It will greatly assist you in the event of a messy and ugly divorce.

If the woman of your dreams refuses to sign a prenuptial agreement, which protects not only you, but her as well — walk away from the relationship! It's not worth the headaches and daily drama you may encounter later. The same principle applies for female professional athletes whose male fiancé refuses a prenup.

Professional Athlete = Instant Financial Target

When Business Deals Go Bad!

Have you ever lost money in a business deal?

You've heard the sad stories. I bet you know a teammate or another athlete who got ripped off by somebody. Or maybe the people you got financially involved with were legit and good people, but the deal just went sour. Either way, you undoubtedly felt the impact of it!

This, unfortunately, happens more often than we think. Resist the temptation to make quick major financial or business decisions of any kind, which may increase your risk factor. Educate yourself and be open-minded to learn about the financial markets and the many products it has to offer. Do your due diligence regarding business propositions.

Ask questions, and don't be afraid to say *NO!*

If something doesn't look right, feel right, sound right, or read right — then don't do the dang thing!

The Athlete Perception Theory (TAPT)™

I created this theory for my *Athlete Career Killer*™ 12-part book series. I'm introducing it here too, and athletes will instantly recognize what it means.

It means avoiding the creation of, and the public perception of having an "entourage." This also deals with *peer pressure* within an "entourage." It's when you may feel like you have to "take care of" your friends from your childhood. You don't, and they should be able to take care of themselves.

Realize that requests for handouts from family and friends will be plentiful once you turn pro. There's nothing wrong with helping a friend or family member in need, but not to the point where it becomes a financial burden to you.

If you're not diligently on top of your finances, maintaining an "entourage" can drain your bank accounts faster than you can smile and say *"unrestricted free agent!"*

Did you happen to notice the above acronym for *The Athlete Perception Theory* — *TAPT*? It was purposely created to sound similar to the word "tapped" — as in tapped out. That's exactly what you'll eventually become if you try to financially support an "entourage."

Certainly, it's all right to be generous to close family and friends every now and then. I'm not saying don't buy your dad and mom their dream house, because they surely deserve it. But don't buy your cousins and homeboys the same stuff you have and allow them to live off of you.

At some point this will put substantial stress on you financially.

Some athletes depend on family members or friends to help them with their finances, and that could be a financially fatal mistake! Avoid hiring family members, friends, or the "friend of a close friend" scenario. It's just not worth the financial risk. Remember, financial professionals should be licensed and legal.

The point is, it's hard to say no to lending money to family and friends you're close to because, if you say yes, the requests will never stop. They may see that as a weakness in you, and keep asking for more dough.

If you're a rookie pro athlete, don't feel that now that you've made it to the "bigs" that you have to impress everyone — including your teammates. You don't have to live beyond your means to impress anyone by driving fancy and expensive cars or buying expensive homes.

Just because you're now a "professional athlete" doesn't mean you should throw your money around irresponsibly.

If you're a veteran athlete who has been through a financial hardship and recovered nicely, become a *mentor* to your younger brethren, and pass along some of your wisdom and insights.

They will thank you for it ten years from now, if not sooner. *I guarantee it!*

Keys to Holding onto Your Wealth

It has been well reported that:
- By the time they have been retired for two years, about 78% of former NFL players have gone bankrupt or are under financial distress because of joblessness, divorce, or from making poor business and money decisions.

- Within five years of retirement, an estimated 60% of former NBA players are broke, as reported by the NBA Player's Association in 2008.

The common reason for these shocking statistics is that many athletes who retire from the game still possess several cars, are still paying mortgages on two to three homes, paying massive amounts of child support each month and, in a lot of cases, are still taking care of family and friends, including their parents.

This takes a major financial toll on them after retirement simply because the big paychecks they were receiving as professional athletes are no longer pouring in anymore. It also takes an emotional toll on retired athletes, who now find they have way too much time on their hands and don't know how to readjust their days accordingly.

Don't let this be you!

Here's the first goal: You want to maintain your wealth. You want to be savvy and accumulate *"generational wealth"* for you and your family for years to come by growing your estate to where your kid's children, and their children, and their children — will be financially set for life.

Here's the second goal: Once you have established a solid game plan for generational wealth, you want to live with what I call *"quiet wealth."*

To me, this means living a quiet, peaceful, happy, drama free lifestyle, without being "gaudy." It also means being charitable in your community – all in complete financial serenity.

Choosing a Financial Planner

Skilled, highly qualified and honest financial planners and advisers aren't hard for athletes to find. The best way to find one is to ask your peers.

Ask a seasoned veteran on your team, the coach, or even the team owner who their planner or adviser is. Seeking out personal references from others you know to be successful is just plain smart. Here's how to find the right financial planner for you.

It's not always easy for professional athletes to decide on the balanced mix of insurance, investments, tax, and estate planning. Generally, you want to seek a financial planner who will suggest broader-based investment recommendations based on extensive knowledge of your financial situation.

After you have a few names of potential candidates, select three. Visit the office of each one and ask for a detailed statement of fees and services, a resumé and references.

Then go back and make comparisons between them.

Make sure you go the extra mile to investigate the person before signing any financial agreements. Make sure they are licensed in their field, have authentic references, and can prove their success on paper, or lack thereof. Now, any company can *"cook the books,"* so be diligent in your search and research.

About Experience

Your financial planner should have, at the very minimum, three years of experience in:
- General principles of financial planning
- Insurance planning and risk management
- Employee benefits planning
- Investment planning
- Income tax planning
- Retirement planning
- Estate planning

About Credentials

Your current financial planner will likely have one of these following certifications or designations:
- CFP®, Certified Financial Planner. The Certified Financial Planner designation is perhaps the most common designation awarded by Certified Financial Planner Board of Standards Inc. (CFP Board) to individuals who meet education, examination, experience and ethics requirements. It generally is regarded as the industry standard for the financial planning profession.
- AIFA®, Accredited Investment Fiduciary Analyst. The AIFA is the first and only professional designation that focuses on the process of conducting fiduciary assessments. The designation is a symbol of ability and knowledge to advise clients of deficiencies in investment processes.
- BCE, Board Certified in Estate Planning. The BCE designation demonstrates the adviser's expertise and commitment to helping individuals plan for the passing of a loved one and their effective transfer of wealth — chiefly how to maximize

passing one's wealth onto a spouse and future generations while mitigating estate taxes.

- CAS, Certified Annuity Specialist. The CAS designation demonstrates the adviser's expertise and commitment to helping individuals work toward their retirement goals with annuities as a suitable option. CAS is fully accredited, and the oldest designation in the annuity industry. It is the only such designation recognized by dozens of Fortune 500 companies.
- CFA, Chartered Financial Analyst®. The CFA charter, awarded by the CFA Institute, is regarded as the designation of professional excellence within the global investment community. The curriculum and examination process are intended to provide candidates with ethical standards of practice, and an in-depth understanding of investment analysis and portfolio management skills.
- CFDP, Certified Financial Divorce Practitioner. The Certified Financial Divorce Practitioner designation is the undisputed professional credential for persons who typically assist either spouse of a divorcing couple to understand their options better and the decisions surrounding their financial scenarios.
- CFS, Certified Funds Specialist. The CFS designation demonstrates the adviser's expertise and commitment to understanding mutual funds — to be able to evaluate and compare financial measurements and benchmarks of the funds when constructing a portfolio. CFS is fully accredited, and the oldest designation in the mutual fund industry — created in 1988.
- ChFC®, Chartered Financial Consultant®. Awarded by The American College, the ChFC® prepares individuals to meet the advanced financial planning needs of individuals, professionals, and small-business owners. The curriculum offers in-depth coverage of key financial planning disciplines, including insurance, income taxation, retirement planning, investments, and estate planning.
- CTS, Certified Tax Specialist. The CTS designation demonstrates the adviser's expertise and commitment to provide ways to reduce taxable income. There are a number of ways to decrease taxable income and reduce tax liability for clients.
- PPC, Professional Plan Consultant. Administered by Financial Service Standards, LLC, the (PPC) designation is awarded to those who successfully complete the 401(k) Service Training Program™. This designation signifies a commitment to education and service excellence in the qualified plan industry.

- QFA, Qualified Financial Adviser. The QFA designation is ideal for those professionals who may wish to attain the coveted CFP® designation, but may lack the bachelor's degree, experience requirements, or the time/money devoted to becoming fully CFP certified.
- RFC, Registered Financial Consultant. The RFC designation is awarded by the International Association of Registered Financial Consultants (IARFC) to those financial advisers who can meet the high standards of education, experience and integrity required of all its members.
- RIS, Retirement Income Specialist. Yes, all professional athletes will face retirement some day! The RIS designation demonstrates the adviser's expertise and commitment to helping individuals plan for a comfortable retirement — chiefly how to maximize income while mitigating risk and taxes.
- RPA, Retirement Plans Associate. The RPA designation is earned by individuals in the group benefits arena who complete an extensive four-course curriculum and successfully pass the examination. The International Foundation is responsible for the overall administration of the program. The Wharton School oversees academic content and standards.

As always, conduct your own thorough due diligence. No one person or team of people, however well trained and skilled, know absolutely everything required to deal in depth with ALL the issues pertaining to your financial matters.

*List courtesy of Agent Broker Training Center.

About Fees and Commissions

Some planners work fee-based only, much like lawyers. Others work exclusively, or almost exclusively on commissions.

Many may charge a combination of fees and commissions. It's your final choice, and yours alone to decide whether the quality of the planner's services are worth the cost. After all, *it's YOUR money!*

What to Ask a Financial Planner

Again, don't be afraid to *ask questions*.

For example:

1. *What experience do you have?*

   Find out how long the planner has been in practice and the number and types of companies with which he or she has been associated. Ask the planner to briefly describe their work experience and how it relates to their current practice. Choose a financial planner who has a minimum of three years of experience counseling individuals on their financial needs. If you're receiving investment advice, it's a good idea to work with someone who has been an adviser through at least one recession or down stock market.

2. *What are your qualifications?*

   The term "financial planner" is used by many financial professionals (and many non-professionals). Ask the planner what qualifies him or her to offer financial planning advice, and whether they hold a financial planning designation such as the Certified Financial Planner or Chartered Financial Analyst marks. Look for a planner who has proven experience in financial planning topics such as insurance, tax planning, investments, estate planning, or retirement planning.

3. *What services do you offer?*

   The services a financial planner offers depend on a number of factors including credentials, licenses and areas of expertise. Financial planners cannot offer insurance or securities products such as mutual funds or stocks without the proper licenses, or give investment advice unless registered with state or federal authorities. *Beware!* Some planners offer financial planning advice on a range of topics but are not licensed and do not offer financial products. Others may provide advice only in specific areas such as estate planning or on tax matters.

4. *How much do you typically charge?*

   The amount you pay the planner will depend on your particular needs, but they should be able to provide you with an estimate of possible costs based on the work to be performed. It's vitally imperative that you ask the planner or adviser to provide you a written breakdown of all fees and commissions, how they are figured, and which ones are fixed and which ones are variable.

5. *What's your investing style: conservative or aggressive?*

   Make sure the planner's viewpoint on investing is not too cautious or overly aggressive for you. They should offer you the right mix and balance of securities for your personal financial status. Some planners also require you to have a certain net worth before offering services.

6. *Will you be the only person working with me?*

    The financial planner may work with you individually, or have others in the office assist him or her. You may want to meet everyone who will be working with you. If the planner works with professionals outside his own practice (such as attorneys, insurance agents or tax specialists) to develop or carry out financial planning recommendations, get a list of their names and do your due diligence on their backgrounds.

7. *How will I pay for your services?*

    As part of your financial planning agreement, the financial planner should clearly tell you in writing how he or she will be paid for services provided.

8. *Are you licensed by your state or FINRA in securities or insurance?*

    Make sure they're licensed, and ask to view it. Also, ask the planner to provide you with a description of their conflicts of interest in writing, if any. For example, financial planners who are employees of banks, insurance companies or investment firms often favor their own company products, even when they are less competitive. The planner may also have relationships or partnerships that should be disclosed to you, such as business he or she receives for referring you to an insurance agent, stockbroker, accountant or attorney for implementation of planning suggestions.

9. *Are you registered?*

    Not all planners are!

10. *Have you ever been publicly disciplined for any unlawful or unethical actions in your professional career?*

    Never be afraid to ask this important question! Your financial future as a current or former professional athlete depends on it! If the person squirms or seems offended by this question — run out the door! Several government and professional regulatory organizations, such as the Financial Industry Regulatory Authority (FINRA), your own state insurance and securities departments, and the CFP Board, keep records on the disciplinary history of financial planners and advisers. Ask what organizations the planner is regulated by, and contact these groups to conduct your due diligence involving a background check. All financial planners who have registered as investment advisers with the Securities and Exchange Commission or state securities agencies, or who are associated with a company that is registered as an investment adviser, *MUST* be able to provide you with a disclosure form called Form ADV, or the state equivalent of that form.

Form ADV contains critical financial information about a registered investment adviser (RIA), and is kept on file with the Securities & Exchange Commission. Many financial planners do not hold securities or insurance licenses, so be persistent in finding the answers to your questions.

11. *Can I get that in writing?*

Ask the planner to provide you with a written agreement that details the services that will be provided. Keep this document in your files for future reference.

12. *What is your opinion of my true financial situation?*

Reexamine your investment goals, time horizon, risk tolerance, and financial circumstances. Have any of these objectives or circumstances changed? If so, will you still be able to meet your long-term financial goals? Allow your planner to assess your true financial situation by providing complete information on your current financial picture.

13. *What about risk in this economic environment?*

Has your risk tolerance changed — or are you just feeling a natural unease following the downturn in the overall market and economy?

14. *Do I need to reconsider my time horizon?*

How long is your time horizon? Are you a young professional athlete just starting out, or are you an established veteran? All things being equal, you can afford to be more aggressive if you have a longer time horizon.

15. *Does my investment strategy need readjusting?*

If you're retiring from the game and withdrawing income from your investment portfolio for living expenses, talk to your financial planner about this next financial phase of your life — living comfortably as a retired or soon to be retired former professional athlete.

If you can answer "yes" to any of the following questions, ask your planner if you may need an adjustment to your investment mix to keep up to date with the following changes, as they apply to you.

- Did you get married or have a child?
- Has there been a divorce, or is your son or daughter getting nearer to needing money for college tuition and expenses?
- Do members of your family need temporary financial assistance?
- Are you now helping to financially support a parent or parents?

16. *What if I haven't invested enough for retirement from sports?*

    Talk to your financial planner about a number of possible strategies to help build up your assets prior to or during your retirement.

17. *Are there any new tax implications for 2010 and beyond?*

    Make sure your planner has a good game plan to legally minimize your taxes.

18. *What's your past performance?*

    Timing of investments often determines performance. When a planner or adviser makes claims — which they sometimes do on their web sites or in brochures — you need to see objective evidence!

19. *What about customer service?*

    Some planners and advisers may frown upon you calling them every time the market has a bad day or a bad week. Once you have an investment strategy in place, be patient, yet firmly persistent. You have a right to know how your money is being handled. Also, ask what kinds of summary statements you will get? What if you call them out of the blue with a tax or risk question? How will it be handled? Make sure whatever arrangement you agree upon is comfortable with all concerned.

20. *What about your ethics?*

    With tens of thousands of financial planners and advisers out there, you don't want one who takes your check intended for investment funds, and "converts it to his or her own use," meaning embezzlement of your hard earned money! The NASD (National Association of Securities Dealers) publishes a monthly list of enforcement actions against brokers and advisers. Thankfully, most of them are honest and legit. There's also the issue of whether the planner or adviser is a fiduciary. This means your interests legally come first.

Remember, *asking questions* is vital to your financial health and well being!

Athlete Investment Options

Recruiting the Right Investment Broker

Remember when you were a high school athlete, and later, if you were fortunate, recruited to play college sports or scouted to be drafted into the pro ranks?

Let's flip that script!

I want you to now be the recruiter who's looking for the same "skills" that scouts and coaches sought in you — but from a financial standpoint.

A carefully selected broker can supply you with valuable investment information and make profitable investment suggestions. If you make the right choice, your broker can be your single most valuable source of help in making good investment decisions.

By the same token, an inept or unresponsive broker can make your life miserable, as well as cost you money.

The first decision you need to make is whether you want a traditional broker, whether you'd prefer to do your own stock and trading research, or get your advice elsewhere and use a brokerage firm only to execute your trades.

Brokers differ in several ways. There are full-service and discount firms, national, regional, and local firms, and firms that operate only online or over the phone. All sell more than stocks; they sell municipal bonds, unit trusts, tax shelters, and annuities, among other products.

But the chief distinction is between full-service and discount firms.

Full-Service Brokers

If you'd rather pay someone else for investment recommendations, then consider researching full-service brokers.

Do you want investment advice and recommendations?

If so, you're likely in the market for a full-service broker. Mostly, these are the high profile national firms with armies of analysts who crank out buy and sell recommendations for a long list of stocks and bonds.

Individual brokers assigned to your account will be called financial consultants or something similar. Rarely are they officially referred to as brokers.

Brokers must be licensed.

Full-service firms offer a wide range of customer services, including research reports, individual advice, asset-management accounts, consolidated account statements, and seminars on retirement planning, tax shelters and other investment-related topics.

Where the full-service brokers separate themselves from the competition is in areas such as stock picking, asset allocation and breadth of research.

The best way to start your search for the full-service broker that's right for you is to talk to people who invest. Who do they use? Why did they choose them? Who does the owner of your football, basketball, baseball, or hockey team use? Ask him or her! *I guarantee* they'll be happy to help you!

They will respect you for coming forth with these questions because it shows you care, are responsible, and are mature enough to want to be an active participant in your own financial future and success as a professional athlete — so don't be shy!

Discount Brokers

If you're the self-serve type of athlete, with the time management, organizational ability, the desire to do extensive company research in considering an investment of your hard earned money, and you have a successful history managing your portfolio, then this may be an option for you.

If you feel comfortable making your own investment decisions and don't need or want a broker's advice, then there's no need to pay for such services. Today, discount brokers offer a myriad of services like stock tickers, libraries of investment information, all-in one accounts, and computer terminals for stopping by their offices to check on the value of your holdings.

But, with discount brokers, you get execution of your order — but no research, no hand holding, no advice! Most firms will make helpful literature available to you, often including research reports from other sources, such as Standard & Poor's, Value Line, and Morningstar.

Salespeople are paid a salary, not commissions. Most discounters also offer a long list of account services identical to those of the full-service brokers, so, again, do your due diligence.

Many discounters are also members of the New York Stock Exchange, with offices in several cities around the country. They have toll-free telephone numbers for distant clients, and most offer online trading.

Discounts for trading stocks, depending on the size of the transaction, can amount to as much as 80% of what you'd pay a full-service broker, although 20% to 30% is more common.

Before you sign on, find out whether there is a minimum charge for trading transactions. Some firms set a $20.00 to $45.00 minimum fee, regardless of the size of the trade. On small trades that could wipe out the savings you might have anticipated.

Investments offer a dangerous draw — enormous rewards with the possibility of awful, financially crippling losses. Athletes love the idea of amassing wealth; however, no one likes to lose their money. The key here is to learn how to invest your money with minimal risks. It's impossible to predict the daily fluctuations of the market.

Also consider Exchange-Traded Funds (ETFs).

What's an ETF?

ETFs, such as the Nasdaq-100 Index Tracking Stock (Nasdaq: QQQQ), Diamonds Trust Series I (NYSE:DIA), which tracks the Dow Jones Industrial Average, and Standard & Poor's depository receipt (SPDRs), (AMEX:SPY) which track the S&P 500 Index, to name a few, allow you to enjoy the benefits of a mutual fund with the flexibility of a stock. Think of an exchange-traded fund as a mutual fund that trades like a stock. Just like an index fund, an ETF represents a basket of stocks that reflect an index such as the S&P 500.

By the way, just in case you didn't know, NYSE is short for *New York Stock Exchange.* And AMEX is short for *American Stock Exchange.*

An ETF, however, isn't a mutual fund; it trades just like any other company on a stock exchange.

Unlike a mutual fund that has its net-asset value (NAV) calculated at the end of each trading day, an ETF's price changes throughout the day, fluctuating with supply and demand. It's important to remember that while ETFs attempt to replicate the return on indexes, there is no guarantee that they will do so exactly.

Because ETFs trade like stocks, you can short sell them, buy them on margin and purchase as little as one share. Another advantage is that the expense ratios of most ETFs are lower than that of the average mutual fund.

When buying and selling ETFs, you pay your broker the same commission that you'd pay on any regular trade.

Never invest any money in securities you cannot afford to lose! Never invest without sound reasoning.

Catching a market high is incredibly rewarding, but market lows are also part of the journey. *Don't make reckless choices.* Smart athletes make their money work harder for them by investing wisely.

Here are eight general tips to investment planning for athletes.
1. Identify and set your financial goals.
2. Understand the different types of investment vehicles.
3. Develop a strategy.
4. Implement your strategy.
5. Monitor the performance of your investment portfolio.
6. Review your investment portfolio.
7. Know that even the best laid plans could still fail.
8. Minimize risk, and don't be afraid to quickly cut your losses before they snowball.

Credit and Debt

How much debt is too much? It depends on how easily you can repay the money and what you borrowed it for in the first place.

You're headed for trouble if you pick up these distress signals:
- You find it more and more difficult each month to make ends meet.
- It's taking extraordinary effort to pay your ordinary expenses.
- You've picked up the habit of paying only the minimum due on your credit card bills each month, and sometimes you juggle payments, stalling one company to pay another.
- You can't save even small amounts, and don't have enough set aside to get you through a financial setback.

Even if you seem to be getting along just fine, you should examine your debt situation occasionally. Pay attention not only to how much you have to pay each month for credit cards and other debt, but also how many months into the future you'll be stuck with those payments.

If you quit using your credit cards today, for example, how long would it take to pay off your non-mortgage debts? Six months? A year or maybe longer? Find this out right now.

Set a debt limit that considers what you can afford today and, just as important, what today's obligations are borrowing from tomorrow.

As an athlete, if debt is a problem, solving it should go to the top of your list of financial priorities! Carrying huge amounts of debt is definitely the equivalent of a ticking time bomb, and is certainly a potential *Athlete Career Killer*™.

How to Get Out of Debt

There are several steps you can take to ensure your credit rating isn't ruined. Whatever the elusive "proper" level of debt may be, a lot of athletes are exceeding it.

Despite generally widespread prosperity in professional sports, athletes have been going broke in record numbers, filing for personal bankruptcy like never before. If you see such drastic action looming in your future, it's better to take some steps now before your credit rating tanks.

Consider rolling your debts into a lower rate loan. Perhaps you can reduce your monthly payments by combining your major debts into a longer term loan at a lower interest rate. This can be an especially rewarding strategy for credit card debt, which hammers you with the highest interest around.

As always, seek the advice and guidance of a licensed certified financial or debt counseling professional. The good news is, if you've paid off your balance on time every month, you probably have a good credit score. And when a professional athlete has good credit, you have more choices.

Switch to a lower rate credit card. Credit card offers are everywhere, and card issuers will gladly arrange for you to roll balances on existing cards into a new account with them, provided your credit rating is still good. Just make sure you don't sign up for a low introductory rate that converts to a high rate after only a few months!

Check your credit record periodically. You can get a *free copy of your credit report* from each of the bureaus every 12 months at AnnualCreditReport.com. You can also get a free credit report if you've been denied credit in the past 60 days. Federal law requires that credit reporting firms provide free reports to people who believe that their credit record is inaccurate because of fraud.

As of this writing, the three major credit-reporting agencies are Equifax; www.econsumer.equifax.com, Experian; www.experian.com, and Trans Union; www.transunion.com.

Come Clean!

If you know things are going to get worse before they get better, call your creditors and spill the beans.

Tell them that you can't pay on time but are determined to pay them back, and you want to set up a payment plan. Could they possibly stretch out the payments for you? Some will. Some will even waive interest and late fees for a period of time to keep charges and fees from skyrocketing.

If you get such an agreement, follow up with a letter to the company describing the terms you discussed. This protects you later if the company decides to change its mind.

Get Help!

If things are looking bleak and you can't handle it alone, consider signing up for National Foundation for Credit Counseling, which operates more than 2,000 local offices.

There, counselors can help you set up a repayment program and negotiate with your creditors for reduced monthly payments and lower, or even waived finance charges. They can then assist you in setting up a more reasonable budget that allows you to make one monthly payment to the service, which then parcels it out to your creditors. There may be a small fee involved.

Save or Pay Down Debt?

Should athletes be putting money into savings or investments, at the same time you're paying off a loan?

The best answer lies in separating good debt from bad debt. It's almost always a good idea to get rid of credit card and other high interest loans before you start setting aside cash.

Tips to Knock Down Debt

1. *Pay off the high-interest debt.* If you have high-interest credit card debt, tackle that first. It doesn't make sense to start saving or investing until you've paid off this debt.
2. *Identify the good debt.* For the most part, it's usually not a good idea to pay off your home mortgage unless you have a lot of extra cash. After all, Uncle Sam refunds part of your interest payment if you itemize your deductions on your tax return. Instead, use your money to invest in liquid assets. However, consider paying off your mortgage and any other debt you might have by the time you retire from the game. You can still live comfortably on less money when those sweet paychecks from your playing days are no longer coming in.
3. *Save and Invest.* Once you've eliminated high-interest debt, start saving as much as you can. One place to begin is your league 401(k). The next best option may be an IRA. In addition to putting money into a retirement account, you need cash that's readily available in an emergency so you don't have to rely on credit cards. Consider setting aside enough money to tide you over for *twelve months* if your paycheck as a professional athlete suddenly stops, like if you make a poor choice and do something foolish, and your league suspends you indefinitely — *without pay!*

Estate Planning for Athletes

Surprisingly, some current and retired athletes *DO NOT* have a will!
Don't let this be you!
Live in peace — make a will!
Don't be foolish and ignore making a will, leaving your entire estate to be decided upon and divided by the courts. If you don't, when you die, your family may be left with legal battles for years to come.

For the record, just because you sit down with a licensed and competent estate planner doesn't mean you're going to die soon. It just means you've matured to the point where you're smarter about your money and more responsible than you ever have been in the past.

Steps to a Good Will

Writing a will is a sobering act that's easy to put off, which is probably why many athletes never get around to it.

Consider for a moment what might happen if you don't leave clear instructions for the distribution of your property after you're gone.

If you die without a valid will, your state will supply one that is ready-made and devised by its legislature.

Like a department store suit, it may fit — and it may not.

The possibilities for trouble when you don't have a will are endless. A hostile relative might be able to acquire a share of your estate, for example, or a relative who is already well off financially might take legal precedence over a more deserving and more needy family member. It makes sense to pay a competent and licensed attorney a reasonable fee to write a document that will lay out your wishes. Do some preliminary research about wills online to help you focus your thinking and get you ready to meet with your estate planning attorney.

Six Steps to Take When Crafting Your Will

1. *Size up your estate.* Start by drawing up a list of your assets — real estate, bank accounts, stocks, bonds, cars, boats, life insurance, profit-sharing and pension funds, business holdings, money owed to you, and the like.
2. *Protect your children.* If you have minor children, you'll have to decide who you want to take care of them if you and your spouse both die. This involves setting up a guardianship, a task that has two principle functions. The first is to provide for the proper care of the children until they reach the age of majority, which is generally 18 years old. The second is to manage the money and property you leave to the children and distribute it to them as you would wish. If you're a divorced athlete, you might be inclined to choose a separate property guardian because the surviving parent typically would get custody of your children. Consider naming backup guardians in case your first choice dies, is incapacitated, or might want to relinquish the job after a few years.

3. *Distribute your property.* Next you'll have to decide how you want your estate distributed. This is obvious and straightforward in many instances, such as leaving everything to your children, or to your spouse if both of you die.
4. *Choose an executor.* Be prepared to name an executor (sometimes called an administrator), whose job it will be to see to the distribution of your estate and make sure any taxes, debts, and other obligations are paid. Choose your executor carefully. Naturally, he or she should be someone you trust — a relative, a longtime and close friend, your lawyer, or anyone you feel is able to take on the responsible task of disposing of your estate. That person should be willing to do the job, so talk to them before you name someone who might later refuse, thus forcing the court to appoint someone you might not have chosen. You also may have to choose someone who will step in as executor if for some reason your first choice can't do it.
5. *Do your due diligence and ask your attorney lots of questions* — because you will surely have many. Write them down if you need to. If your estate is substantial, as most are with professional athletes, consult an attorney who specializes in estate planning. Insurance policies, investments, and home equity could make your estate larger than you think it is.
6. *Change it if you want.* If your situation changes in the future, you can always amend the will.

Changing Your Will Later

Life as a professional athlete is ever-changing, and so are your estate planning needs.

After you've created your will and an estate plan, you'll most likely need to revisit them at key points in your life as your circumstances change.

Here are seven situations in which you'll want to reevaluate your will.

1. *You Get Married.* Your new spouse doesn't automatically become your chief heir. Most states give a spouse one-third or one-half of an estate. If you don't have any children, your parents or siblings would get the rest. To leave all your property to your spouse, you'll need a will. You cannot disinherit a spouse without her consent. If you are living with someone but are not married and you want your significant other to inherit any of your property, you definitely need a will.

2. *You Become a Parent (again).* Obviously, the big question is how your children will be cared for if both you and your spouse die. Consider using trusts, perhaps in your will, to handle assets that would go to your children. Talk with your attorney to determine if executing a durable power of attorney naming your spouse or someone else to act for you in financial matters when you can't, would be in your best interest. Durable power remains effective even if you become mentally unable to handle your own affairs.

3. *You Approach Retirement.* If you've been blessed to play professional sports for a long period of time, and are considering retirement from the game, your assets have probably grown substantially, so tax planning could save your heirs thousands in federal estate taxes. As you know, in sports, injuries can happen at any time. If you're a younger athlete in the prime of your career and an injury forces you to retire, the same principle applies.

4. *You Get Divorced.* Review absolutely everything. The people in your life are changing. So must your estate plan. You need a new will altogether, because in most states a divorce automatically revokes the provisions of a will that apply to a former spouse. In some states a divorce revokes the entire will. Get with your licensed estate planning attorney to help you set up trusts to control the assets you plan to leave to your children. And revise any living trusts to remove your former spouse as a beneficiary or trustee after a divorce. Do likewise with a durable power of attorney or a living will. Also, unless restricted by a divorce decree, change the beneficiaries on your life insurance, pensions, and IRA.

5. *You Remarry.* You and your new spouse may have to plan for families from prior marriages, and for children you have together. Consider a *prenuptial agreement*, should you want to keep assets separate and nullify your inheritance rights to each others estates. More about prenups later. You'll want to provide for your new spouse and still be certain your children, if any, are taken care of. To do this, your attorney may talk to you about a Qualified Terminable Interest Property trust — QTIP, for short. This trust can be set up in a will to give your spouse the income from the trust property and some rights to principal. But when she dies, the assets go to beneficiaries you have chosen, like your children.

6. *Your Career Has Ended and You Move to Another State.* If you retire from the game and move to another state, or any time you move to a new state, for that matter

(active athletes, too), have your estate planning documents reviewed in light of that particular state's laws and your current needs.

7. *Your Spouse Dies.* This loss can leave you emotionally vulnerable to financial mistakes. Avoid selling your house or making other drastic changes for at least several months. Seek expert advice from your attorney. There may be tax benefits to disclaiming some of your inheritance in favor of alternate beneficiaries, such as your children, if your spouse's estate is subject to the federal estate tax and you have enough assets of your own, including liquid assets. You should consider getting a new will and, if needed, a revocable living trust. Execute a new durable power of attorney and a living will (which expresses your wishes in case of an illness that leaves you permanently incapacitated). Put these in a safe place, and tell people who need to know and whom you trust, where they are.

Tax Planning

As your life and athletic career changes, so do the set of tax rules that affect you.

The Internal Revenue Code now reaches into nearly every nook and cranny of your life as an athlete, from beginning to retirement. The tax bill athletes owe each spring is based on the saving, investing, spending, business and other personal decisions you make during the year.

That's why you must be aware of your opportunities to embrace, and pitfalls to avoid, as your life as a taxpayer evolves. The fact that federal income taxes are among most families' biggest annual expenditures trumpets the importance of tax planning for athletes. Talk to a competent, skilled and licensed tax attorney to learn more.

Steps to Hiring a Tax Pro

Professional athlete tax returns can be complicated.

Athletes should hire a year round, highly skilled and certified tax professional for tax planning, like a certified public accountant (CPA), or a certified public accountant/personal financial specialist (CPA/PFS).

Picking the appropriate type of tax planner is the easy part. Actually finding the right person to do the job can be tough.

If you're thinking about enlisting the help of a professional tax planner for the first time, or are searching for someone new because you're not satisfied with the service you're getting from someone else, follow these steps:

1. Get a referral. Ask your friends, family, teammates, coaches, team executive personnel, and your league, whether they can recommend a certified tax professional. Then narrow your list of recommended tax professionals down to two or three candidates, who you will then visit for an interview.
2. Interviewing candidates. Interview them in person. If they aren't willing to give you a few minutes of their time on the phone — or they want to charge you for the initial interview — look elsewhere. You want somebody who is willing to listen to you, hear what you're saying, and answer your questions in plain terms that you can clearly understand.

What to Ask

1. *How long have you been in practice?* You want someone who has been preparing returns long enough (i.e. several years) to anticipate problems or IRS challenges.
2. *What are your credentials?* Anyone can hang out a sign claiming to be a tax preparer, because there are no licensing requirements. Look for an enrolled agent, accredited tax adviser (ATA), accredited tax preparer (ATP), certified public accountant (CPA) or CPA/PFS. Only a CPA can have the PFS, personal financial specialist designation. Check your state's licensing board and professional associations to assure that he or she is licensed, is a member in good standing, and has had no disciplinary action taken against him or her.
3. *Do you have any specialties?* This is important to ask if you have a specific need. For example, if you own and operate a business in the off-season, you need someone who knows business accounting. Or, if you have rental property, look for someone who has experience handling this sort of tax situation.
4. *How much will you charge?* A tax preparer should be able to provide you with an estimate. Find out if he or she charges an hourly rate or flat fee, and whether that fee will cover everything or will there be add-ons for planning meetings and calls throughout the year.
5. *Will you file my return in a timely manner?* And will you have time to meet with me throughout the year?

6. *Will you represent me before the IRS if a problem arises?* If the answer is no, run out the door! If you are ever audited, you want someone who will defend your return.

Advice for Young Athletes

Are you a young athlete planning a trip down the aisle?

Make a date to discuss your financial future with her first. If you're planning to say "I do" soon, save yourself some arguments later by talking about your finances now.

More important than the wedding gown, cake, flowers, or the invitations, is preparing for your financial future together.

Sit down with her, discuss your goals and expectations on a *mature* level, and come up with a plan for an effective merger of your financial lives.

It may not sound romantic, but do it anyway! Quarreling over money is one of the biggest causes of marital discord and divorce for athletes, and anyone else for that matter.

Ten Questions to Ask Before Saying "I Do"

1. *Where would you like to be in five or ten years?* This question is the best way to start a money conversation. For example, does one of you want to go back to school, start your own business, or own a vacation home? And, if you plan to raise a family, how many children and when? Discussing these important issues together will help you set priorities and identify savings goals.
2. *What are our assets and liabilities?* Before you can create an effective strategy to reach your goals, each person should fill out a net worth worksheet detailing his or her assets and liabilities. Once you know where you stand right now, it's much easier to move forward. Consult a licensed financial planner to help with your planning. And if you haven't discussed it already, now may also be a good time to bring up a prenup. A prenuptial agreement spells out how assets will be distributed in the event of a divorce. Divorce happens! It's simply a common part of life in our society. With about one-third of first marriages and half of second marriages ending in divorce, it makes sense to protect your financial interests as a young professional athlete, or any professional athlete.

3. *Should we keep our finances separate or combine them?* Some couples relish the unity and trust that joint accounts foster, while others prefer more freedom and autonomy by maintaining separate accounts. Or you can have both. Some couples set up a joint account for household expenses, while keeping separate accounts for personal spending. The key is to find a system that works for both of you.

4. *What about our investments?* Whether or not you choose to combine your investment accounts is, again, entirely up to you. Nevertheless, it's important to view your portfolios as a whole to make sure you aren't overlapping. If you both hold shares of the same stock, for example, you could be placing yourselves at risk should anything happen to the company. Check for overlap by making an appointment to sit down with your licensed financial planner.

5. *How will we handle daily spending decisions?* One of the first tasks newlyweds should tackle is creating a budget. Sit down together and discuss how much you expect to spend on groceries, clothes, vacations, eating out and other household expenses. The word *"budget"* doesn't have to be a bad word to be avoided for the young professional athlete. Think of it as a means to reaching your goals. You should also take this time to discuss other spending issues, such as how much each of you can spend without consulting the other. You probably don't want to discuss every $50.00 purchase, but you also don't want to come home from practice one day and *unexpectedly* find a new Rolls Royce in the driveway either. For example, I just looked up the price online for a base *2010 Rolls Royce Phantom Coupe.* The asking price — $408,000. *S-u-r-p-r-i-s-e!*

6. *Who will be responsible for paying the bills and preparing the taxes?* Discuss early about who'll be doing this. Have a game plan for success. No matter who ends up handling the bills in your marriage, make sure each partner knows where to find all the different account information, including web sites, passwords and bill due dates in case anything should happen, and the other person needs to take over the responsibilities.

7. *What is your tolerance for financial risk?* One of the biggest culprits in marital money disputes is a mismatch of risk tolerance. You may be the type of young professional athlete who doesn't mind taking an investment risk here and there, figuring you're still early into your career. But your future spouse may be much more conservative and cautious than you are. Try to compromise on financial strategies that both of you can live with. If you still can't reach an amicable

agreement, you might seek investment advice from a neutral third party, such as a licensed financial planner.

8. *What are our insurance options?* Adding a spouse to your health insurance may be cheaper than maintaining separate plans. Consider your specific health needs, then look at the costs and benefits of each person's plan. Combining your auto-insurance coverage may likely also save you money. You'll want to make sure you have enough homeowners or renter's insurance to protect your combined possessions. What about life insurance? Do you need it? If you already have a policy, either privately or through your league, do you need to change your beneficiary information?

9. *How does your credit report look at the time of marriage?* The good news is that simply marrying a person with bad credit won't drag down your stellar record. What's yours is yours and what's hers is hers. So, for example, if you apply for a car loan by yourself, your spouse's credit report shouldn't be a factor. However, when it comes to applying for joint financing, like buying a house together, lenders will consider both your credit and payment histories. It's better to know ahead of time of any potential problems than to receive the shocking news in the mortgage lender's office that you're stuck with a higher interest rate, don't qualify for as much money as you'd planned, or that you're being turned down for the loan entirely.

10. *How will we handle existing debt?* Make a pact to pay off your debts soon. Start with the balances that carry the highest interest rates. You may choose to work individually or collectively to pay off debts you accrued before the wedding, but don't add each others names to your obligations. Also, consolidating your own student loans, if any, to lock in today's record-low rates is a good move — but, again, don't merge your loans with your spouse's. The commingled debt would be nearly impossible to untangle should you ever divorce, and if one of you were to default, the other would be left holding the bag.

Secrets to Marital and Money Bliss

Communication and compromise are critical to resolving money disputes with your spouse or significant other. But you also need practical money management techniques to better react to common marital issues.

One common conflict is — spending too much! Sometimes a spender is in conflict with a saver, and sometimes two spenders stroll hand in hand to the brink of bankruptcy.

In either case, each of you would benefit by writing down your goals — a new house, a Caribbean vacation? Make sure you're both in agreement and stay on track.

Once you see where you stand in dollars and cents, one of you may be convinced that you need to spend less, or the other may feel more comfortable about spending more. (Hopefully both will agree to spend less!)

20 More Money Tips for Athletes

Let's focus this section using pro hockey athletes as examples.

I also love hockey! I've been a huge fan since I was 12!

1. *Don't let your signing bonus change your life.* Athletes drafted in the first or second round to the NHL can receive a signing bonus in the range of several hundred thousand U.S. dollars, and more, for example, but the majority of those athletes will not immediately go to the NHL.

2. *Manage your spending.* You'll only get paid for seven months out of the year. With a big check coming in every two weeks, it's tempting for young athletes to buy big ticket items and live an expensive lifestyle. But NHL athletes only get paid from October to April (excluding playoffs, bonuses and awards). Many draw on a line of credit to carry them through.

3. *You'll probably have to fund 50 years of retirement!* Most NHL athletes will play for less than 15 years, and retire in their late twenties or early thirties. Those who are injured will have even shorter careers. You have to start saving early and invest carefully to make your money last throughout your lifetime.

4. *Careful tax planning can make a huge difference.* For most people, taxes are their single largest expense. The multiple filing requirements of a professional cross-the-border athlete can make tax planning very complex. An athlete's country of residence can dramatically impact the overall taxes you pay. Many Canadian resident athletes take advantage of significant tax savings by setting up a Retirement Compensation Arrangement (RCA).

5. *Fluctuations in foreign exchange can have a big effect on your finances.* Most athletes are paid in U.S. dollars. If you rent, buy or sell property in Canada or overseas, changes in the value of the Canadian dollar can have a big impact.

ATHLETE CAREER KILLERS

6. *Before you buy your dream house, evaluate the impact of where you own property.* In Canada, as of this writing, mortgage interest is only deductible if the property is used for investment purposes. For U.S. residents, interest on up to $1,000,000 (U.S.) of the mortgage on the main home or a second home can be tax-deductible. Consult your licensed tax professional for more specifics.

7. *Practice saying NO!* As a professional athlete, you will be asked to fund business and investment ideas, and make donations. Other people will ask you for money regularly, like family members and friends. Don't be afraid to tell anyone NO!

8. *Endorsement income can offer tax advantages.* Canadian resident athletes who receive endorsement income could consider setting up a Canadian corporation to take advantage of lower corporate tax rates. You will need professional advice for this advanced strategy.

9. *Protect your assets from lawsuits.* High-income and high-net-worth athletes are more likely to be subject to lawsuits. You should consider strategies to protect your wealth, such as setting up a domestic or foreign trust.

10. *Insurance and estate planning.* Consider protecting your family's future through insurance and estate planning. Ensure there is adequate disability insurance. Also, some forms of life insurance can provide tax free investment growth. To ensure your family is provided for, it is important to make a will and plan to minimize U.S. estate tax, as well as probate tax. One common strategy is to set up a revocable living trust to hold U.S. real estate assets in order to avoid U.S. state probate tax. Seek professional advice.

11. *Follow where your spending takes you.* Often athletes will look at their accounts and wonder, where did it all go? Take stock and inventory of what you are spending and keep a running account for every dollar. This will allow you to see areas of your life that may be draining your wallet for no good reason at all.

12. *Learn to master the art of delaying gratification.* Wait before buying expensive items. Think about the money you have and how you want to spend it. Postpone making major expenditures until after your first completed year in professional hockey.

13. *Learn to live below your means.* Follow the example of smart wealth and spend less than you earn. Write a monthly household budget and stick to it. Devise a personal financial plan with your financial planner for yourself and your family. This offers you the opportunity to create true sustaining wealth.

14. *Look for opportunities to buy items on sale.* Wealthy athletes like buying items on sale too!
15. *Save at least 15% of your annual salary,* and don't touch it!
16. *Pay your taxes in full every year.* Except if you live in Florida, where there are no state taxes.
17. *Create an emergency fund.* Hopefully you'll never need it, but life happens sometimes.
18. *Have money automatically deducted.* Have funds from your paycheck directly deposited into a separate account only for your mortgage payment, or have your mortgage payment automatically deducted from that account by your mortgage lender.
19. *Review your insurance coverage.* Too many young athletes are talked into paying too much for life and disability insurance, whether it's by adding coverage to car loans, buying whole-life insurance policies when term-life makes more sense, or buying life insurance when you have no dependents. It's important that you have enough insurance to protect your dependents and your income in the case of death or disability, so find out what's right for you.
20. *Keep good records.* If you don't keep good records, you're probably not claiming all your allowable income tax deductions and credits. Set up a system now, and use it all year. It's much easier than scrambling to find everything at tax time, only to miss items that might have saved you money.

For all athletes — if financial hardship ever comes your way at some point in your athletic and post-career, know that if you remain positive, keep a good attitude, and commit to continually educating yourself about the financial world we live in, you *CAN* carve opportunity from financial adversity.

Play Hard. Do Good. Be Money Savvy.™

Chapter 10
COLLEGE ACADEMICS

No pull — No play.™

"If you don't pull your own weight in the classroom — you don't play!"
– David L. Brown

Game Resumé™

College athletics and academics automatically go hand-in-hand.

Unfortunately, negative perception and stereotyping creates the false impression that a student has to be either smart or athletic. In order for a student to feel well-rounded, it's best if they perform well in both areas.

Colleges and universities are held accountable for the success of student-athletes in the classroom, as well as their progression toward graduation. However, the problem of chronic and severe academic under-performance by many student-athletes starts long before they set foot on a college campus.

As a student-athlete, you aspire to take your game to the next level. *Your game film is your resumé.*

If you're academically ineligible to play, you can't build a solid resumé for pro scouts and coaches to truly evaluate your *Total Talent Package*™ (TTP).

If your grades are poor, you can't get on the field and court.

Your game resumé is then severely diminished. If this happens, you risk the possibility of not even being drafted, which greatly decreases your potential value, as well as future financial opportunities.

In the NFL, for example, if you have a minimal resumé of collegiate game film, it serves as a negative trickle-down effect. Here's how: it may cause you to have a lower draft grade, which could mean not being drafted at all. You then become a rookie free agent, meaning you weren't drafted and can sign with any team. Now your chances of making an opening day roster are limited — at best, and you also find yourself at the low end of the rookie salary scale.

Additionally important, student-athletes who aspire to make it to the NFL or NBA must have the mental capacity to absorb and execute *complex* play books and game plans — quickly. In football, it's called *FBI -- Football Intelligence*. Thus, the reason you hear coaches say they want *"smart football players,"* and *"smart basketball players."*

In this chapter I'll show student-athletes how important it is to perform well in the classroom on a consistent basis, and have that success carry over onto the field and court.

Classroom Struggles

Many student-athletes coming out of high school recruited to play football and men's basketball on the college level may be under-prepared for the academic rigors of the schools they choose to attend.

Unfortunately, a lot of the student-athletes are either first-generation college students, come from a low socioeconomic backgrounds, where academics weren't viewed as a high priority, or a family that didn't have the best resources available.

This can create academic disappointment and be harmful to a student-athlete's self-esteem and their image of themselves as scholars.

Students who have never been confident with their academic ability can be permanently damaged under those and other circumstances that set the stage for future academic failure. The purpose of college is to provide a student-athlete an excellent education, but many athletes have other interests ahead of academics — like playing professional sports.

Schools offer student-athletes valuable and important resources, but many don't take advantage of the programs or use them to their full capacity.

Admittedly, there are increasing time demands and personal pressures on the Division-1A student-athlete in today's era of *"big business"* college sports. Among the main pressures is the fact that college student-athletes are often viewed as celebrities.

Increased demands from the NCAA *(National Collegiate Athletic Association)* and the pressure to create successful athletic programs that generate high revenue are also factors. Dealing with the pressures of the ins and outs of a student-athlete's daily schedule can make important things, like time management and acceptable GPAs, a huge challenge.

Many athletes who arrive on a college campus immediately look forward to their professional sports careers.

Unfortunately, many of them aren't aware of the grim statistics. A student-athlete has a greater chance of becoming a brain surgeon than an NFL quarterback. Fewer than 1 in 75 NCAA men's basketball players, 1 in 50 NCAA football players, and 1 in 100 women's basketball players are drafted into the professional ranks.

(*Statistics courtesy of Visions, Iowa State University Alumni Association online edition*).

With many student-athletes coming out of college early to play in the NFL and NBA, some may say college athletes don't care about getting their degrees and only care about trying to get to the next level and getting paid. I'm here to tell you that the majority of college athletes I talk to locally do care about the academic side of things, especially in our current economy here in the Mahoning Valley of northeast Ohio, comprising of the Youngstown-Warren areas.

Student-athletes who turn pro may feel like they can always go back and earn their degrees later, and many do. You just have to want it bad enough. You have to be skilled at putting distractions aside. It certainly helps when you have a great support system in place, like family, coaches, and staff, so that your main focus is on going to class first, and playing football, basketball, baseball or hockey, second.

The successful strategy to live by for a college student-athlete is to strive to successfully complete your course work during the week — and *play hard* on Saturday, or Friday night if you're a high school senior student-athlete.

Don't be afraid to challenge your teammates in regard to their academics. Simply saying, *"Hey, man — you gotta step it up in class,"* sends a message that you're not only holding yourself responsible and accountable — but them, too!

In the last two years, the NCAA has ratcheted up its standards for initial eligibility and progress toward a degree. Coaches and those in athletic departments across the country have become even more meticulous when it comes to academic progress.

The NCAA keeps close tabs via the *Academic Progress Rate* (APR). The APR is calculated by measuring the academic eligibility and retention of student-athletes by team each term, and on a year-to-year basis. Under the rules of APR, academic progress will be calculated for each individual student athlete, and a cumulative APR will be calculated for each sports program. Each team must maintain a minimum APR over four years or incur penalties from the NCAA. Penalties can include loss of scholarships, probation, and bans on participation in championships.

For example, for college football or men's basketball programs, an APR of 925 (out of 1000) calculates to an approximate graduation success rate of about 60%.

Also, the NCAA may issue warnings to programs that don't meet the goals. The APR system seems to have been universally accepted and has helped student-athletes and school athletic departments focus on what's most important to the department and to the institution — *student success*.

I also strongly encourage student-athletes to work closely with the Office of Residence Life (ORL) at their respective school. This is normally a department of Student Affairs. Residence Life programs generate and maintain a campus environment that facilitates the physical well-being of students, and emphasizes opportunities for personal and intellectual growth, self-governance, social and cultural programming, independence, and informal interaction with faculty members, and more. Its purpose is to strive for student, faculty, and staff cooperation and collaboration.

Six Keys to Academic Success

1. Individual academic counseling available to all student-athletes.
2. Learning centers that provide skill development, social awareness, and learning disability support.
3. Developing skills for life by promoting character building as an important part of the educational process.
4. Implement social programs geared toward off the field and court education, such as personal conduct, alcohol use and abuse, responsible sexual behavior, education regarding guns, drugs, clubbing, domestic violence on and off campus, drinking and driving, and more.
5. Programs where student-athletes serve as mentors and go into their local community to talk to younger people about their own experiences, how they have overcome challenges, and speak about the "intangibles" necessary to do things "the right way."
6. Covering other topics such as resumé building and writing, nutrition, financial planning, money management, and fiscal responsibility.

The bottom line for student-athletes — Focus on YOU!

Focus on *you* as an individual first and foremost. When you feel you're on solid ground in that department, then turn your attention to your academics. Forget about what the percentages say, and what the critics are talking about. Handle YOUR academic and athletic business, and the rest will eventually take care of itself.

It shouldn't be about your race either. Your race should never be an obstacle in your pursuit of earning a good education. Make it about you — the individual — with *no excuses.* You may have come from a family of limited resources. You may have had a difficult childhood. You may not have been afforded the rights and privileges of others in the past, but realize and understand that it's exactly that — in the past!

Today is a new day, a new opportunity toward a new attitude in making the decision to be accountable and responsible — for YOU!

If you had a tough past, use it as a motivator to rise above it. Don't wait for someone or something else to change. YOU CHANGE first. When you change your attitude, your thoughts, and your overall mindset — you can change your whole life!

True stories abound of men and women who had the courage to rise above difficult circumstances to become successful college and pro athletes, entertainers, musicians, business leaders, business owners, religious figures — even Presidents of the United States.

If they can do it — so can YOU! Decide today that you are going to live your life to a higher standard — no matter who or what comes your way.

And when you make it to the top — come back and become a *mentor* for another student-athlete, and teach him or her how to do things "the right way," like you did!

Ineligibility Stinks!

Many colleges and universities offer admission to student-athletes who have known learning disabilities.

They are then provided with appropriate academic accommodations under guidelines governed by state and federal law. If an athlete has a learning disability, emotional or psychological issues, that's an entirely different circumstance that warrants special assistance.

Many student-athletes excel academically at the college level, many others do not. Some receive clear evidence that they are doing poorly, such as getting low grades on exams or other course work. Others simply suspect or fear that they are doing poorly.

For example, a student-athlete may have difficulty understanding reading assignments, or he may feel confused by instructors' lectures.

> *Tip:* Never be afraid to ask your teachers or professors questions if you don't understand something. I know, peer pressure is sometimes difficult to ignore, and you may feel embarrassed to seek help.

Avoid those feelings as best you can, and find the courage within yourself to raise your hand and say, *"I don't get it. Could you please explain that again?"*

If you know you're struggling in a course, such as math or writing, act on it! *Don't wait* until it's too late to constructively deal with the situation. Discuss receiving extra help, like getting a tutor or joining a study group. If you are a college freshman student-athlete, meet with your freshman adviser or a college adviser.

If your academic performance, or lack thereof, is keeping you awake at night, know that you're certainly not alone. Many student-athletes share this experience, even though they may not talk about it. You simply may need to readjust your attitude and expectations.

Recognize that college courses are much more difficult than high school courses, and the pace is *MUCH* faster. Missing even one class can leave you way behind. Poor academic performance carries serious consequences. This often causes you to become ineligible to play the sport you love, and later be placed on academic probation — temporarily or permanently halting your college athletic career.

Academic Probation

Student-athletes can be placed on probation for any of the following reasons, and more.
- Earning two or more grades below C in any quarter.
- Having a cumulative GPA below 2.00 on all work attempted, especially for sophomores, juniors, and seniors.
- Failing to maintain a C average in your major field of study.

ATHLETE CAREER KILLERS

If you receive notice that you're on academic probation, be sure to set up a meeting with a college adviser. The adviser can help you explore reasons for poor performance and discuss what you can do differently in order to raise your grades going forward.

If you find yourself on probation and you don't correct the academic deficiency within the period of probation, normally the subsequent quarter, you may be dismissed from your college or university, and not be able to play football or basketball.

> *Note:* Academic integrity at any college or university is of the utmost importance. If a student-athlete is found guilty of dishonesty in doing academic work, such as plagiarism, for example, or having someone else do the work for you, you may receive a failing grade in that course and be suspended or permanently excluded from the university.

Don't drop the ball in the classroom. Remember, any academic setback is an opportunity for a great comeback!

Time Management

Student-athletes have told me — it's all about time management. Consistently meeting your academic obligations is about planning ahead and having good time management skills. Take advantage of your school's student services support programs. They can assist you if you need some individual guidance by providing counselors or private tutors.

Also, check out study hall programs. The truth is, for many student-athletes, balancing class work and practice is difficult, forcing you to enlist help — and that's okay! You should never be embarrassed or feel ashamed for seeking out these services if you know you need them. Your academic and athletic future depends on it.

Twenty Time Management Tips

1. *Get organized.* Have an organized workplace. This will keep you from constantly trying to find your work, and reduce distractions. Both can waste time, especially during those times the residence halls or your apartment are noisy. Consider using an appointment calendar for everything, including listings of study time. Use "to do" lists for each day and week.

2. *Plan ahead.* Determine how long class assignments and tasks will take. See if big tasks can be broken down into smaller tasks, which may be easier to schedule (such as studying for exams and visiting the library as part of an assignment to write a term paper).
3. *Prioritize your tasks.* Use an A-B-C rating system for items on your "to do" lists, with A items being the highest priority. But don't postpone the small tasks. A sense of accomplishment is good; however, overlooked small tasks can become larger and more difficult ones.
4. *Avoid overload.* Take short breaks during study and work periods. Don't put everything off until the last minute. Don't "cram" for exams.
5. *Do the most difficult work first.* Read for comprehension, rather than just to get to the end of a chapter. Read the syllabus as soon as you get it, and note all due dates on your calendar.
6. *Be flexible.* The unexpected happens (sickness, car troubles, etc.); you need to be able to fit it into your schedule. Know how to rearrange your schedule when necessary, and know who to ask for help when needed.
7. *Have vision and purpose.* Don't forget the "big picture." Have and follow a personal, educational, and athletic career mission statement. Are your activities ultimately helping you achieve your goals? What's important to you? What do you value most?
8. *Don't be a perfectionist.* Trying to be perfect sets you up for defeat. Nobody can be perfect. Difficult tasks usually result in avoidance and procrastination. You need to set achievable goals, but they should also be challenging.
9. *Learn to say "No."* For example: Your girlfriend wants you to see a movie with her tonight. Your buddies call a bit later and want you to go with them to a party, but tonight you were going to study and do laundry. You really aren't interested in seeing a movie or going to a party, and you want to say no, but you hate turning people down (peer pressure). Politely saying "No" should become a habit. It frees up time for the things that are most important.
10. *Prioritize some more.* Prioritizing your responsibilities and engagements is very important.
11. *Combine several activities.* Another suggestion is to combine several activities into one time spot. For example, while commuting to class, listen to taped notes. Or, while showering, make a mental list of the things that need to be done that day.

12. *Don't procrastinate!* Don't fall into the trap of putting off the things that you should be doing now. What makes a big difference for your success is your ability to recognize procrastination reasons, like fear of failure — or fear of success.
13. *Identify the best time to study.* Everyone has high and low periods of attention and concentration on any given day. Are you a "morning person" or a "night person?"
14. *Get some rest.* When you're fresh, you can process information more quickly and save time as a result.
15. *Study in shorter time blocks.* This keeps you from getting fatigued. This type of studying is efficient because while you're taking a break, your brain is still processing the information.
16. *Have fun!* Include time for socializing in your schedule. You need to have a social life, and you also need to have balance in your life.
17. *Eat properly.* Running on empty makes your day seem longer, and your tasks seem more difficult.
18. *Review your notes every day.* You'll reinforce what you've learned, so you need less time to study. You'll also be ready if your professor calls on you in class, or gives a pop quiz.
19. *Let friends know your schedule.* If phone calls are proving to be a distraction, for example, tell your friends that you take social calls from 7:00 - 8:00 p.m. It may sound silly, but it helps.
20. *Keep it all in perspective.* Setting goals that are unrealistic sets you up for failure. While it's good to set high goals for yourself, be sure not to overdo it. Set goals that are difficult, yet attainable.

NCAA Intervention

When you enroll in a college or university program, the NCAA is keenly interested in this one question — *can a student-athlete be successful at his respective college or university?*

Over the last few years, the NCAA has intervened and created firm standards for academic performance among member institutions.

Programs with incentive and disincentives have been created to reward sport teams that do well academically, while penalizing those that do not. Their goal is to encourage improvement of academic performance of all student-athletes on all sports teams.

The NCAA requires member institutions to distribute graduation rates to prospective student-athletes and/or their parent(s) or guardian(s) to ensure athletes and their families are made aware of the academic reputation of the institutions they are considering.

Recruits considering various universities should answer two important questions: which institution will provide the best academic experience, and second, which will provide the best athletic experience?

Barriers

One of the most common barriers toward academic success for student-athletes is — *peer pressure!*

Any reluctance toward seeking counseling can be either internal, like being an introvert, or external, like succumbing to peer pressure and stress.

External Barriers

Forces beyond the control of student-athletes may also contribute to the under utilization of counseling and student services.

Barriers from the college or university may inhibit the help-seeking behavior of student-athletes. Institutions may assume a cautious role and choose not to offer additional support services to their student-athletes for fear of violating NCAA sanctions.

The perception of student-athletes as being over-privileged has many programs cautious that they are not viewed as providing too many benefits to student-athletes. Universities may assume that the athletic department and programs will handle issues and concerns of athletes.

Team Commitments

Practice and competition may dramatically reduce the amount of free time a student-athlete has available for seeking needed academic services. This is on top of the demands academic schedules place upon them. They may be unable to sacrifice athletic or academic time to seek help for personal problems and often, by default, turn to their coaches and teammates for the help and support they need.

A working knowledge of barriers that might factor into a student-athlete's decision to seek counseling can help counselors better respond to their unique challenges and concerns. Counselors can help you overcome internal barriers to seeking help by promoting the connection between mental and physical health.

The counselor should be sure to focus on several areas key to successful therapy:
1. Establishing rapport with the student-athlete helps develop a sense of team that translates well into their everyday lives.
2. Encouraging students to share their problems and openly engage in conversation sessions, should be an early goal.
3. Stressing confidentiality due to the factors previously mentioned.

However, you can lead a horse to water, but you can't make him drink. Thus, the individual student-athlete must have the desire and open-mindedness to receive legitimate academic assistance.

In other words, you certainly must apply yourself!

Yet, many times a student-athlete can't do that on their own, or just don't know how. That's when student services come into play.

Academic Skills Help You Succeed in Sports

Many sports rely on logic and memorization, two very important components of math and other school courses.

By improving your math skills through studying and doing your homework/course work, you will be exercising your brain to work fast in the problem solving situations you face during most team sports, such as football and basketball.

These sports require players to interact and think fast to reach the final goal — winning. Math and reading assignments help prepare students to think logically and quickly in these and other real-life situations.

Academics Teach Focus

Academics also help athletes to stay focused.

Learning to study and do homework while on a noisy bus on the way to or from a game will certainly teach you how to block unnecessary distractions.

This is a valuable skill for all student-athletes. The practice of blocking out distractions while studying will serve you well in the classroom and elsewhere.

Skills for Now — Skills for Later

Did you know? As of this writing, college basketball athletes only need to pass six hours in fall to remain eligible for the second half! Obviously, the schools are using the athletes and the athletes are using the schools right back, making it exceedingly difficult for student-athletes to focus on academics at the end of a semester.

Performing well academically will motivate you to succeed in life.

The vast majority of elementary through high school student-athletes are not going to become professional athletes. This means that you need to start to prepare today for whatever career you choose for tomorrow.

Even if you have what it takes to become a professional athlete, you will greatly benefit from your degree of choice, and the math, reading, and writing skills you attained that are necessary to complete personal tasks such as paying bills, balancing bank accounts, paying taxes, and understanding financial markets, among other things.

If an injury, for example, forces the end your athletic career, you will always have the skills and education you need to have a successful life after sports.

Your college degree will serve you well — long after your athletic career is over!

What Parents Can Do

The importance of academics for student-athletes must start early and — *AT HOME!*

The foundation that fathers and mothers set early on will ultimately determine the attitudes of their child student-athletes when they reach the collegiate level.

Where should it all begin? *In elementary school!*

More can be done at the elementary and high school levels in continuing to encourage academic excellence from those involved in extracurricular activities, not just athletics specifically. The key for parents of student-athletes in helping them with the transition into college is choosing the right college or university that offers a balance of both academics and athletics.

Parents can create a list of questions for a potential school, such as, what is the school's academic reputation? Does the school offer support services, such as a writing center, academic advising center, and computer facilities?

Data has shown the individual student-athlete has suffered from an educational system that has not prepared him or her well for institutions of higher learning.

Their training through the educational system has left a number of students with inadequate skills necessary for academic success in college. At the same time, academic excellence is oftentimes not encouraged or viewed as important in the home.

Set Priorities

The first thing a parent can help their young student-athlete with is setting priorities. Sit down together and list the important elements in your child's life. Explain to him/her that family comes first, schoolwork second, and sports third.

Be realistic. Inform them that sports are going to take a lot of time and energy.

Parents must allow children who want to play sports to pursue their athletic hopes and dreams, but should not forget that education comes first. When student-athletes have a great support system in place at home, it helps them put all the distractions in proper perspective and allows them to focus.

Get Real

Once priorities have been established, you and your child should work out daily, weekly, and season-long schedules. First, make a list of your child's after-school activities, athletic and otherwise, in order of importance. Then decide how much time will be required for each activity — such as homework, guitar lessons, practice, games, and driving to and from all of the activities.

Once you have a realistic view of what you are dealing with, help your child work out a schedule that makes time for everything, including having fun!

Consider setting aside a fixed period every day for homework. During that time, *turn off* the TV, cell phones, computer, video and hand-held games *(Pokemon, Nintendo, PlayStation, and Xbox 360 can wait until later)*.

If your child finishes their homework, he can use the remaining time to read or work on future assignments. Also, encourage your child to tackle their most difficult homework assignments first, ideally before late afternoon practices, so they will remain fresh and energized for learning.

Communicate

Combined and consistent communication among parents, athletes, and teachers is essential for striking a balance between school work and sports.

Parents should let coaches know as soon as possible if their young athlete has to miss a practice or a game — for a doctor's appointment, makeup test or quiz, religious holiday, or simply spending quality time with a parent, for example. Coaches should also try to adjust their schedules accordingly also.

Parents can serve as good role models by setting priorities at home and sticking to them. Athletes who do well in their scholarly pursuits should also be viewed as role models.

Parents should urge schools to continue to give special awards to student-athletes who maintain high grade-point averages.

A Privilege, Not a Right

Student-athletes must meet their responsibilities, including keeping up their school work.

Participation in a school's sports program is a privilege, not a right. A high school counselor, for example, can meet with parents and students before the season begins and outline the expectations for students and suggest ways in which parents can help their children succeed, academically and athletically.

Balancing the demands of school and sports isn't easy. But your child will benefit by developing good time-management skills. These skills will not only help your child study better and play better, but they will also serve your child long after his or her days as a student-athlete are over.

Five Tips for Parents of Young Athletes

1. Let the coach know about your child's other commitments, if any.
2. Encourage your child to get homework done early, after coming home from school.
3. Set aside a certain period every day for quiet study.
4. Watch for signs of burnout, like falling grades, diminished interest in other activities, and fatigue.
5. Work with coaches and school officials to minimize sports interference with academics.

Looking Ahead

Athletics has a history of importance in American society.

Across the country, newspapers and websites have devoted entire sections, and television programs have created entire channels dedicated to covering the latest updates on sports.

Attention has not always been solely about games and competitions. The spotlight has recently been redirected to academics.

Shining light on the area of academics may not only increase the number of athletic departments offering specialized academic support services and monitoring strategies, but may also increase the academic success of individual student-athletes.

Pressure placed on athletes to win may have a detrimental effect on the student's commitment to be successful in the classroom, giving them the perception that athletics are more important. Recognizing areas of potential struggle might be valuable in helping facilitate academic services for them.

Perhaps it is not just a matter of academic support services and study halls; rather the trend is directly related to role conflicts and adjustments to collegiate life student-athletes commonly experience.

The NCAA has been *proactive* in establishing programs to try to help ensure student-athlete success.

Besides the thrill of competing and learning how both wins and losses parallel many of life's lessons, the single largest associated benefit of athletic competition for scholarship athletes is the opportunity to earning a valuable degree.

Components and Resources

Although the following components of an academic support system are certainly not inclusive, the items listed below are fundamental and essential to the development of a good academic support system.

- *Student-athletes.* The better the academic quality of the students involved, the easier the job of academic support. But standardized test scores and high school grades cannot measure a student's desire or maturity. A poor high-school grade point average and low standardized test scores can be transformed into good college grades through dedication and an athlete's naturally competitive spirit.

However, student-athletes can also be somewhat pampered or sheltered before college, and the rigors of athletic demands and poor time management can contribute to academic underachievement.

- *Faculty.* Faculty members are the true first line of communication regarding a student-athlete's academic performance. If communication and trust are fostered, everyone benefits.
- *Athletic counselors.* Roles of athletic counselors vary, often involving eligibility issues, personal counseling and academic advice, and simply being a positive supporter. Athletic counselors should meet regularly with all student-athletes. Listening skills, trust, and respect are key ingredients to a successful relationship between a student-athlete and a counselor.
- *Tutors.* Tutors can play a huge role in the academic success of student-athletes. Careful screening, knowledge of subject, clear and concise tutoring rules, a system of checks and balances that can be enforced and monitored, and regular evaluations are critical elements for success. Make sure tutors understand and maintain ethical standards of their college or university. Tutors must NOT be tempted to do coursework for an athlete! Unfortunately, this does happen.
- *Computer resources.* Maximizing academic success without adequate computer support is difficult. The ready availability of computers for student-athletes to use to complete academic assignments can be critical.
- *Nurturing a study environment.* Successful academic support centers tend to have a dedicated study area where student-athletes can study in a quiet environment with easy access to both computers and tutors.
- *Nutrition.* A healthy diet equals a healthy mind and body!

<u>College athletes and agents</u>. Current NCAA rules permit student-athletes to have advisers, but those advisers/agents are NOT allowed to be part of ANY negotiation process, like negotiating a future endorsement agreement with a sports gear company, taking money from an adviser or agent, or an adviser/agent doing favors for you and your family in clear violation of NCAA rules, for example. And if they are doing this, which does continue to happen, unknowingly to the athlete or not, you could be found in violation of NCAA rules and lose your remaining eligibility.

Beware! If something doesn't feel right...just say *"No thanks!"*

I strongly believe this entire book would make a tremendously valuable and beneficial required college course, or as an elective, for student-athletes as part of a curriculum of an undergraduate program, whereby student-athletes would be required to pass the courses in order to graduate.

This book would also be available in college and university student bookstores.

The courses would be taught at the Division-1A level, Department of Sociology. Sociology is the study of the dynamics and consequences of social life.

It would include in-depth discussion about the issues that face college and professional athletes.

Speakers (myself included) would be brought in to share their stories, experiences, successes and failures as a tool to help student-athletes understand and appreciate the opportunities you have.

As an author, public speaker, consultant, character coach and mentor, I know how important it is to give our young student-athletes tools that better prepare them for — *THE REAL WORLD* — through continued education and awareness.

Let's change the way college athletes think about academics!

Play Hard. Study Hard.™

Chapter 11
3RD DOWN AND GOD

#1 Spiritual Guide for Athletes™

"When you talk to God — don't talk to Him about how big your problems are. Talk to your problems about how big your God is!"
– David L. Brown

Life's 3rd Downs

Reading this chapter won't change your life. Applying it will.

I saw a quote on a church sign one day while driving in my city.

"Never give the devil a ride. He'll want to do the driving."

How true!

When athletes encounter 3rd downs in life, as we all inevitably do, you still have options. When you're at that moment of truth, you're at 3rd down. You have an opportunity to advance forward. You can choose to do the right thing, or not.

Choose the right thing, it's first down — life is good. Make a poor choice — now it's 4th down and your opportunities become limited.

In football, championship winning teams consistently convert on 3rd down. Don't put yourself and your career in a 4th down meltdown, no matter what sport you play. Don't give up your power, your dreams, and possibly your freedom. Have the right attitude — make the right choice on 3rd down and let God guide you.

Your success in life and sports is built on the foundation of character, and character is the result of hundreds and hundreds of choices you make that gradually turn who you are at any given moment into who you want to be.

If your decision making process is not based on good character, moral conduct and spirituality, you could be labeled as being a "character" instead of having it. Character isn't something you are born with and can't change, like who your biological father and mother are. It's something you must take responsibility for forming.

The really amazing thing about character is that, if you're sincerely committed to making yourself into the person and athlete you want to be, you'll not only create those qualities, you'll strengthen them and re-create them in abundance, even as you're drawing on them each and every day. That's why building your spiritual character is vital to becoming all you can be as a person and an athlete.

This chapter addresses the hope for athletes on all levels to address your spiritual thoughts and feelings as it relates to your life and athletic career.

Who Are You?

This is a powerful question most of us ask ourselves at some point in life. What is it that you should do with your life? What is your purpose in life, your passion?

This chapter helps you discover — or strengthen, what the meaning of your life is, and helps you realize how to find purpose of life, and how to live your passion through Jesus Christ.

To find your purpose, you must first realize that you have choices.

What is the collective spirit of your past, present, and future? What's your MVP — Most Valuable Purpose — or Most Valuable Passion? Why are you here, and what did God put you on this earth to achieve as an athlete and human being?

Having a purpose in your life is like a spiritual experience.

- Realize what you value in life.
- Figure out what your passion is.
- Get an idea what your purpose in life could be.

Open your eyes and your heart to a side of life and sport that is often downplayed — the side of love, generosity, and gratitude, and the belief in God. Through Him, you can continue to build a career and life around honor, dedication, persistence, passion, love, and connection to the divine guidance within each of you.

A fundamental message that your purpose in life is to love — to give love and receive love, to contribute your heart and soul to your "game," and to honor the passion and dreams that live at the core of who you are.

A life of purpose or a purpose driven life?

That satisfying and fulfilling way to live that we all seek eludes many athletes. Lacking a life mission and direction, we chase material goods, money, and power, yet yearn for the satisfaction and fulfillment of living a life of meaning, a life of internal reward and satisfaction.

What is success? Success is the steady progression toward a worthy ideal. Success is making good choices in your life. Success is the ability to love, enjoy your work, and have fun in your life. Success is making a difference, a positive difference. Success is making the world a little bit better because you existed. And success begins with purpose.

One of the keys to success is the belief in a mission. A mission is your purpose for living. A mission supersedes goal setting. A mission gives your life meaning. All men and women who are successful and high achievers are people who seem to lose themselves in a commitment that is bigger than they are; they are turned on by a purpose or a mission.

We ask ourselves, "Who am I?" "Why am I here?" and "What is my life all about?" We look for answers that give us direction and knowledge that provides a life plan. Instead, we're advised to ask, "What do I want?" but get confused by the multitude of "material wants" that marketers bombard us with each and every day.

The following questions will assist you in discovering and articulating your passions.

1. What do I most often give to others?
2. What do I have the most fun doing?
3. What do others look to me for?
4. What am I most often complimented on?
5. What do the people closest to me say my passions are?
6. What ideas, things, places and/or people am I most inspired by?
7. What do I love to do that makes the world a better place or in some way contributes to the lives of others?
8. What is the most profound experience I would like someone to receive as a result of any interaction with me?
9. What is the most important quality or guidance that I did NOT receive enough of as a child?
10. How does it feel when I create or share that quality or guidance with someone else?

Observe — Accept — Change

Without judging yourself, take a moment and look around at your surroundings.

You have created this environment, consciously or subconsciously. It mirrors who you are right now, not who you wish to be, nor who you could be, but who you are now. What does it tell you about YOU? If what you see in your surroundings suggests inner states of being that surprise, shock, or disappoint you, don't judge them as wrong or bad.

Accept them, and acknowledge that the life you're manifesting is not the life you'd like to create, and then move on to thoughts of how to create what you really do want. And keep working to master a quiet mind. One of the keys to finding your purpose in life is to be able to understand yourself better.

How would you describe yourself?

Are you a risk taker? Are you persuasive, intuitive, or excitable? Are you cautious, controlled, or fact-oriented? Are you relaxed, friendly, or conciliatory?

By answering these questions it helps you to better understand your motives and what excites you.

Some other important questions to ask yourself:
- What activities are most important to me?
- What things would I most like to change about my life?
- What would I do if I had no limitations and knew I could not fail?
- How would I like to be remembered when I leave this life?

Some athletes today have lost their way, and their focus. They have wandered.

They have wandered away from their own path of heart, passion and spirituality. They've lost sight of the adventure and challenge in doing what excites them. Many other athletes do follow their hearts, do pursue their passions, and do remain true to their dreams with passion and focus. In so doing, they provide a model that the world desperately needs.

It's playing the sport you love that brings pleasure, and continuing to learn, grow, and evolve. Discovering your purpose means finding out who you are and striving to be that person all the time. Once you've developed a purpose for your life, it becomes easier to set and achieve your goals, because you will know what you really want.

You will have goals that allow you to do what you really enjoy, and when this happens you will have already become a success. This is not to say that you won't have challenges and problems. You will. But when you're doing things the right way, with the right attitude, facing those problems and challenges will be much easier.

Athletes have a unique set of authentic gifts which can only truly flourish when you associate with like-minded people who cherish you and accept you for who you are. Find the teams, teammates, coaches, friends, and relationships with whom you belong. Don't stop until you do.

Ask yourself these questions:

- Am I on the right team?
- Does it feel like home for me?
- Do I hang out with people who bring out my highest, best self?
- Do I like myself when I'm with friends and teammates?
- Do I experience myself as an awesome human being with the people currently in my life?

If your answers are yes, congratulations — you are on a path to fulfillment, joy, contribution, and spirituality.

If your answers are no, or you're just not sure, it is time to begin the most important search of your life. You are not an island. You are co-created in the presence of those who walk the path of life with you. To realize the full potential of your life, you need "family," who honor and love you. Find your home. It's worth everything.

Consider that dedication and persistence are the trademarks of success and the access to fulfilling your dreams. Athletes are masters at this. You don't quit, and you persevere through setbacks, injuries, and disappointing performances.

When you persist, you triumph. When your dedication is true, you prevail. It's important to see the connection between persistence and dedication.

Dedication is the fire that fuels persistence. Look at the lives of the athletes you most admire — what they've accomplished, and what they have endured to become who they are. Their lives have not been without challenges, for there are challenges in any life path.

The winners are those who persist, who do not see trials as roadblocks to their dreams, but only as "This is what I must deal with today." In the face of setbacks and poor performance, you will discover the strength of your dedication and spirituality.

Be crystal clear on your dreams. Hold these dreams powerfully in your heart, and imagine yourself fulfilling them confidently, brilliantly, joyfully, and spiritually. Your ability to summon persistence when you most need it hinges on the strength of your faith and dedication.

Purpose

Someone once said there are two great days in life – the day you are born and the day you discover why you were born.

Success is knowing your purpose in life and working toward that purpose each day.

Consider the wonderful and popular story of a hammer. It's designed to hit nails. That's what it was created to do. Now imagine that the hammer never gets used. It just sits in the toolbox.

The hammer doesn't care.

But now imagine that same hammer with a soul, a self-consciousness. Days and days go by with him (or her) remaining in the toolbox.

He feels funny inside, but he's not exactly sure why. Something is missing, but he doesn't know what it is.

Then one day someone pulls him out of the toolbox and uses his claw to pull construction staples from wooden boards. The hammer is exhilarated. Being held, being wielded, pulling out a bunch of staples — the hammer loves it.

At the end of the day, though, he is still unfulfilled. Pulling staples from boards was fun, but it wasn't enough.

Something is still missing. In the days that follow, he's used often. He gently bangs a hubcap back into place, blasts through some drywall, knocks a table leg back into place. Still, he's left unfulfilled.

He longs for more action. He wants to be used as much as possible to knock things around, to break things, to blast things. He figures that he just hasn't had enough of these events to satisfy him.

Then one day someone uses him on a *NAIL!*

Suddenly, the lights come on in his hammer soul. He now understands what he was truly designed for. He was meant to hit nails. All the other things he hit and pulled pale in comparison.

He now knows what his hammer soul was searching for all along.

We are created in God's image for a relationship with him. Being in that relationship is the only thing that will ultimately satisfy our souls. Until we come to know God, we may have had many wonderful experiences, but haven't hit a nail. We've been used for some noble purposes, but not the one we were ultimately designed for, not the one through which we will find the most fulfillment. A relationship with God is the only thing that will quench our soul's longing.

Jesus Christ said, "I am the bread of life. He who comes to me will never go hungry, and he who believes in me will never be thirsty." Until we come to know God, we are hungry and thirsty in life. We try to "eat" and "drink" all kinds of things to satisfy our hunger and thirst, yet they remain.

We are like the hammer. We don't realize what will end the emptiness, the lack of fulfillment in our lives.

Usually, when we keep God out, we try to find fulfillment in something other than Him, but we can never get enough of that thing. We keep "eating" or "drinking" more and more, erroneously thinking that "more' is the answer to the problem, yet we are never ultimately satisfied.

Our greatest desire is to know God, to have a relationship with God. Why? Because that's how we've been designed.

Have you hit a nail yet?

Here are ten tips for hitting that nail:

1. Apply life purpose in the here and now.
2. Have a clear and complete vision of the dream (two, five, or even ten years down the line).
3. Have a practical plan for how to get there, and take the practical steps.
4. One need not know all the steps or exactly how to realize complete success.
5. As long as the first few steps are outlined and taken, the rest will become clear along the road to fulfilling your highest passion.
6. Consider what is "uniquely" you and what you offer.
7. When you help others, how do you do it? What effect does it have on others? Do you help others discover their own truth?
8. Ask yourself, "How did I arrive at my purpose?"
9. Be true to yourself, discovering your authenticity and your unique way of achieving a self-determining life, doing your own thing, finding and following your own passion.
10. Learn self-love first and everything else will take care of itself.

Remember...God's got your back. Never take Him for granted.

Many athletes kneel and pray after scoring a touchdown, or gather in a group prayer after a hard-fought game. Some athletes look up to the sky and point upward, as if to acknowledge God. Others thank God after winning the game.

Either way, they are competitors who attribute success to their religious faith. For athletes who maintain their Christian principles on and off the field, the stereotype they sometimes carry is that of a timid, weak competitor, which is far from the truth.

For some athletes, it's easy to lose your self control in a game. But know that faith will help keep you focused. Mental toughness can provide the winning edge. Never see your faith as keeping yourself from winning, rather view it as the reason you are winning, on and off the field and court.

And yet, some people still consider such athletes weak because they hold onto their faith in a secular world. Athletes aren't "soft" because they're Christians. Athletes who live and play by faith understand that playing aggressive is fine, but when the game is over you move on and remember that in the end...it's just a game.

In many ways, sports represent the very best of the human spirit. And yet, some may find it odd to suggest a connection between sports and spirituality, as though these are two completely distinct facets of human life, without any bearing upon each other whatsoever.

The connection between sport and spirituality might seem hard to see at first. But there is a pronounced — though usually hidden — psychic and spiritual aspect to sport, which the best sportsmen and sportswomen are familiar with, even though they may not use the word "spiritual" to describe it.

It's possible to say that, depending on your definition of spirituality, the desire to experience spiritual well-being is one reason we play sports.

Sport is important because it's one of the most readily available ways of generating the state of being "in tune." It's a state of being that athletes experience when your attention is completely absorbed in an activity and you become oblivious of your surroundings. It's what you experience when you fully concentrate and make powerful mental efforts, and when you perform challenging, stimulating, creative activities.

It allows you to take control of your own consciousness and step beyond that which is considered a "normal state."

Make a Change

Imagine for a moment that you're building a house.

You hire a contractor, but he never consults the blueprints drawn up by your architect or designer. He works without a plan. An unwise move, because the contractor needs to know where to lay the foundation, erect the walls and place the windows.

Only then will the home look the way it was intended.

The same can be said of life. How can you try to build your life without first consulting the great architect of life, the one who created us for a wonderful purpose? The Bible says, "We know that God causes everything to work together for the good of those who love God and are called according to His purpose for them." (Romans 8:28)

Furthermore, there is more to be gained by living according to God's plan. True fulfillment and meaning in life is found in God. By asking Jesus, God's son, to be the biggest part of your life, you will discover the very purpose for which God created you.

There is no thing and no one else who can do this; no religion, no philosophy, no person. Just Jesus. He said of Himself, "I am the way, the truth and the life. No one comes to the Father except through me." (John 14:6)

Power to change is about one thing — knowing God.

Here are four principles to help you discover how you can begin a relationship with God and experience power to change.

1. God loves you and offers a wonderful plan for your life.
2. God created you. Not only that, He loves you so much that he wants you to spend eternity with Him. Jesus said, "For God so loved the world that He gave his only Son so that everyone who believes in Him will not perish, but have eternal life." (John 3:16)
3. Jesus came so that each of us could know and understand God in a personal way. Jesus alone can bring meaning and purpose to your life.
4. All of us are sinful and separated from God. Therefore, we cannot know and experience God's love and plan for our life. The fact is, we need Jesus. The Bible says, "…all fall short of God's glorious standard." (Romans 3:23)

Though God intended for us to have a relationship with Him, we naturally want to do things our own way. We're stubborn, selfish, and frequently unable to follow through on our promises. Try as we might, we just keep stumbling. Deep down, our attitude may be one of active rebellion or passive indifference, but it's all evidence of what the Bible calls sin, an old archery term which literally means "missing the mark."

The Bible says the result of sin in our lives is death, spiritual separation from God. (Romans 6:23) Although we may try to reach God through our own effort, we inevitably fail.

In the Zone

Athletes often speak of being *"in the zone."* These are moments when suddenly everything "clicks" and you shift to a higher level of performance and become capable of astounding feats.

Without even trying very hard, everything seems naturally and inevitably perfect. Time moves slower than normal, and is often the main reason why an athlete is capable of such astounding feats.

He or she has more time to play with, more time to anticipate his opponents' actions and to position yourself. Experiences like these are usually temporary, but it seems that the best athletes are always *"in the zone"* to a degree, or at least have the ability to step into it.

Why is it that sport has this seeming power to generate spiritual states of being *"in the zone?"*

Perhaps the best answer is to compare it to a more traditional method of inducing spiritual states, the practice of meditation. We can look at meditation as a method of intensifying — and purifying — what you could call our "consciousness energy."

This is the energy of our being, our vitality or life force. In our daily lives there is a constant outward flow of this energy. It's used up by the "thought chatter" that continually runs through our minds, by the efforts we make to absorb and process the massive amount of sensory information we're bombarded with every day, and to perform the activities which our lives are filled with.

As a result, there's usually little of this energy left inside us. When we meditate, all this changes. By sitting in a quiet room, on your own, and closing your eyes, you have already "plugged" three of the normal ways in which consciousness energy drains away (processing information, interacting with other athletes and activity).

As you concentrate, this "thought chatter" naturally fades away until — hopefully — it stops altogether, and you experience a sense of complete mental stillness and peace.

There is now a higher than normal level of consciousness energy within you. You have retained it rather than letting it get away from you. Your consciousness energy is no longer being monopolized by your instincts, emotions, desires and mental activity.

Therefore, it's able to rise to the highest level, resulting in a spiritual state of being…*"in the zone."*

Your Spiritual State

Sport can be a kind of spontaneous spiritual practice.

And for those who, for cultural or social reasons, don't have the opportunity or the desire to follow an actual spiritual path, it's probably very significant in this regard, since it's a way of adding a spiritual dimension to your lives.

Even if we do follow a spiritual path, activities like sport should still be important to us.

In the end, the connection between sport and spirituality reminds us of what spiritual teachers have always insisted: that instead of just being "spiritual" for the half an hour or so that we sit down to meditate, we should try to integrate spirituality into every aspect of our lives. Even the most mundane aspects of our lives are potentially divine and offer us the opportunity to taste spiritual well-being.

What are the signs that you are living your life with passion and purpose? How can you tell if you're on the right track, on the way, or got it going on?

You'll know when…

- You're totally obsessed with what you're doing. Time just flies by, and you're on a "high" when you're doing the "thing" you love. To you it's not "work" at all because you're enjoying every moment and spending your time doing exactly what excites and makes you happy. It's what gets you "bursting" out of bed in the morning, and when you're away from it you can't wait to get back to it.
- You're totally hyper-focused and in a trance-like state when you're doing what you love. You feel like you've been transported elsewhere, and your immunity to distraction is on "high." Often, you may not hear people around you speaking to you, and only realize when you find yourself being roused and brought back to the sound of the words, "Are you listening to me? Hey, did you hear what I just said?"

- You've got a strong underlying belief, all the while, that this IS definitely what you're meant to do.
- You keep a strong clear vision afloat all the time of where you want to get to, even when you're tired and exhausted, events and circumstances aren't flowing, things seem to not be going your way, and people are against you.
- You just keep going when the going gets tough, and keep getting up and on with it.
- You surprise even yourself at your unfailing persistence to keep going, and feel propelled by this inner life force that is driving you.
- Despite the hurdles, trials, tribulations and frustrations, you look back with a smile, knowing that you've really enjoyed the experience anyway. You know deep down inside that you're going somewhere worthwhile and what you're doing has meaning and purpose.
- Things just seem to fall into place easily, and just happen "serendipitously." People appear, telephone calls come, offers of support and guidance are present, new relevant resources are introduced to you. You stop for a moment, and you're in the right mindset to see and understand what's happening. You then smile and muse with sincere pleasing satisfaction.
- You see that what you do makes a real difference in the lives of others beyond what you imagined. You give real value. Their feedback says it all, and you're constantly amazed with great humility.
- Sometimes you have a clear vision of what you want, but the pathway there isn't always clear. As chapters unfold and phases roll out and define themselves in your life, ones you didn't even expect, you stay open to guidance.

Doesn't it make sense that if you LOVE what you're doing you'll do it more often, more easily, and keep getting better at it?

When you do that, the value you give to others will grow amazingly and exponentially. The key is to start doing what you love NOW. Take action! Make yourself immune to distraction! Get on track and be committed, have good judgment — and make good choices!

Granted, success may not find you overnight, but over the course of time it's entirely possible, and it's happening all the time.

If others can do it, so can you!

There will be nothing more satisfying than turning your calling, purpose, and passion into a rewarding and prosperous athletic career that you love doing, every single day, and to live the life you were meant to live.

How cool is that? *Very cool.*

Accept Him

Jesus is God's solution to the problem of human imperfection and evil. Because of Jesus' death on the cross, we don't have to be separated from God any longer.

Jesus paid the price for our sin, and in so doing, bridged the gap between us and God. Instead of trying harder to reach God, we simply need to accept Jesus and his sacrifice as the one way to God.

Jesus said, "I am the resurrection and the life. Those who believe in me, even though they die like everyone else, will live again. They are given eternal life for believing in me, and will never perish." (John 11:25-26)

Not only did Jesus die for our sin, He rose from the dead. (1 Corinthians 15:3-6) When He did, He proved beyond doubt that He can rightfully promise eternal life, that He is the son of God and the only means by which we can know God.

Yet, just having knowledge about God's plans and purposes isn't enough. We need to consciously accept Jesus Christ as the payment for our sin and welcome Him into our life.

It is not enough just to know these three truths...

1. We must individually accept Jesus Christ as Savior and Lord, then we can know and experience God's love and plan for our life. The Bible says, "But to all who believed Him and accepted Him, he gave the right to become children of God." (John 1:12)

2. We accept Jesus by faith. The Bible says, "God saved you by His special favor when you believed. And you can't take credit for this; it is a gift from God. Salvation is not a reward for the good things we have done, so none of us can boast about it." (Ephesians 2:8,9)

3. Accepting Jesus means first believing that Jesus is who He claimed to be, then inviting Him to take the control of our lives and make us into new people. (John 3:1-8) Jesus said, "I'm standing at the door and I'm knocking. If anyone hears my voice and opens the door, I will come in." (Revelation 3:20)

How will you respond to God's invitation? What will you do with the claims of Jesus Christ?

Consider these two principles:

Self-directed Life
- Self is on the throne.
- Jesus is outside the life.
- Interests are directed by self, often resulting in frustration.

Christ-directed Life
- Jesus is in the life and on the throne.
- Self is yielding to Jesus.
- Interests are directed by Jesus, resulting in harmony with God.

Which direction best represents your life as a person and athlete? Which direction would you like to have representing your life?

Choosing to submit your life to God is the most significant decision you can ever make.

This choice involves more than simple intellectual agreement that Jesus is God and that He died on the cross to pay the penalty for your sins.

Becoming a Christian also requires that you commit the rest of your life to God, to do what He asks of you and to live in accordance with His principles.

This decision is not something to be taken lightly. It requires sacrifice and a total re-orientation of your life around God rather than yourself.

As Jesus said, "If anyone would come after me, he must deny himself and take up his cross daily and follow me." (Luke 9:23)

If you feel you are ready to make this commitment, you can do so right now by telling God you are sorry for your past mistakes, putting your trust in Him, and asking Him to make you into the person He created you to be.

This step involves faith. You probably still have a number of unanswered questions at this point. You must be willing to make the decision based on what you know right now and trust God to fill in the details later. The precise words you use to commit yourself to God are not important. He knows the intentions of your heart.

Your prayer can be as simple as *"Help!"* or it can focus on an issue that is specific to your situation.

If you are unsure of what to pray, use the following sample prayer to get started.

> *"Jesus, I want to know you. I want you to come into my life. I'm sorry for the things I've done that have broken my relationship with God. Only You can give me the power to change and become the person You created me to be. Thank you for forgiving my past mistakes and for giving me eternal life with God. I give my life to You. Please do with it as You wish. Amen."*

However – action speaks louder than words.

By praying the above prayer, or one similar to it, you have just taken a giant step toward making God the center of your life. What follows is a lifelong journey of change and growth as you get to know God better through Bible reading, prayer and interaction with other Christians.

If you prayed the prayer above and invited Jesus into your life, you've become a Christian, which simply means, "Christ in one."

Congratulations...and may God bless you always.

"David-isms"

David-isms are spiritual words of wisdom and otherwise, from author, David L. Brown.

"Don't just exist, survive, then die. Make a difference. Leave a legacy."

"He is who He says He is. He does what He says He's going to do — so just keep the faith."

"Each and every new day is an opportunity to be better than you were yesterday."

"Don't sweat the little stuff! There will be plenty of 'Big Stuff' you will have to deal with in the course of your life, so save your energy for those."

"It's not a 'stroke of genius' — it's a stroke of J-E-S-U-S!"

"It's about giving God a high-five, a fist-bump, a jumping or standing chest bump, or a jumping full body bump. It's about acknowledging Him, praising Him, and thanking Him for all your blessings, big and small, to appreciate them all, even in troubled times, and not take any of them for granted."

"You work hard to "get." You don't "get" without the work."

P.O.I.S.E = "The PATIENCE to overcome OBSTACLES that can INTERFERE with your ability to be a SUCCESS in EVERYTHING you do."

On making good choices: "It's not always about making 'big' choices and decisions. It's like depositing your money into your savings account and reaping the rewards of compound interest. You can deposit a little bit here and there, maybe more on some days. The more you put in, even in small amounts, the more you'll have in the end. Making good 'small' choices and decisions will serve you well when the 'big' ones come around."

"Uncertainty is often uncomfortable -- sometimes painful. When you can't see the road ahead it can be stressful. However, uncertainty also has an upside. It's the fertile ground that's needed to foster creativity, growth, progress, and success. Not being able to see the road ahead means you've got an opportunity to CREATE it. Uncertainty gives you a choice -- to be paralyzed by fear or to be inspired to action. The more often you're able to put inspiration to action in the face of doubt -- to do something that builds momentum, the better positioned you'll be for long-term success."

To college student-athletes: "Think about your life as a whole, and realize four-years, or sometimes less, of being a student-athlete is a mere microcosm when compared to the entirety of your life expectancy. Make the most of your college careers -- make it count. Those years go by really fast."

"An athlete getting into trouble is like being upside down on your mortgage. You owe more than it's worth, and if you don't make your payments, the bank will foreclose on you. When an athlete is upside down, and your career has more questions than answers, if you don't do the rights things afterward to make it right, your team and league may eventually foreclose on your athletic career."

"Before you take one step inside that night club, bar, strip club, or late night party, reflect on the potential dangers and consequences and ask yourself...is it really worth it? Like taking out the trash in your home, you must focus on keeping your mental and emotional "house" free of trash also. Are any emotional issues of the past hindering you from making good decisions in your life and career?"

Athletes making mistakes: "We all make mistakes at various points in our lives. No one is perfect. However, when you're a public figure like today's athletes are, fair or not, your mistakes are MAGNIFIED."

"When you play hard and do good, you win."

"When you work hard and do good, you win."

"When you live right and do good, you win."

"Play Hard. Be Good.™"

"Think big. Give big. Do good. Live well."

"Want to be an all-star? Be viewed as an all-star by what you do on AND off the field and court!"

"Your attitude is the control center of your entire life."

"Stop. Think. Do the right thing."

"The key to happiness: Quality of life. Not quantity of strife."

"Have you ever stopped and watched a turtle go about its business? When our lives are going 100 miles an hour, turtles teach us to slow down and reflect on what really matters. Forget about stopping to smell the roses...stop and watch a turtle!"

On the subject of character in sports and life: "It's not about being perfect. It's about making good choices."

"Current and future athletes should not be judged solely by their athletic talents, skills, and accomplishments, but by the substance of their character, on and off their playing surface."

"Jesus is the greatest coach and motivational speaker of all time. His playbook (the Bible) confirms that, if you believe in it and follow his words."

"Everything you do and say is a direct reflection of who you are."

"I don't believe in the term 'self-made.' No one achieves success by themselves and without the help of others. Someone, somewhere along the way believed in you and me, after or before we believed in ourselves."

"I don't believe in the term 'late bloomer.' I believe God places all of us in the right place, at the right time, for the best benefits in our lives...in His due season. It took me nearly forty-eight years to discover my true passion; what God put me on this earth to do -- write."

On peer pressure: "Just be yourself and have faith in the rest."

"Help God shower you with His abundant blessings and favor. Help Him help you by keeping the faith and making good choices in your sports and personal life. Remember, it's about C.H.O.I.C.E — Courage. Honesty. Opportunity. Integrity. Competition. Excellence."

"Some say change must start from the ground up. That may be true for some things. For me, God inspires change from head to toe, beginning with our mind and how we think about things, the choices we make each day, and the attitude we carry along with it."

"Our actions, as a result of displaying good judgment and making good choices, basically amount to two things. They are either worthy or they're worthless. Wouldn't you rather strive to make worthy decisions rather than worthless decisions that will discredit your good name, your family, your friends, your team and your league? Do the right things in your life that will result in worthiness instead of worthlessness."

"I once met a woman who told me she had no health insurance, no auto insurance, and not much money. I encouraged her to keep the faith and remain in a spirit of hope, and know that she still had…*'Jesus insurance.'* He will provide a way."

"Don't wait for a miracle; be the miracle. It is within you."

"I often ask God, 'God, don't just show me 'The Way,' show me 'Your Way, because I know Your Way is truly The Way.'"

"It's been said by some that wisdom is not knowledge. Wisdom shines light on knowledge. Wisdom causes you to do the right thing when you don't know what to do."

"In Hollywood, bad publicity is often considered 'good publicity' and welcomed when a star makes the headlines for doing something bad or outrageous. It doesn't work that way in sports."

Regarding faith and character:
1. Everywhere you want to be (*Visa*).
2. Don't leave home without it (*American Express*).
3. When it absolutely, positively has to be there overnight (every day and night) (*FedEx*).

"I believe, as a nation, we've gotten ourselves into trouble with the longtime sports axiom of 'boys will be boys.' We have allowed ourselves to become too comfortable and too tolerant with this misguided ideology. I believe it sends the wrong message to our young males, who then become young men still believing in the myth. It's time to discredit that old saying. Enough is enough, and we don't have to accept those same old attitudes anymore."

"When I realize and recognize a blessing from our Heavenly Father, I simply say, 'Bravo, Jesus…bravo!'"

"In life, sometimes you have to sacrifice to end the strife and restart your life."

"There will always be haters, doubters, naysayers, negative people, non-believers, procrastinators, etc., with bad attitudes who will want you to agree with their way of thinking. Don't let them sing you a lullaby. Stay focused and do the right thing for you."

"Prayer is like good home cookin'. You can't get enough of it, and you're always coming back for more."

On athletic maturity: "Grow your mind, grow your game, grow your spirituality, grow as person."

"When I know things are going well in my life and I can feel the momentum of it all, I say, 'Work it, Jesus...work that!'"

"When things are going good in your life, it's not just good...it's OH MY GOD GOOD!"

"Thank you, God, for all your blessings, big and small. With all my heart, I appreciate them all -- Amen."

David-isms on How to Draft Character for Your Team:

Every successful owner, coach, and athlete knows that team dynamics change each season.

The following are advice from general managers and athletic directors on drafting athletes with character and good moral conduct.

"A GM (general manager) may assemble and strive to retain the strongest core of talent possible, but even in the midst of such stability, team dynamics will still fluctuate. How your team acquires players with character either through free agency, trades, or via the draft will ultimately determine how the team deals with adversity and how it handles success."

"How you assemble and integrate new team members depends on an accurate assessment of your team's current needs, as well as long term requirements, which should be based on the character of the players a team brings into your team culture. Before you lead your team to victory and success, decide on constructing a team with as many high character athletes as you can possibly find."

"The true test of an athlete's character will actually come in the aftermath of his/her mistake. Will they make genuine changes, or will the same habits and mindset continue to cloud their decision making? Only time will tell. Apologies are nice, but talk is cheap.

Your actions afterward will determine your true courage to change and transform yourself."

"This is what true professionals do. They produce and do things the right way on and off the field and court, regardless of the circumstances they may face. That's character."

On success: "For your dreams to come true, give God an opportunity in your life."

"In general, athletes are *NOT* bad people. They are good people who sometimes make *BAD* choices. I believe their decision making process can be corrected with education, awareness, and an aggressive change in mindset."

"It is my hope for athletes on all levels, young and old, male and female, to achieve a personal best for yourself. Good character is a way of living…a higher standard. It's also a way of sharing and a way of giving. When you work hard, play hard and do good…you win, regardless of what the scoreboard reads."

"The truth is, *Athlete Career Killers*™ never go away. They will always be there…waiting for you. It's up to you whether you decide to allow them into your life — or not."

"Remember…you can't keep a good man or woman of God down!"

Pray Hard. Do Good.™

Chapter 12
RECRUITING VIOLATIONS

The Truth Will Set You Free – or Will it?

These days in college athletics, if someone so much as sneezes and you don't say *"bless you,"* it could very well get you, your coach, or athletic department in deep trouble!

In fact, a former high-profile running back who currently plays for the NFL's New Orleans Saints gave back the 2005 Heisman Trophy he won as a USC Trojan due to alleged violations while attending the university.

The athlete has not admitted any wrongdoing.

His high profile basketball counterpart at USC was also in the news for being investigated for violations in early January, 2010. The school implemented self-imposed sanctions on their basketball program as a result for violating NCAA rules.

Recruiting violations and alleged cheating in the NCAA have become a major topic in college sports, specifically college football and men's basketball. Athletes are becoming ineligible to play, coaches are being reprimanded, fired, and are resigning more so than ever before.

Fans, athletes, coaches, and media across the country are wondering which program will be hit next, and who specifically might come under intense scrutiny.

What's the problem?

Has the game been victimized by opportunistic agents, recruiters, runners and hangers-on looking to collect on the next NBA super-star? Is the NCAA doing enough to combat the problems?

What are the real issues and concerns?

To get the answers, I went straight to the sources. I interviewed two high-profile head coaches in football and basketball, representing two power conferences. I agreed to their request for *full anonymity*, and I asked them to give their opinions and recommendations about their sport.

And boy did they have opinions!

Basketball Head Coach Interview:

Q: *Many issues seem to stem from summer recruiting. What's the worst part of it?*

> A: Summer recruiting is pretty intense, competitive and time consuming, not just for the coaches, but for the athletes and their families also. Oh yeah, and I hate runners too!

Q: *Explain what a "runner" is in basketball.*

> A: (Laughing)...I call runners "creepers." These are people who are basically 'street agents' that do the dirty work befriending players, especially players with pro potential, hoping to cash in later when that player gets to the NBA. Some of the runners work independently while others are directly associated with agents.

Q: *What do runners do for, or provide to athletes?*

> A: Geez, you got another hour to kill, David? From my own personal knowledge and experience, runners, or 'creepers' as I call them, give players money, give their family members money to cover normal expenses like rent, electric bill, sometimes they provide a mortgage payment, a car payment, you name it. It's not always cash either. It could be gifts too. Of course all of this is in direct violation of NCAA rules and regulations.

Q: *You said "from my own personal knowledge and experience..." does that mean you have seen runners give cash or gifts to athletes or their family, and turned the other cheek?*

> A: No, no! Never. I like my job too much. But I have certainly chased off a few in my time, and still do. I do make it a point to warn my players and their family and friends about what's going on. Creepers are like cockroaches jam packed in a tiny box. Once you open that lid, they all come crawling out...and they seem to multiply too (laughing). Makes your skin crawl because they can put young men's athletic careers in jeopardy.

Q: Speaking of families, what's the toughest part of talking with them?

> A: You sit down in the kitchen or the living room with a kid's parents and you look them in the eye and promise a father and a mother that you'll be there for her son during his journey. But the reality is, as soon as I get on campus I have so many other obligations to take care of, the kid is pretty much left on his own for an extensive period of time, except for occasional follow-up conversations. So we have to do a better job of placing these kids in the hands of good orientation programs, upper-class mentors, and do a better job of evaluating their progress both academically and socially. Then there's the high probability of a kid being "one and done," (meaning a student-athlete has a one-year college basketball career) which is also not good for our game.

Q: How much sleep do you lose at night worrying about who your star athlete is hanging out with or what agent might be talking to him?

> A: Well, I can't be there with him 24\7, nor do I want to be, but it is a concern. One of the things I want to learn about a kid when I meet his family during a recruiting stop, is to find out as much as I can about his character and how he was raised. I ask his parents what type of people did he hang out with in high school and if he ever got into any trouble. I'll tell you another thing, a lot of kids who are freshman, sophomores and juniors in high school should go straight to summer school. Many just aren't ready or mature enough for the college level. We do our best to maintain a clean program, but what exactly does clean really mean? Right now as I'm talking to you and without my knowledge, one of my assistant coaches could be on the phone innocently returning a call from a kid's dad or mom who had a general, sincere question about the recruiting process. Is returning a phone call to a kid's parent in violation of NCAA rules and regulations? It may be! But does that one innocent phone call make our entire program dirty? No. I can't police everyone one hundred percent of the time.

Q: On the topic of maturity, how much of that factors into a young student-athlete taking money, gifts, or other things from a coach, agent or recruiter?

A: Before a kid even gets to the college level, and parents sometimes won't want to admit this, many talented players are spoiled from the time they start elementary school. They are coddled, enabled, and no one has the guts to tell them "no." Some parents have told me, "I know my son is talented. You know my son is talented. Other coaches are calling me too. What are you going to do for me if you want my son to play basketball at your school?" Some parents feel entitled. When a kid sees that attitude from his parents, he adopts an attitude of entitlement too. So a lot of times when you hear about a kid getting into trouble for talking to an agent or coach, the parents are most likely aware of it and signed off on it beforehand, yet it's the kid, the coach, and the college or university who takes the blame and suffers the penalties from the NCAA. Parents should be held accountable too and many of them encourage misconduct because, depending on their economic situation at home, find it nearly impossible to resist the temptation. Parents may say "no thanks" to money as an offer to help the family, but some coaches, agents and recruiters are relentless. They will keep knocking on a parent's door, keep calling them, keep texting them, until the temptation is just too strong to ignore. It happens all the time. Once a kid sees that the parents are on board, to him the sky's the limit on what he will accept from a coach or agent.

Football Head Coach Interview:

Q: *If you were the president of the NCAA, what would you change?*

A: Simplify things! I know it seems that simplicity should be a simple thing to integrate, but it's true. The NCAA rules and regulations on recruiting violations, academic misconduct, improper contact with players, penalties, sanctions, is just too broad. I think the NCAA should break it down into smaller segments with essential topics of concern in bullet points, then send it out to everyone as a "special report," or as a weekly or bi-weekly newsletter. To sit down and try to decipher an entire segment of any current rule or regulation makes me feel like I should have gone to school to become a lawyer instead of a being a head coach. If I can't make sense of it, how do you expect a student-athlete to? And it's not just me and my players. People in my athletic department don't understand half the stuff that's in their either. I'm sure that's a common thread. The NCAA is the only authoritative show in town in collegiate athletics. They're not going to reform themselves any time soon, but obviously changes need to be made.

Q: *What's your opinion on APRs (Academic Progress Rate – a system of academic checks and balances. It holds schools accountable for both their graduation rates and academic success.)?*

A: I think coaches should be held responsible for keeping abreast of their kids and their academic performance. But student-athletes have to do their part too. We can't hold their hands and go to their dorm rooms every morning to make sure they're up and getting ready for class. We as coaches can only do so much. It has to be a collective effort of the player, coach, his family, professors, student services and support, the community and everybody else.

Q: *In today's society of modern technology and athletics, what's good about it and what don't you like?*

A: Everybody has a cell phone, right? So how do you regulate the number of times you can call a recruit? These days I can get into trouble if I call a kid too often, or text him, tweet him, email him, or even say hello on his blog or Facebook page. This social media thing is crazy. I can't control that, and the NCAA can't control it either. So to cover my butt I contact my athletic department and compliance director first to make sure what I can and can't do. But even with that, mistakes can and do happen. Then you have to differentiate between a minor NCAA rule violation and a secondary rule violation. It becomes awfully confusing for coaches, the players and their families, agents and everyone else. Recruiting is a very competitive thing. Most coaches are honest, ethical and above-board. There are coaches out there who knowingly try to gain an advantage over the rest of us. And let's not forget about the dishonest agents and other recruiters out there. There are bad apples in every industry. You'll never be able to weed them out 100%.

ATHLETE CAREER KILLERS

Q: College football head coaches are a pretty prestigious and powerful group. If you knew a fellow coach was cheating, would you turn him in to the NCAA?

A: I don't walk around looking for cheaters. I think if you cheat, eventually you will get caught. I've got enough to worry about with my own program. The majority of coaches at Division 1 schools are doing things the right way. As long as another school doesn't try to steal my players, I give others the benefit of the doubt. But let's not be ignorant of the facts, cheating has been going on as long as the game has been played. It still happens. People are just being more creative about it these days. Some get away with it, some get caught.

Q: Looking ahead, what's your forecast?

A: I'm hopefully and cautiously optimistic things will become more transparent. Today, the game is a lot more regulated and scrutinized than at any point in my coaching career. Our sport's image has taken a beating in the media. The public wants answers and they're mad as hell about the crap that's been going on. As a whole I think there are more good things about our game than bad ones. I just want more clarity from everybody involved, but there's so much money at stake, it's difficult to tell what's real and what's not, who's got integrity and who doesn't. As an institution of collegiate athletics, we also have to do a better job of policing our own student-athletes and departments as best we can.

Q: The NCAA has an Agent, Gambling and Amateurism Activities staff (AGA). Their job is to investigate potential rules violations. What's your take on agents?

A: Well, now the NCAA is exploring the idea of our players having agents and advisers. If it's done in transparent way, and it doesn't interfere with my preparations and other obligations as a head coach, I see no problem with agents talking to my players. I believe the NCAA means well and is trying to correct a lot of things. But good intentions don't always equate to actually getting results. I want my players to be informed about their future options just as any head coach would. We have to come up with a better system to regulate agents and impose penalties and fines upon them if they are guilty of any misconduct. The NCAA does have an oversight committee and it's in the early stages of being researched so we'll see how it goes.

Q: *As you know, coach, under current NCAA rules, there is nothing that prohibits an athlete from speaking with or getting advice from an agent. Is that okay with you?*

A: I don't have a problem with that. As I said before, as long as it doesn't diminish or interfere with what we are trying to accomplish as a team, and that's winning games, or comprise the integrity of our university or the player himself. Many agents take advantage of a kid's 'youthfulness' in not knowing about the business side of it and try to get a kid to commit to being their client. I think the dishonest and crooked agents should be posted on billboards in every college town in the country and on campuses, with a photo of their face plastered and a caption that reads 'NCAA's Most Wanted.'

Q: *Those type of guys could potentially become Coach Career Killers™, if they haven't already. Okay, so maybe there should be a specific location on campus where athletes, coaches, agents and\or advisers can meet to openly discuss that athlete's professional potential and future. What are your thoughts on that, coach?*

A: Good point. It would be better than an agent inviting a kid to a lavish party in order to fill his ear with a bunch of promises, or going to a kid's house and tainting his parents and family members. I don't think I want that meeting to occur in my coach's office. That's too obvious. How 'bout we hold the meetings in the college chapel conference room? Seriously though, you make a good point, but I would want to meet with everyone in a room with lots of glass walls where we could be seen by people walking by. Keep things transparent. Will agents go for that? I doubt it. Just like coaching, the agent business is just as competitive.

Q: *In the NFL, the Player's Association implies a strict no-contact rule for agents when it comes to college athletes, unless they declare for early eligibility in the draft. However, the NBA Player's Association does not. Your thoughts?*

A: I think the NFL has it right, for the most part. Without that rule in the NBA, it opens the door to the proverbial bottomless pit when it comes time to punish an agent. I hope the NBA will re-evaluate that one sooner rather than later. But if you punish an agent, who's going to lay down the law? What legal jurisdiction are they under? The NCAA has no legal rights to impose punishments on agents, to the best of my knowledge. It's a tough road to haul. The problem with agents is that my players generally won't get into trouble for just talking to an agent. I mean, we do live in a free country; but at the same time when an agent is offering a kid or his family money and gifts, that's where the problems start.

Q: *So how can we change things?*

A: Be honest about things and be accountable. I talk to my players all the time about being informed and that's their right and responsibility. If one of my players is ready to turn pro after being in my program for only two years, more power to him to reach out there and achieve his goals and dreams. But do it the right way, the smart and well-informed way. Don't just get blinded by all the potential dollars signs that are being thrown around out there. I mean, in my opinion, the agents aren't going away any time soon. Right now there's just an over saturation of agents and runners relative to college players. We might as well face reality and make it legal for an agent to advise a student-athlete and stress transparency and clarity because it's going to continue to happen behind closed doors, on street corners, at parties, at a parent's house anyway, so let's bring the thing out into the open, have all the parties involved sit down together, the coaches, players, agents, and of course the NCAA, and structure it from there. Otherwise, it's like playing Russian Roulette with a kid's college career, my coaching career, the integrity and the reputable ethics of my university. Will I still be coaching when and if that type of transparency happens? I'm not optimistic about that, to be honest.

Q: *Last question, coach. There is an organization out there for agents called the Uniform Athletes Agent Act. It's law in about 39 states to date. According the information I gathered from the Associated Press, here's what they determined the UAAA amounted to back in year 2000, in a quick excerpt:*

"... provides for the uniform registration, certification, and a mandated criminal history disclosure of sports agents seeking to represent student athletes who are or may be eligible to participate in intercollegiate sports, imposes specified contract terms on these agreements to the

benefit of student athletes, and provides educational institutions with a right to notice along with a civil cause of action for damages resulting from a breach of specified duties."

In layman's terms, the law allows schools to actually sue agents who damage the university, many times from a financial standpoint, by interacting with an athlete illegally.

Have you ever heard of the organization? If so what are your thoughts on it in regard to being a road map of ethics for agents?

Oh, and if you ever get bored some weekend, you can read the full report at http://www.law.upenn.edu/bll/archives/ulc/uaaa/aaa1130.htm

> A: (Laughing) You thought you'd throw the old coach a curve on that one, didn't you, David? I just might check out the website, but I may need a lawyer to translate all the legal jargon. Well, I have heard about them. I'd like to see what the current success rate and percentages are, and what penalties and fines, if any, have been imposed on agents. It seems to me that this isn't a very well-known or talked about organization from an agent's perspective. I've never heard about it from an actual agent before. If an agent is getting sued, he surely wouldn't want me to know about it. To be quite honest, it sounds like one of those 'shell' companies that get formed just for the legal aspect of it, but never really do anything.

David L. Brown: Well, actually, this from the *Associated Press*; it says they did an investigation and concluded that schools rarely, if ever, sue agents for damages. In the end, the UAAA is hardly ever utilized to punish a bad agent. The *Associated Press* stated that twenty-four states reported taking no disciplinary or criminal action against sports agents, and were unable to determine if state or local prosecutors had pursued such cases. Others described the laws as being enforced a few times, or rarely -- an indication of what a low priority they are.

Coach: Exactly.

David L. Brown: Thanks, coach.

Coach: Thank you, David, good talking to you.

Chapter 13
DEPRESSION & ANXIETY
(Bonus Chapter)

Depression can kill!

Among athletes, depression can be a serious issue if not addressed immediately and in the right way. It's not necessarily going to be obvious when someone, even an athlete you're very close to, is suffering from depression.

Depression doesn't discriminate.

A Denver Broncos wide receiver reportedly took his own life after it was reported he may have been distraught over a recent knee injury, causing him to have surgery and miss the 2010 season. The second-year pro was found dead in his home in Colorado Monday, September 20, 2010, in an apparent suicide from a self-inflicted gunshot wound to the head.

He was twenty-three.

Depression, fear, anxiety, peer pressure, and pressure to live up to your own expectations or the perception of expectations from others, can hit athletes and anyone else who, on the surface, have everything going for them.

This includes young *NFL, NBA, NHL, Major League Baseball*, college and high school players who have their whole lives ahead of them.

Depression isn't always logical or rational, but it's powerful, it's misunderstood and it's more widespread than most people imagine.

One of the best ways to combat depression is talking about it with someone you trust. If you are a friend or family member of an athlete, focus on *listening intently* to the words he or she uses in normal conversation.

Such statements like, *"Well, maybe I should just kill myself,"* should be taken seriously as a key warning sign of potential suicide, even if the person says it jokingly.

Be supportive and never feel like you're invading their privacy. Let the person know you are there for them if they want to talk more in-depth about their feelings. Once a person senses that you're okay with talking about suicide, they tend to open up more about the issues they may be facing.

Professional sports leagues offer ample services to help athletes cope with their issues – personal, financial, family or otherwise. The leagues and teams provide those under the umbrella of its player development programs.

It includes free counseling sessions and trained staff who are around every team on a regular or semi-regular basis. There are also life skills classes, both mandatory and voluntary, taught on a regular basis.

You would be wise to develop an identity outside of being a high school, college or professional athlete.

If your sole identity and self-worth is wrapped up in you being an athlete, where you can easily be replaced due to injury, poor choices off the field and court, or lack of production, what's going to happen when you don't have sports any longer?

I acknowledge it's often difficult to get athletes to ask for help. This *"gladiator"* mentality could hurt – or kill you.

It can be equally tough for friends and family members of professional athletes to directly address a potential problem. Many times, the athlete is providing a roof over that person's head, or extra money in their pocket, which may prevent them from intervening for fear of straining the relationship.

Even for teammates, it's difficult to put a hand on your buddy's shoulder and say, *"Hey, man, I think you need some help."*

Many outside observers may think the money a professional athlete makes provides a comfortable "buffer" against the pressures they endure. The truth is, many times a lot of money for an athlete in their 20s has just the opposite effect, which may add to already enormous pressure.

If you know of anyone who may be showing signs of depression, elevated anxiety, or abnormal isolation, or who may be vulnerable to them, please have them contact *(or you can contact)* your local suicide hotline or a mental health professional.

It could save a life.

Play Hard. Do Good. Talk About It.™

Off-topic note: A future Hall-of-Fame quarterback with the Minnesota Vikings found himself on the front page headlines and over the internet. But this time, it was not due his heroics on the football field.

The long-time NFL QB is currently being investigated for allegedly sending inappropriate photographs and text messages to a former New York Jets sideline reporter when he played for the team in 2008.

He could face suspension, as of this writing.

NFL Commissioner Roger Goodell, during a live chat with fans from the league website in late October, 2010, said "workplace conduct" is the main focus in the investigation into allegations of improper behavior against the Vikings QB.

Goodell also said the NFL is "working hard" on the development of a workplace conduct training program for all teams and expects to roll it out by the end of the 2010 season.

Always remember to treat everyone with respect and focus on making good choices each and every day.

Is it gonna be YOU?

Are you going to be the next athlete I read and hear about in a negative way?

I hope not.

Someday, somewhere, you and I may meet. It could be anywhere -- at an event or function, before your game, after your game, at a youth football or basketball camp, or sometime in the off-season.

After we introduce ourselves, I'll ask you one simple question:

So...did YOU make a good choice today?

NEVER allow your lifestyle and social life to have a negative impact on your life and athletic career.

You must maintain your focus, even in a world where it's easy to lose focus.

I would like to also dedicate this book to you (write your name below).

X_____

Kudos to you! You made the right choice by reading this book.

It means that you care and you're serious about making good decisions in your life and athletic career -- and that's important. The world needs more athletes and people like you.

I applaud you. I thank you.

Play Hard. Live Right.™

About the Author

David L. Brown is the foremost expert and leader in helping athletes avoid lifestyle disaster and embarrassing headlines off the field and court. *Athlete Career Killers*™ is the first book dedicated to providing step-by-step solutions for improving Player Personal Conduct™ in sport, and is the world's #1 guide that could save your life and athletic career.

Mr. Brown is Founder & CEO of Character Athletic, Ltd. He is also founder of Athlete Safety Academy™ (ASA), Athlete Safety Experts™ (ASE), University of Integrity™, and Parkway Press™.

He is a public and professional speaker, athlete safety expert and coach, consultant, and mentor.

David L. Brown's Workshops/Seminars:

Athlete Career Killers™: A Workshop/Seminar Created for Professional and College Athletes.

Play Hard. Do Good.™ : A Workshop/Seminar Geared toward Youth and High School Athletic Programs, Groups, Organizations and Associations.

University of Integrity™: A Workshop/Seminar Designed for Coaches, Recruiters, Agents, and Athletic Directors.

Personal Biography

Early Seventies – In junior high I received honors as a wrestler. I was voted an all-star while playing first base and right field on a team coached by my late dad. I also enjoyed playing my favorite sport — football — on a team with my brother. We lived in a beautiful little beach town in South Haven, Michigan.

During off seasons, to hone my skills in basketball, I attended Hoosier Basketball Camp at Lake James, Angola, Indiana, three years in a row in 1974, 1975, and 1976. Following the conclusion of the 1975 camp, I was honored to be named an all-star, and was the recipient of the "Pride" award, given to the player who exhibited the most effort and intensity during camp.

That same year I was voted by the camp counselors to receive the Tom Saylor Award, which recognizes the player who demonstrates an excellent attitude and rapport with other campers, shows intense desire to improve oneself, and is exemplary in sportsmanship and conduct. It was quite an honor.

The camps were great fun, and I got to meet, chat with, and get autographs from some of the all-time great players like Bob Lanier, Jerry Sloan, and Bob Love, and college coaches like Fred Schaus of Purdue, Johnny Orr of Michigan, and Tex Winter of Northwestern.

Late Seventies – After my sophomore year in high school, while I still lived in Michigan, my dad worked in a steel mill as a metallurgist and foreman. Shortly thereafter, a lot of plants in our area were beginning to close down permanently due to a bad economy. Unfortunately, Dad's plant succumbed to the poor economy and announced the plant would be closing its doors for good. It was tough on my dad and our family. We loved the area in South Haven, had made long friendships, and both my dad and mom were active in the community.

Dad, or "Pops," as we often called him, had to make some tough choices back then. It was, either keep his family in the area and find another job, or go where the jobs were. He ultimately accepted a pretty good job offer out of state in the New Castle, Pa. area. Our family later relocated to New Wilmington, Pa., a small, quiet town just up the road from New Castle, and home to the Westminster Titans and Westminster College, a private liberal arts college.

At Wilmington High School, I was active in football, basketball, and track & field. I was a 6'-3', 200 pound safety and wide receiver on the football team. After completing my two year stint in New Wilmington, I was honored to graduate as a two-time all tri-county defensive back, and in 1977 was also voted most valuable defensive back.

On the basketball team at Wilmington, I was a center, and considered a "rugged rebounder." I manned the middle, and successfully held my own against taller opponents due to smarts, strong fundamentals, and athletic ability. I played on a few all-star teams, and enjoyed the experiences. In track, I ran 100, 200, 440 meters, and the long jump.

In my senior high school year, I was recruited in football, my best and favorite sport, by the likes of Ohio State, Wisconsin, Louisville, Virginia Tech, and West Virginia University to name a few. *I actually still have all those recruitment letters!* My dad, family, and I loved traveling to the cities and touring the campuses. I was classified by college scouts and coaches as a "Blue Chip" athlete coming out of high school.

I was focused on football, track, and basketball, but I lost my focus in the classroom. I was a bright kid, I just didn't apply myself like I should have. Instead, I focused on sports and girls, like many seventeen year olds do.

So, in 1979, after the disappointment of not being able to play for a major college or university, I opted to sign to play football at a local school, Slippery Rock State College, which is now known as Slippery Rock University, or The Rock, now in NCAA Division II. I majored in communications.

The highlight of my brief football career at The Rock was the September 29, 1979 game at the famed Michigan Stadium in Ann Arbor, playing Shippensburg.

We lost that game, but it was a great experience.

I later returned to college and earned an English degree from Penn State University.

www.ingramcontent.com/pod-product-compliance
Lightning Source LLC
Chambersburg PA
CBHW081453040426
42446CB00016B/3229